DAX Formulas for PowerPivot

by

Rob Collie

Holy Macro! Books
420 Captain Blyth Place
Merritt Island, FL 32953 USA

DAX Formulas for PowerPivot

Author: Rob Collie

Layout: Tyler Nash

Technical Editor: Scott Senkeresty

Cover Design: Shannon Mattiza 6'4 Productions & Jocelyn Hellyer

Indexing: Nellie J. Liwam

Published by: Holy Macro! Books, 420 Captain Blyth Place, Merritt Island, FL 32953 USA

Distributed by: Independent Publishers Group, Chicago, IL

First Printing: November 2012. Printed with corrections June 2013. Printed in USA

ISBN: 978-1-61547-015-0 Print, 978-1-61547-212-3 PDF, 978-1-61547-332-8 ePub, 978-1-61547-112-6 Mobi

LCCN: 2012949097

Table of Contents

Acknowledgements

Bill Jelen – for tremendous support, encouragement, and humor. I never could have navigated the waters of the book trade without your assistance and fair treatment.

David Gainer - for teaching me half of everything valuable that I know, and teaching me to trust the other half. Three lifetimes would not be long enough to repay you. WWDD (What Would Dave Do?) – most impactful role-playing game of all time :)

Ken Puls – for crystallizing the need for me to write this book. All is right with Nature now – we are back to a state where there is nothing about Excel known to Rob and unknown to Ken.

Zeke Koch - for being so "insanely" awake and uncompromising (in a good way), and for letting some of that rub off on me. WWZD was the only other instance of the "WW" game I ever played.

The late Heikki Kanerva - for taking a chance on me, supporting me, and advocating for me. You are missed.

David Gonzalez - for encouraging me to go talk to Heikki.

Jeff Larsson - for helping me survive (barely!) the campaign of 1997-1999.

David McKinnis - for the tour of the Word97 Tools Options dialog, "a monument to the spineless backs of program managers everywhere."

Ben Chamberlain, Malcolm Haar, and Chetan Parulekar - for helping me understand that I was actually helpful (cue the Sally Field acceptance speech) and helping an insecure guy find his first footing.

John Delo - for patching OLE32 in RAM, the single greatest "stick save" in the history of software. Also for being a worthy adversary, and for taking the fountain dunking like a man. (The champagne squirtgun in the eyes was a crafty defense, well played).

Jon Sigler - for being next in line sticking his neck out for me.

Richard McAniff - for ovens and steaks, and more wisdom than I appreciated at the time.

Robert Hawking and Juha Niemisto - for patiently welcoming yet another green program manager to the complexities of your world.

Amir Netz - for sending me that "you should come look at our new project" email in 2006, and for encouraging me to start the blog in 2009.

David Kruglov - for reinforcing what Amir said, and for getting me into that SharePoint conference.

Maurice Prather – for introducing me to David K, for bailing us out big time as we were leaving town, and generally just being a great friend. I still owe you a long-overdue explanation for a few things.

Donald Farmer, TK Anand, Ariel Netz, Tom Casey, John Hancock – for supporting me in a VERY difficult time, and for giving me a precious eight-month window during which I found my new place in the world.

Donald "Tommy Chong" Farmer, again – for being such an amazingly good sport and good human throughout, even after switching teams.

Kasper de Jonge - for incredible transcontinental assistance and kinship, for saying nice things about my hoops game after trouncing me, for moving to the US and taking over the Rob Collie chair at MS (!), for reviewing the book, and for providing some much-needed screenshots there at the end.

Denny Lee – for critical support on occasions too numerous to list. Quite simply the man, eh?

Marianne Soinski - for teaching a certain 12 year old underachiever how to write, to REALLY write, and for forgiving (in advance!) the writing sins I would later commit in these pages and on the blog.

The Sambreel Crew – mas tequila por favor.

Lee Graber – wow, we've come a LONG way since sitting at that conference table staring at each other in confusion.

Howie Dickerman, Marius Dumitru, and Jeffrey Wang – for fielding my questions over the years, even (especially!) when they were user error.

Howie Dickerman, again – for also reviewing the book, on a short deadline.

Marco Russo and Alberto Ferrari, aka "The Italians" – for providing that next level of teaching, at and beyond the frontiers of my comprehension.

David Churchward, Colin Banfield, and David Hager – the all-stars of guest blogging. You are all too modest to admit the extent of your own skill and contribution.

Dany Hoter and Danny Khen – for a truly pragmatic, open-minded, and humble frame of mind. For seeking input in a world where everyone's walkie-talkie is stuck on SEND. It really stands out.

Eran Megiddo – for retroactively helping me to digest some of life's starkest truths.

Chad Rothschiller, Eric Vigesaa, Allan Folting, Joe Chirilov – I smile every time I think of you guys. Friendly, smart, witty monsters of the software trade. You all helped me more than I helped you.

Mike Nichols – Mexico.

Greg Harrelson – for starting that fantasy football league in 1996, inadvertently leading to my Excel obsession.

Joe Bryant – for writing the trendsetting article "Value Based Drafting," which really, REALLY spun me into full Excel addiction.

Dennis Wallentin - for excellent gang signs, for being a great human, and for fighting through.

Dick Moffat - for opening my eyes to the slide in Excel's credibility as a development platform.

Mary Bailey Nail – for weathering the artillery barrage, for forcing me to discover the GFITW, and for guaranteeing that all "year over year" biz logic I encounter in the future will seem like child's play.

Dan Wesson – for welcoming a "spreadsheet on steroids" into the scientific world, and for enjoying it. Also, for introducing the word "anogenital" into my tech talks – the most guaranteed laugh generator of all time.

Jeff "Dr. Synthetic" Wilson – for your determination and feedback.

Scott Senkeresty – for sticking around through many distinct phases of Rob over the past sixteen-plus years, and for reviewing this book more carefully and enthusiastically than I could have ever expected of anyone (in raw form no less!)

The rest of the crew at Pivotstream – for having the courage and foresight to bet the farm on PowerPivot three years ago, and for supporting me in this book project.

Tyler Nash – for patiently processing endless rounds of revisions.

Pandora - no one's jazz is smoother than yours.

The crew at Cedar-Fairmount Starbucks - for a steady supply of caffeine and social interaction over the past few years.

Phoenix Coffee - for inventing the Stuporball. You were the coffee mistress of bookwriting – please do not tell Starbucks.

RJ and Gabby Collie – for being proud of your dad. I never would have guessed how cool that would feel. Also, for being such thoughtful young people in general.

Jocelyn Collie – for sticking close during the move, for accepting and appreciating your goofball husband "as-is," for inspiring my switch from defense to offense, for school mornings, and for always knowing where everything is.

Supporting Workbooks and Data Sets

When I first committed to write the book, I decided that I would not attempt a companion CD or similar electronic companion of samples, data sets, etc.

I made that decision for two reasons:

1. I've found that when I am able to say something like "take a look at the supporting files if this isn't clear," that provides me too easy of an escape hatch. Treating the book as a purely standalone deliverable keeps me disciplined (or more disciplined at least) about providing clear and complete explanations.
2. Companion materials like that would have delayed release of the book and made it more expensive.

But as I neared completion of the book I realized that I could still provide a few such materials on an informal basis, downloadable from the blog.

So I will upload the original Access database that I used as a data source, as well as the workbook itself from various points in time as I progressed through the book:

http://ppvt.pro/BookFiles

Note that this will be a "living" page – a place where you can ask for clarification on the files, suggest improvements to them, etc. As time allows I will modify and improve the contents of the page.

A Note on Hyperlinks

You will notice that all of the hyperlinks in this book look like this:

http://ppvt.pro/<foo>

Where <foo> is something that is short and easy to type. Example:

http://ppvt.pro/1stBlog

This is a "short link" and is intended to make life much easier for readers of the print edition. That link above will take you to the first blog post I ever published, which went live in October of 2009.

Its "real" URL is this:

http://www.powerpivotpro.com/2009/10/hello-everybody/

Which would *you* rather type?

So just a few notes:

1. **These short links will *always* start with http://ppvt.pro/** – which is short for "PowerPivotPro," the name of my blog.
2. **These links are case-sensitive!** If the link in the book ends in "1stBlog" like above, typing "1stblog" or "1stBLOG" will *not* take you to the intended page!
3. **Not all of these links will lead to my blog** – some will take you to Microsoft sites for instance.
4. **The book does not rely on you following the links** – the topics covered in this book are intended to be complete in and of themselves. The links provided are strictly optional "more info" type of content.

Introduction

My Two Goals for This Book

Fundamentally of course, this book is intended to train you on PowerPivot. It captures the techniques I've learned from three years of teaching PowerPivot (in person and on my blog), as well as applying it extensively in my everyday work.

Unsurprisingly, then, the contents herein are very much instructional – a "how to" book if ever there was one.

But I also want you to understand how to maximize PowerPivot's impact on your career. It isn't just a better way to do PivotTables. It isn't just a way to reduce manual effort. It's not just a better formula engine.

Even though I worked on the first version of PowerPivot while at Microsoft, I had no idea how impactful it would be until about two years after I left the company. I had to experience it in the real world to see its full potential, and even then it took some time to overwhelm my skeptical nature (my Twitter profile now describes me as "skeptic turned High Priest.")

This is the rare technology that can (and will) fundamentally change the lives of millions of people – it has more in common with the invention of the PC than with the invention of, say, the VCR.

The PC might be a particularly relevant example actually. At a prestigious Seattle high school in the early 1970's, Bill Gates and Paul Allen discovered a mutual love for programming, but there was no widespread demand for programmers at that point. Only when the first PC (the Altair) was introduced was there an opportunity to properly monetize their skills. Short version: they founded Microsoft and became billionaires.

But zoom out and you'll see much more. *Thousands* of people became millionaires at Microsoft alone (sadly, yours truly missed that boat by a few years). Further, without the Altair, there would have been no IBM PC, no Apple, no Mac, no Steve Jobs. No iPod, no iPhone, no Appstore. No Electronic Arts, no Myst. No World of Warcraft. **The number of people who became wealthy as a result of the PC absolutely dwarfs the number of people who had anything to do with inventing the PC itself!**

I think PowerPivot offers the same potential wealth-generation effect to Excel users as the PC offered budding programmers like Gates and Allen: your innate skills remain the same but their value becomes many times greater. Before diving into the instructional stuff in Chapters 2 and beyond, Chapter 1 will summarize your exciting new role in the changing world.

And like many things in my life, the story starts with a movie reference ☺

1- A Revolution Built on YOU

Does This Sound Familiar?

In the movie *Fight Club*, Edward Norton's character refers to the people he meets on airplanes as "single serving friends" – people he befriends for three hours and never sees again. I have a unique perspective on this phenomenon, thanks to a real-world example that is relevant to this book.

A woman takes her seat for a cross-country business flight and is pleased to see that her seatmate appears to be a reasonably normal fellow. They strike up a friendly conversation, and when he asks her what she does for a living, she gives the usual reply: "I'm a marketing analyst."

That answer satisfies 99% of her single-serving friends, at which point the conversation typically turns to something else. However, this guy is the exception, and asks the dreaded follow-up question: "Oh, neat! What does that *mean*, actually?"

She sighs, ever so slightly, because the honest answer to that question always bores people to death. Worse than that actually: it often makes the single-serving friend recoil a bit, and express a sentiment bordering on pity.

But she's a factual sort of person, so she gives a factual answer: "well, basically I work with Excel all day, making PivotTables." She fully expects this to be a setback in the conversation, a point on which she and her seatmate share no common ground.

Does this woman's story sound familiar? Do you occasionally find yourself in the same position?

Well imagine her surprise when this particular single-serving friend actually becomes **excited** after hearing her answer! He lights up – it's the highlight of his day to meet her.

Because, you see, on this flight, she sat down next to me. And I have some exciting news for people like her, which probably includes you :-)

Excel Pros: The World is Changing in Your Favor

If you are reading this, I can say confidently that the world is on the verge of an incredible discovery: it is about to realize how immensely valuable you are. In large part, this book is aimed at helping you reap the full rewards available to you during this revolution.

That probably sounds pretty appealing, but why am I so comfortable making bold pronouncements about someone I have never met? Well, this is where the single-serving friend thing comes in: I have met **many** people like you over the years, and to me, you are very much 'my people.'

In fact, for many years while I worked at Microsoft, it was my **job** to meet people like you. I was an engineer on the Excel team, and I led a lot of the efforts to design new functionality for relatively advanced users.

Meeting those people, and watching them work, was crucial, so I traveled to find them. When I was looking for people to meet, the only criteria I applied was this: you had to use Excel for ten or more hours per week.

I found people like that (like you!) all over the world, in places ranging from massive banks in Europe to the back rooms of automobile dealerships in Portland, Oregon. There are also many of you working at Microsoft itself, working in various finance, accounting, and marketing roles, and I spent a lot of time with them as well (more on this later).

Over those years, I formed a 'profile' of these 'ten hour' spreadsheet people I met. Again, see if this sounds familiar.

Attributes of an Excel Pro:

- They grab data from one or more sources.
- They prep the data, often using VLOOKUP.
- They then create pivots over the prepared data.
- Sometimes they subsequently index into the resulting pivots, using formulas, to produce polished reports. Other times, the pivots themselves serve as the reports.
- They then share the reports with their colleagues, typically via email or by saving to a network drive.

- They spend at least half of their time re-creating the same reports, updated with the latest data, on a recurring basis.

At first, it seemed to be a coincidence that there was so much similarity in the people I was meeting. But over time it became clear that this was no accident. It started to seem more like a law of physics – an inevitable state of affairs. Much like the heat and pressure in the earth's crust seize the occasional pocket of carbon and transform it into a diamond, the demands of the modern world 'recruit' a certain kind of person and forge them into an Excel Pro.

 Aside: Most Excel Pros do not think of themselves as Pros: I find that most are quite modest about their skills. However, take it from someone who has studied Excel usage in depth: if you fit the bulleted criteria above, you are an Excel Pro. Wear the badge proudly.

I can even put an estimate on how many of you are out there. At Microsoft we used to estimate that there were 300 million users of Excel worldwide. This number was disputed, and might be too low, especially today. It's a good baseline, nothing more. But that was **all** users of Excel – from the most casual to the most expert. Our instrumentation data further showed us that only 10% of all Excel users *created* PivotTables.

'Create' is an important word here – much more than 10% *consume* pivots made by others, but only 10% are able to *create* them from scratch. Creating pivots, then, turns out to be an overwhelmingly accurate indicator of whether someone is an Excel Pro. We might as well call them Pivot Pros.

You may feel quite alone at your particular workplace, because statistically speaking you *are* quite rare – less than 0.5% of the world's population has your skillset! But in absolute numbers you are **far** from alone in the world – in fact, you are one of approximately thirty million people. If Excel Pros had conferences or conventions, it would be quite a sight.

 I, too, fit the definition of an Excel Pro. It is no accident that I found myself drawn to the Excel team after a few years at Microsoft, and it is no accident that I ultimately left to start an Excel / PowerPivot-focused business (and blog). While I have been using the word 'you' to describe Excel Pros, I am just as comfortable with the word '**we.**'

As I said up front, I am convinced that our importance is about to explode into the general consciousness. After all, we are already crucial.

Our Importance Today

As proof of how vital we are, here's another story from Microsoft, one that borders on legend. The actual event transpired about ten years ago and the details are hazy, but ultimately it's about you; about us.

Someone from the SQL Server database team was meeting with Microsoft CEO Steve Ballmer. They were trying to get his support for a 'business intelligence' (BI) initiative within Microsoft – to make the company itself a testbed for some new BI products in development at that time. If Steve supported the project, the BI team would have a much easier time gaining traction within the accounting and finance divisions at Microsoft.

In those days, Microsoft had a bit of a 'prove it to me' culture. It was a common approach to 'play dumb' and say something like, "okay, tell me why this is valuable." Which is precisely the sort of thing Steve said to the BI folks that day.

To which they gave an example, by asking a question like this: "If we asked you how much sales of Microsoft Office grew in South America last year versus how much they grew the year before, but only during the holiday season, you probably wouldn't know."

Steve wasn't impressed. He said, "sure I would," triggering an uncomfortable silence. The BI team **knew** he lacked the tools to answer that question – they'd done their homework. Yet here was one of the richest and most powerful men in the world telling them they were wrong.

One of the senior BI folks eventually just asked straight out, "Okay, **show** us how you'd do that."

Steve snapped to his feet in the center of his office and started shouting. Three people hurried in, and he started waving his arms frantically and bellowing orders, conveying the challenge at hand and the information he needed. This all happened with an aura of familiarity – this was a common occurrence, a typical workflow for Steve and his team.

Those three people then vanished to produce the requested results. In Excel, of course.

Excel at the Core

Let that sink in: the CEO of the richest company in the world (and one of the most technologically advanced!) relies **heavily** on Excel Pros to be his eyes and ears for all things financial. Yes, I am sure that now, many years later, he has a broad array of sophisticated BI tools at his disposal. However, I am equally sure that his reliance on Excel Pros has not diminished by any significant amount.

Is there anything special about Microsoft in this regard? Absolutely not! This is true everywhere. No exceptions. Even at companies where they claimed to have 'moved beyond spreadsheets,' I was always told, off the record, that Excel still powered 90% of decisions. (Indeed, an executive at a large Microsoft competitor told me recently that his division, which produces a BI product marketed as a 'better' way to report numbers than Excel, uses Excel for **all** internal reporting!)

Today, if a decision – no matter how critical the decision, or how large the organization– is informed by data, it is overwhelmingly likely that the data is coming out of Excel. The data may be communicated in printed form, or PDF, or even via slide deck. But it was *produced* in Excel, and therefore by an Excel Pro.

The message is clear: today we are an indispensable component of the information age, and if we disappeared, the modern world would grind to a halt overnight. Yet our role in the world's development is just getting started.

Three Ingredients of Revolution

There are three distinct reasons why Excel Pros are poised to have a very good decade.

Ingredient One: Explosion of Data

The ever-expanding capacity of hardware, combined with the ever-expanding importance of the internet, has led to a truly astounding explosion in the amount of data collected, stored, and transmitted.

Estimates vary widely, but in a single day, the internet may transmit more than a thousand *exabytes* of data. That's 180 CD-ROMs' worth of data for each person on the planet, in just 24 hours!

However, it's not just the volume of data that is expanding; the number of *sources* is also expanding. Nearly every click you make on the internet is recorded (scary but true). Social media is now 'mined' for how frequently a certain product is mentioned, and whether it was mentioned positively or negatively. The thermostat in your home may be 'calling home' to the power company once a minute. GPS units in delivery vehicles are similarly checking in with 'home base.'

This explosion of volume and variety is often lumped together under the term 'Big Data.' A few savvy folks are frontrunning this wave of hype by labeling themselves as 'Big Data Professionals'. By the time you are done with this book, you might rightfully be tempted to do the same.

There's a very simple reason why 'Big Data' equals 'Big Opportunity' for Excel Pros: human beings can only understand a single page (at most) of information at a time. Think about it: even a few hundred rows of data is too big for a human being to look at and make a decision. We need to summarize that data – to 'crunch' it into a smaller number of rows (i.e. a report) – before we can digest it.

So 'big' just means 'too big for me to see all at once.' The world is producing Big Data, but humans still need Small Data. Whether it's a few hundred rows or a few billion, people need an Excel Pro to shrink it for human consumption. The need for you is only growing.

 For more on Big Data, see http://ppvt.pro/SaavyBigData.

Ingredient Two: Economic Pressure

The world has been in an economic downturn since 2008 and there is little sign of that letting up. In general this is a bad thing. If played properly, however, it can be a benefit to the Excel Pro.

Consider, for a moment, the BI industry. BI essentially plays the same role as Excel: it delivers digestible information to decision makers. It's more formal, more centralized, and more expensive – an IT function rather than an Excel Pro function – but fills the same core need for actionable information.

A surprising fact: paradoxically, BI spending increases during recessions, when spending on virtually everything else is falling. This was true during the dot-com bust of 2000 and is true again today.

Why does this happen? Simply put: when the pressure is on, the value of smart decisions is increased, as is the cost of bad ones. I like to explain it this way: when money is falling from the sky, being 'smart' isn't all that valuable. At those times, the most valuable person is the one who can put the biggest bucket out the window. However when the easy money stops flowing, and everyone's margins get pressured, 'smart' becomes valuable once again.

 Insights are the key

Up to this point, I have used terms like 'crunched data,' 'reports,' 'Small Data,' and 'digestible information' to refer to the output produced by Excel Pros (and the BI industry). Ultimately though, the decision makers need *insights* – they need to learn things from the data that help them improve the business.

I like to use the word 'insights' to remind myself that we can't just crunch data blindly (and blandly) and hand it off. We need to keep in mind that our job is to deliver insights, and to create an environment in which others can quickly find their own. I encourage you to think of your job in this manner. It makes a real difference.

Unlike BI spending, spending on spreadsheets is *not* measured – people buy Microsoft Office every few years no matter what, so we wouldn't notice a change in 'Excel spending' during recessions. I suspect, however, that if we could somehow monitor the number of hours spent in Excel worldwide, we would see a spike during recessions, for the same reason we see spikes in BI spending.

So the amount and variety of data that needs to be 'crunched' is exploding, and at the same time, the business value of *insight* is increasing. This is a potent mixture.

All it needs is a spark to ignite it. And boy, do we have a bright spark.

Ingredient Three: PowerPivot

The world's need for insights is reaching a peak. Simultaneously, the amount of data is exploding, providing massive new insight opportunities (raw material for producing insights). Where is the world going to turn?

It is going to take an *army* of highly skilled data professionals to navigate these waters. Not everyone is cut out for this job either – only people who *like* data are going to be good at it. They must also be trained already – there's no time to learn, because the insights are needed now!

I think you see where I am going. **That army exists today, and it is all of you.** You already enjoy data, you are already skilled analytical thinkers, and you are already trained on the most flexible data analysis tool in the world.

However, until now there have been a few things holding you back:

1. **You are already very busy.** Many of you are swamped today, and for good reason. Even a modestly complex Excel report can require hundreds of individual actions on the part of the author, and most of those actions need to be repeated when you receive new data or a slightly different request from your consumers. Our labor in Excel is truly "1% inspiration and 99% perspiration," to use Edison's famous words.

2. **Integrating data from multiple sources is tedious.** Excel may be quite flexible, but that does not mean it makes every task effortless. Making multiple sources 'play nicely' together in Excel can absorb huge chunks of your time.

3. **Truly 'Big' Data does not fit in Excel.** Even the expansion of sheet capacity to one million rows (in Excel 2007 and newer) does not address all of today's needs. In my work at Pivotstream I sometimes need to crunch data sets exceeding 100 million rows, and even data sets of 100,000 rows can become prohibitively slow in Excel, particularly when you are integrating them with other data sets.

4. **Excel has an image problem.** It simply does not receive an appropriate amount of respect. To the uninitiated, it looks a lot like Word and PowerPoint – an Office application that produces documents. Even though those same people could not *begin* to produce an effective report in Excel, and they rely critically on the insights it provides, they still only assign Excel Pros the same respect as someone who can write a nice letter in Word. That may be depressing, but it is sadly true.

The Answer is Here

PowerPivot addresses all of those problems. I actually think it's fair to say that it completely wipes them away.

You are the army that the world needs. You just needed an upgrade to your toolset. PowerPivot provides that upgrade and then some. I would say that we probably needed a 50% upgrade to Excel, but what we got is more like a 500% upgrade; and that is not a number I throw around lightly.

 Imagine the year is 1910, and you are one of the world's first biplane pilots. One day at the airfield, someone magically appears and gives you a brand-new 2012 jet plane. You climb inside and discover that the cockpit has been designed to mimic the cockpit of your 1910 biplane! You receive a *dramatic* upgrade to your aircraft without having to re-learn how to fly from scratch. That is the kind of 'gift' that PowerPivot provides to Excel Pros.

I bet you are eager to see that new jet airplane. Let's take a tour.

2- What Version of PowerPivot Should You Use?

Three Primary Versions

By the time you are reading this, there will have been three different major releases of PowerPivot:

1. **PowerPivot 2008 R2** – I simply call this "PowerPivot v1." The "2008 R2" relates back to a version of SQL Server itself and has little meaning to us.
2. **PowerPivot 2012** – unsurprisingly I call this "PowerPivot v2." Again the 2012 relates to SQL Server, and again, we don't care that much.
3. **PowerPivot 2013** – to be released with Excel 2013. I will probably end up calling this "PowerPivot 2013"

The first two are available from PowerPivot.com, whereas the third is shipped with Excel 2013.

Of the three, I will be using v2 (PowerPivot 2012) in this book. v2 offers many improvements over v1, but there are a number of reasons why 2013 is not widely adopted yet.

Quirky Differences in User Interface: v2 vs. 2013

The concepts covered in this book are 100% applicable to 2013 even though the screenshots and figures all have the v2 appearance.

The differences between v2 and 2013 are "cosmetic" – formulas and functions behave the same for instance. But sometimes "cosmetic" can mean "awkward."

And there is definitely something awkward about 2013 that they need to fix. Put simply, it's more awkward to find and edit your formulas in 2013 than it is in v1 and v2. I've been in discussions with my former colleagues at Microsoft about this, and they understand it, but are not yet ready to announce a fix.

OK, I got that off my chest. Let us continue :-)

2013 PowerPivot only available in "Pro Plus" Version

Microsoft really surprised me at the last minute, just as 2013 was officially released. It was quietly announced that PowerPivot would only be included in the "Pro Plus" version of Office 2013. This is NOT the same thing as "Professional" – Pro Plus is only available through volume licensing or subscription and is not available in any store.

And unlike with 2010, there is no version of PowerPivot that you can download for 2013. If you don't have Pro Plus, you simply can't get PowerPivot.

For more on this issue, see http://ppvt.pro/2013ProPlus

32-bit or 64-bit?

Each of the three versions of PowerPivot is available in two "flavors" – 32-bit and 64-bit. Which one should you use?

 On PowerPivot.com, 32-bit is labeled "x86" and 64-bit is labeled "AMD64."

If you have a choice, I *highly* recommend 64-bit. 64-bit lets you work with larger volumes of data but is also more stable during intensive use, even with smaller data volumes. I run 64-bit on all of my computers.

For example, I have a 300 million row data set that works fine on my laptop with 4 GB of RAM, but with 32-bit PowerPivot, *no* amount of RAM would make that possible. (In fact, it would not work even if I cut it down to 20 million rows).

So if you have a choice, go with 64-bit – it offers more capacity and more stability. That said, you may not have that luxury. You have to match your choice to your copy of Excel.

 You *cannot* run 64-bit PowerPivot with 32-bit Excel, or vice versa!

So the first question you need to answer is whether you are running 32-bit or 64-bit Excel.

In Excel 2010, you can find that answer here, on the Help page

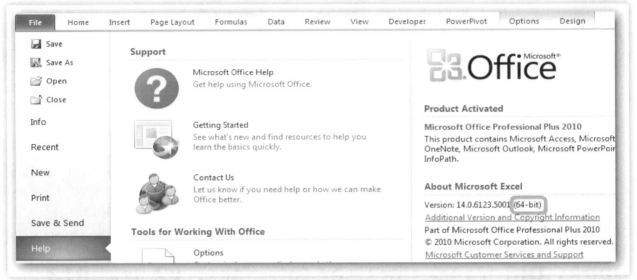

Figure 1 Finding whether your version of Excel is 32-bit or 64-bit

If you are running 32-bit Excel, fear not: most people are. I actually can think of no reason to run 64-bit Office except PowerPivot itself, so the 64-bit trend is really just getting started. (Who needs 64-bit Outlook, Word, and PowerPoint? No one does).

 Certain Office addins only run in 32-bit, so double check that before you decide to unin-stall 32-bit Office and switch to 64-bit.

Office 2010 or Newer is Required

No, sadly you cannot run PowerPivot with Excel 2007 or earlier versions.

There were very good technical reasons for this, and it was not an attempt by Microsoft to force people into Office 2010. Remember, the PowerPivot addin is free, and it would have been better for Microsoft, too, if PowerPivot worked with 2007.

If you are curious as to the reasons behind the "2010 or newer" requirement, see this post:

http://ppvt.pro/PP2007

A Note About Windows XP

On the more recent versions of Windows (Vista, Win7, and soon Win8), the PowerPivot window has a ribbon much like Excel does:

Figure 2 The PowerPivot window has a ribbon on most versions of Windows

But on Windows XP, the PowerPivot window has an old-style menu and toolbar:

Figure 3 On Windows XP, the PowerPivot window has a traditional menu and toolbar

All of the screenshots in this book are taken on Windows 7, and therefore show the ribbon in the PowerPivot window.

If you are using Windows XP and would like a "translation" guide, Microsoft has one here:

http://ppvt.pro/XP2Ribbon

3- Learning PowerPivot "The Excel Way"

PowerPivot is Like Getting Fifteen Years of Excel Improvements All at Once

PowerPivot was first released in 2009, but development began *fifteen years* prior to that, in 1994. Back then, it was called Microsoft SQL Server Analysis Services (SSAS). Actually, SSAS is very much alive and well as a product today – it remains the #1-selling analytical database engine in the world. SSAS was/is an industrial strength calculation engine for business, but targeted at highly specialized IT professionals.

In late 2006, Microsoft architect Amir Netz launched a secret incubation project (codename: Gemini) with an ambitious goal: make the full power of SSAS available and understandable to Excel Pros. A few months later he recruited me to join the effort (he and I had collaborated before when I was on the Excel team). Gemini was eventually released under the name PowerPivot in 2009.

 Continuing with the "biplane and jet" metaphor, think of SSAS as the jet plane, and Project Gemini (PowerPivot) as the effort to install an Excel-style cockpit and instrument panel so that Excel Pros can make the transition.

The key takeaway for you is this: **PowerPivot is a much, *much* deeper product than you would expect from something that appeared so recently on the scene.**

This actually has two very important implications:

1. **It is very hard to exhaust PowerPivot's capabilities.** Its long heritage means that a staggering number of needs have been addressed, and this is very good news.

2. **It is very helpful to learn it in the right sequence.** When touring the cockpit of your new jet, much will be familiar to you – the SUM() function is there, so is ROUND(), and even our old friend RAND(). But there are new functions as well, with names like FILTER() and EARLIER() and CALCULATE(). Naturally you want to start with the simplest and most useful functions, but it is hard to know which ones those *are*.

That second point is very important, and worth emphasizing.

Learn PowerPivot Like You Learned Excel: Start Simple and Grow

When you were first introduced to Excel (or spreadsheets in general), you likely started simple: learning simple arithmetic formulas and the "A1" style reference syntax. You didn't dive right into things like pivots until later. (In fact pivots didn't even exist in the first few versions of Excel).

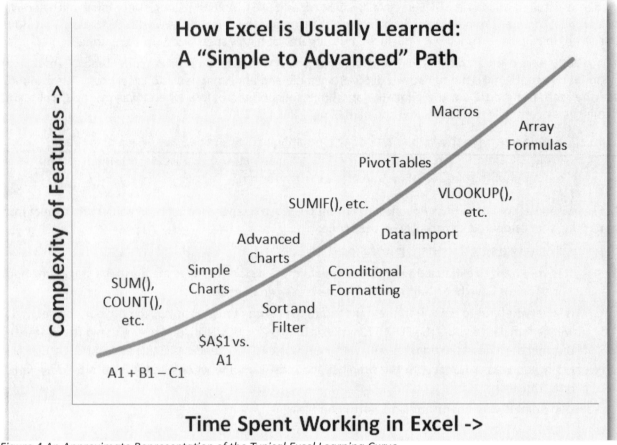

Figure 4 An Approximate Representation of the Typical Excel Learning Curve

You started with the simple stuff, got good at it, and only *then* branched out to new features. Incrementally, you added to your bag of tricks, over and over.

PowerPivot is no different. There are simple features (easy to learn and broadly useful) and advanced features (harder to learn and useful in more specific cases).

I have carefully sequenced the topics in this book to follow the same "simple to advanced" curve I developed and refined while training Excel pros over the past few years. The result is an approach that has proven to be very successful.

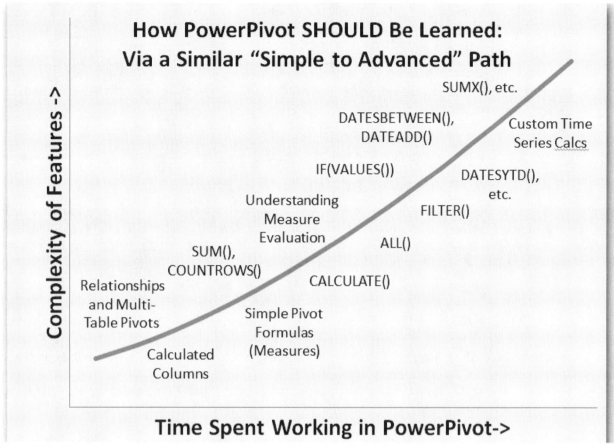

Figure 5 The learning curve I advocate to Excel Pros as they adopt PowerPivot

I highly recommend that you proceed through the book "in order." You will see that the chapters in this book are organized in roughly the order pictured above.

When to Use PowerPivot, and How it Relates to Normal Pivot Usage

I hear this question a lot. Simply put, PowerPivot is useful in any situation where you would normally want to use a pivot. Whether you have 100 rows of data or 100 million, if you need to analyze or report on trends, patterns, and/or aggregates from that data, rather than the original rows of data themselves, chances are very good that PowerPivot has something to offer.

When you use a traditional (non Power-) pivot, your workflow in Excel generally looks something like this:

1. **Grab data** from one or more sources, typically landing in Excel worksheets (but sometimes directly in the "pivotcache" in advanced cases).

2. **If multiple tables of data are involved,** use VLOOKUP() or similar to create integrated single tables

3. **Add calculated columns** as needed

4. **Build pivots** against that data

5. **Either use those pivots directly** as the final report/analysis, or build separate report sheets which reference into the pivots using formulas

Our guiding philosophy on PowerPivot was "make it just like Excel wherever possible, and where it's not possible, make it 'rhyme' very closely with Excel." Accordingly, the 5-step workflow from above looks like this in PowerPivot:

1. **Grab data** from one or more sources, landing in worksheet-tables in the PowerPivot window.

2. **Use relationships to quickly link multiple tables together**, entirely *bypassing VLOOKUP()* or similar tedious formulas.

3. **Optionally supplement that data with calculated columns and measures**, using Excel functions you have always known, *plus some powerful new ones*.

4. **Build pivots** against that data

5. **Either use those pivots directly** as the final report/analysis, or *convert pivots into formulas* with a single click for flexible layout, or you can still build separate report sheets which reference into the pivots using formulas.

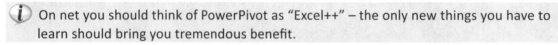 On net you should think of PowerPivot as "Excel++" – the only new things you have to learn should bring you tremendous benefit.

What This Book Will Cover in Depth

Simple Guideline: the more "common knowledge" something is, the less pages I am going to spend on it. I figure, for instance, that the button you use to create pivots is not worth a lot of ink. That topic, and many others, has been covered in depth by Bill Jelen's first PowerPivot book, http://ppvt.pro/MRXLPP **By contrast, the formula language of PowerPivot needs a lot of attention**, so it receives many chapters and consumes most of the book.

But even in topics that are relatively straightforward, I will still point out some of the subtleties, the little things that you might not expect. So for instance, in my brief chapter on Data Import, I will call provide some quick tips on things I have discovered over time.

And what is this "DAX" thing anyway? "DAX" is the name given to the formula language in PowerPivot, and it stands for Data Analysis eXpressions. I'm not actually all that fond of the name – I wish it were called "Formula+" or something that sounds more like an extension to Excel rather than something brand new. But the name isn't the important thing – the fact is that DAX *is* just an extension to Excel formulas.

OK, let's load some data.

4- Loading Data Into PowerPivot

No Wizards Were Harmed in the Creation of this Chapter

I don't intend to instruct you on how to use the import wizards in this chapter. They are mostly self-explanatory and there is plenty of existing literature on them. Instead I want to share with you the things I have learned about data import over time.

Think of this chapter as primarily "all the things I learned the hard way about data import."

That said, all chapters need to start somewhere, so let's cover a few fundamentals...

Everything Must "Land" in the PowerPivot Window

As I hinted in previous chapters, all of your relevant data MUST be loaded into the PowerPivot window rather than into normal Excel worksheets. But this is no more difficult than importing data into Excel has ever been. It's probably easier in fact.

Launching the PowerPivot Window

The PowerPivot window is accessible via this button on the PowerPivot ribbon tab in Excel:

Figure 6 This button launches the PowerPivot window

 If the PowerPivot ribbon tab does not appear for you, the PowerPivot addin is either not installed or not enabled.

One Sheet Tab = One Table

Every table of data you load into PowerPivot gets its own sheet tab. So if you import three different tables of data, you will end up with something like this:

Figure 7 Three tables loaded into PowerPivot. Each gets its own sheet tab.

You Cannot Edit Cells in the PowerPivot Window

That's right, the PowerPivot sheets are read-only. You can't just select a cell and start typing.

You can delete or rename entire sheet tabs and columns, and you can add calculated columns, but you cannot modify cells of data, ever.

Does that sound bad? Actually, it's a good thing. It makes the data more trustworthy, but even more importantly, it forces you to do things in a way that saves you a *lot* of time later.

Everything in the PowerPivot Window Gets Saved into the Same XLSX File

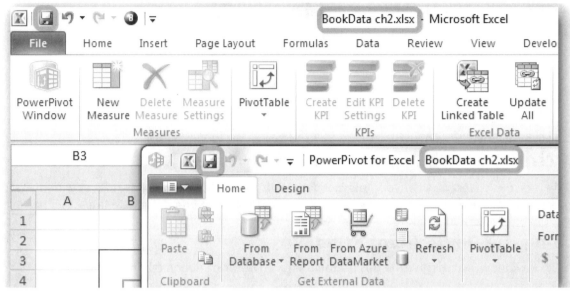

Figure 8 Both windows' contents are saved into the same file, regardless of which window you save from

> *(i)* Each instance of the PowerPivot window is tightly "bound" to the XLSX (or XLSM/XLSB) you had open when you clicked the PowerPivot Window button in Excel. You can have three XLSX workbooks open at one time, for instance, and three different PowerPivot windows open, but the contents of each PowerPivot window are only available to (and saved into) its original XLSX.

Many Different Sources

PowerPivot can "eat" data from a very wide variety of sources, including the following:

- From normal Excel sheets in the current workbook

- From the clipboard – any copy/pasted data that is in the shape of a table, even tables from Word for instance

- From text files – CSV, tab delimited, etc.

- From databases - like Access and SQL Server, but also Oracle, DB2, MySQL, etc.

- From SharePoint lists

- From MS SQL Server Reporting Services (SSRS) reports

- From cloud sources like Azure DataMarket and SQL Azure

- From so-called "data feeds"

So there is literally something for everyone. I have been impressed by PowerPivot's flexibility in terms of "eating" data from different sources, and have always found a way to load the data I need.

For each of the methods above, I will offer a brief description and my advice.

Linked Tables (Data Source Type)

If you have a table of data in Excel like this:

CalendarYear	MonthNumberOfYear	SalesTerritoryRegion	EnglishProductSubcategoryName	Budgeted Sales
2001	7	Australia	Mountain Bikes	71510
2001	7	Australia	Road Bikes	190248
2001	7	Canada	Mountain Bikes	4183
2001	7	Canada	Road Bikes	15429
2001	7	France	Mountain Bikes	7916
2001	7	France	Road Bikes	31825
2001	7	Germany	Mountain Bikes	4384
2001	7	Germany	Road Bikes	36068

Figure 9 Just a normal table of data in a normal Excel sheet

You can quickly grab it into PowerPivot by using the "Create Linked Table" button on the PowerPivot ribbon tab:

Figure 10 This will duplicate the selected Excel table into the PowerPivot window

Advantages

- This is the quickest way to get a table from Excel into PowerPivot

- If you edit the data in Excel – change cells, add rows, etc. – PowerPivot will pick those changes up. So this is a sneaky way to work around the "cannot edit in PowerPivot window" limitation.

- If you add columns, those will *also* be picked up. I call this out specifically because Copy/Paste (below) does *not* do this, and I frequently find myself wishing I had used Link rather than Copy/Paste for that reason.

Limitations

- **You cannot link a table in Workbook A to the PowerPivot window from Workbook B.** This only creates a linked table in the PowerPivot window "tied" to the XLSX where the table currently resides.

- **This is *not* a good way to load *large* amounts of data** into PowerPivot. A couple thousand rows is fine. But ten thousand rows or more may cause you trouble and grind your computer to a halt.

- **By default, PowerPivot will update its copy of this table *every* time** you leave the PowerPivot window and come back to it. That happens whether you changed anything in Excel or not, and leads to a delay while PowerPivot re-loads the same data.

- **Linked Tables cannot be scheduled for auto-refresh** on a PowerPivot server. They can only be updated on the desktop. (This is true for PowerPivot v1 and v2. I believe this is no longer true in 2013 but have not yet tried it myself).

- **You cannot subsequently change over to a different source type** – this really isn't a limitation specifically of linked tables. This is true of every source type in this list: whatever type of data source is used to create a table, that table cannot later be changed over to use another type of data source. So if you create a PowerPivot table via Linked Table, you cannot change it in the future to be sourced from a text file, database, or any other source. You will need to delete the table and re-create it from the new source.

It is often very tempting to start building a PowerPivot workbook from an "informal" source like Linked Tables or Copy/Paste, with a plan to switch over and connect the workbook to a more robust source (like a database) later. Resist this temptation whenever possible! If you plan to use a database later, load data from your informal source (like Excel) into that database and then import it from there. The extra step now will save you *loads* of time later.

Tips and Other Notes

- **To work around the "large data" problem,** I often save a worksheet as CSV (comma separated values) and then import that CSV file into PowerPivot. I have imported CSV files with more than 10 million rows in the past.

- **To avoid the delay** every time you return to the PowerPivot window, I highly recommend changing this setting in the PowerPivot window to "Manual"

Figure 11 Change the Update Mode to Manual

Pasting Data Into PowerPivot (Data Source Type)

If you copy a table-shaped batch of data onto the Windows clipboard, this button in the PowerPivot window will light up:

Figure 12 This button could have been named "Paste as New Table"

Advantages

- **You can paste from any table-shaped source** and are not limited to using just Excel (unlike Linked Tables)

- **You can paste from other workbooks** and are not limited to the same workbook as your PowerPivot window

- **Pasted tables support both "Paste/Replace" and "Paste/Append"** as shown by the buttons below:

Figure 13 These paste methods can come in handy

Limitations

- **Suffers from the same "large data set"** drawback as Linked Tables.

- **You can never paste in an additional column.** Once a table has been pasted, its columns are fixed. You can add a calculated column but can never change your mind and add that column you thought you omitted the first time you pasted. This becomes more of a drawback than you might expect.

- **Not all apparently table-shaped sources are truly table-shaped.** Tables on web pages are notorious for this. Sometimes you are lucky and sometimes you are not.

- **Cannot be switched to another data source type** (true of all data source types).

Importing From Text Files (Data Source Type)

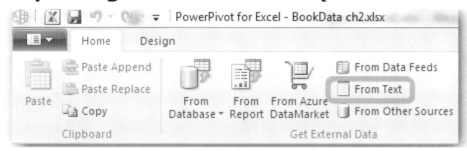

Figure 14 The text import button in the PowerPivot window

Advantages

- **Can handle nearly limitless data volumes**

- **You can add new columns later** (if you are a little careful about it, see below)

- **Text files can be located anywhere** on your hard drive or even on network drives (but not on websites, at least not in my experience). So some backend process might update a text file every night in a fixed location (and filename), for example, and all you have to do is refresh the PowerPivot workbook the next day to pick up the new data.

- ***Can* be switched to point at a different text file,** but still cannot be switched to an entirely different source type (like database).

Limitations

- **No reliable column names** – unlike in a database, text files are not robust with regard to column names. If the order of columns in a CSV file gets changed, that will likely confuse PowerPivot on the next refresh.

- **Cannot be switched to another data source type** (true of all data source types).

Databases (Data Source Type)

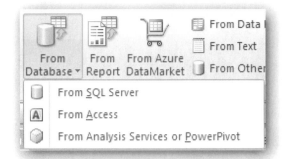

Figure 15 The Database import button in the PowerPivot window

Advantages

- **Can handle nearly limitless data volumes**

- **You can add new columns later**

- **Can be switched to point at a different server, database, table, view, or query.** Lots of "re-pointability" here, but you still can't switch to another data source type.

- **Databases are a great place to add calculated columns.** There are some significant advantages to building calculated columns in the database, and then importing them, rather than writing the calculated columns in PowerPivot itself. This is particularly true when your tables are quite large. We will talk about this later in this chapter.

- **PowerPivot really shines when paired with a good database.** There is just an *incredible* amount of flexibility available when your data is coming from a database. More on this in the following two links.

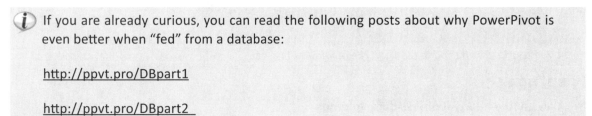

  If you are already curious, you can read the following posts about why PowerPivot is even better when "fed" from a database:

  http://ppvt.pro/DBpart1

  http://ppvt.pro/DBpart2

Limitations

- **Not always an option.** Hey, not everyone has a SQL Server at their disposal, and/or not everyone knows how to work with databases.

- **Cannot switch between database types.** A table sourced from Access cannot later be switched over and pointed to SQL Server. So in reality, these are separate data source types, but they are similar enough that I did not want to add a completely separate section for each.

- **Cannot be switched to another data source type** (true of all data source types).

Less Common Data Source Types

SharePoint Lists

These are great when you have a data source that is maintained and edited by human beings, especially if more than one person shares that editing duty. But if your company does not use SharePoint, this isn't terribly relevant to you.

Only SharePoint 2010 and above can be used as a PowerPivot data source.

The Great PowerPivot FAQ is an example of a public SharePoint list, where myself and others from the community can record the answers to frequently-asked questions, which are then shared with the world. It is located here:

http://ppvt.pro/TheFAQ

Reporting Services (SSRS) Reports

This is another example of "if your company already uses it, it's a great data source," but otherwise, not relevant.

 Only SSRS 2008 R2 and above can be used as a PowerPivot data source.

Cloud Sources Like Azure DataMarket and SQL Azure

Folks, I am a huge, huge, HUGE fan of Azure DataMarket, and they improve it every day. Would you like to cross-reference your sales data with historical weather data for every single store location over the past three years? That data is now easily within reach. International exchange rate data? Yep, that too. Or maybe historical gas prices? Stock prices? Yes and yes. There are *thousands* of such sources available on DataMarket.

I don't remotely have space here to gush about DataMarket, so I will point you to a few posts that explain what it is, how it works, and why I think it is a huge part of our future as Excel Pros. In the second post I explain how you can get 10,000 days of free weather data:

http://ppvt.pro/DataMktTruth

http://ppvt.pro/DataMktWeather

http://ppvt.pro/UltDate

SQL Azure is another one of those "if you are using it, it's relevant, otherwise, let's move on" sources. But like DataMarket, I think most of us will be encountering SQL Azure in our lives as Excel Pros over the next few years.

"Data Feeds"

Data Feeds are essentially a way in which a programmer can easily write an "adapter" that makes a particular data source available such that PowerPivot can pull data from it.

In fact, SharePoint and SSRS (and maybe DataMarket too, I forget) are exposed to PowerPivot via the Data Feed protocol – that is how that source types were enabled "under the hood."

So I am mentioning this here in case your company has some sort of custom internal server application and you want to expose its data to PowerPivot. The quickest way to do that may be to expose that application's data as a data feed, as long as you have a programmer available to do the work.

For more on the data feed protocol, which is also known as OData, see:

http://www.odata.org/

Other Important Features and Tips
Renaming up front – VERY Important!

The names of tables and columns are going to be used everywhere in your formulas. And PowerPivot does NOT "auto-fix" formulas when you rename a table or column! So if you decide to rename things later, you may have a lot of manual formula fixup to do.

And besides, bad table and column names in formulas just make things harder to read. So it's worth investing a few minutes up front to fix things up.

I *strongly* recommend that you get into the habit of "import data, then immediately re-name before doing anything else." It has become a reflex for me. Don't be the person whose formulas reference things like "Column1" and "Table1" ok?

Don't import more columns than you need

I will explain why in a subsequent chapter, but for now just follow this simple rule:

 If you don't expect to use a column in your reports or formulas, don't import it. You can always come back and add it later if needed, unless you are using Copy/Paste.

Table Properties Button

This is a very important button, but it is hiding on the second ribbon tab in the PowerPivot window:

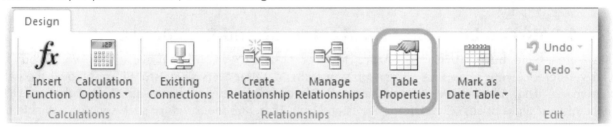

Figure 16 For all data source types other than Linked Tables and Copy/Paste, you will need this button

This button is what allows you to modify the query behind an existing table. So it's gonna be pretty important to you at some point. I know someone who used PowerPivot for two months before realizing that there was a second ribbon tab!

When you click it, it returns you to one of the dialogs you saw in the original import sequence:

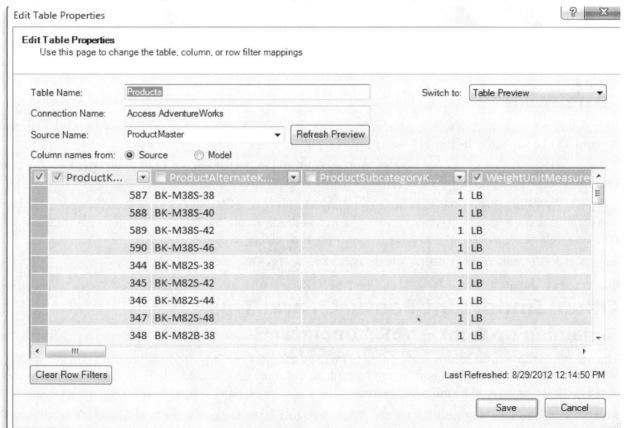

Figure 17 Here you can select columns that you originally omitted, or even switch to using a different table, query, or view in a database

Table Properties button. Don't leave home without it.

Existing Connections Button

Also located on the second ("Design") ribbon tab:

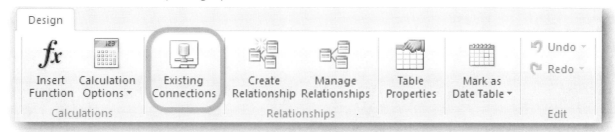

Figure 18 This button will also come in handy

Clicking this brings up a list of all connections previously established in the current workbook:

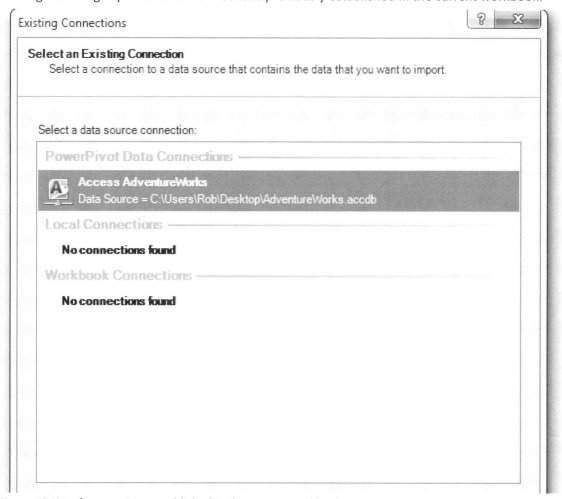

Figure 19 List of connections established in the current workbook

This dialog is important for two reasons:

1. **The Edit button lets you modify existing connections.** In the screenshot above, you see a path to an Access database. If I want to point to a different Access database, I would click Edit here. Same thing if I want to point to a different text file, or if I want to point to a different SQL Server database, etc.

2. **The Open button lets you quickly import a new table from that existing connection.** I *highly* recommend doing this rather than starting over from the "From Database" button on the first ribbon tab. You get to skip the first few screens of the wizard this way, AND you don't litter your workbook with a million connections pointing to the same exact source.

5- Intro to Calculated Columns

Two Kinds of PowerPivot Formulas

When we talk about DAX (the PowerPivot formula language, which you should think of as "Excel Formulas+"), **there are two different places where you can write formulas: Calculated Columns and Measures.**

Calculated Columns are the less "revolutionary" of the two, so let's start there. In this chapter I will introduce the basics of calculated columns, and then return to the topic later for some more advanced coverage.

Adding Your First Calculated Column

You cannot add calculated columns until you have loaded some data. So let's start with a few tables of data loaded into the PowerPivot window:

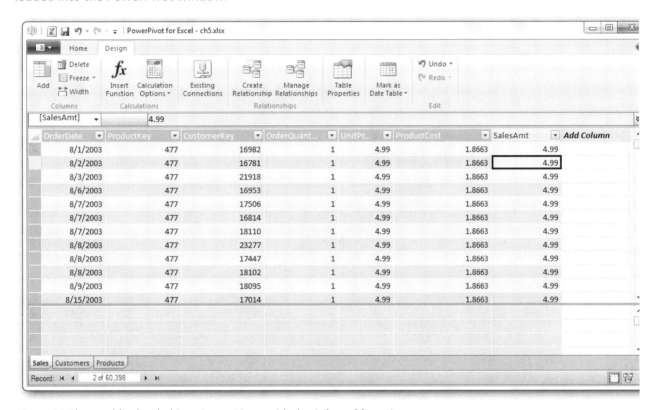

Figure 20 Three tables loaded into PowerPivot, with the Sales table active

Starting a Formula

You see that blank column on the right with the header "Add Column?" Select any cell in that blank column and press the "=" key to start writing a formula:

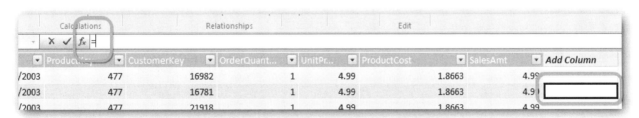

Figure 21 Select any cell in the "Add Column", press the "=" key, and the formula bar goes active

Referencing a Column via the Mouse

Using the mouse, click any cell in the SalesAmt column:

Figure 22 Clicking on a column while in formula edit mode adds a column reference into your formula

Referencing a Column by Typing and Autocomplete

I am going to subtract the ProductCost column from the SalesAmt column, so I type a "-" sign.

Now, to reference the ProductCost column, I type "[" (an open square bracket). See what happens:

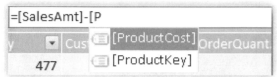

Figure 23 Typing "[" in formula edit mode triggers column name autocomplete

I can now type a "P" to further limit the list of columns:

Figure 24 Typing the first character of your desired column name filters the autocomplete list

Now I can use the up/down arrow keys to select the column name that I want:

Figure 25 Pressing the down arrow on the keyboard selects the next column down

And then pressing the up arrow also does what you'd expect:

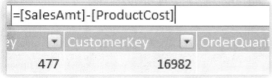

Figure 26 The up arrow selects the next column up

Once the desired column is highlighted, the <TAB> key finishes entering the name of that column in my formula:

=[SalesAmt]-[ProductCost]

Figure 27 <TAB> key enters the selected column name in the formula and dismisses autocomplete

Now press <ENTER> to finish the formula, just like in Excel, and the column calculates:

=[SalesAmt]-[ProductCost]

erKey	OrderQuant...	UnitPr...	ProductCost	SalesAmt	CalculatedColumn1
16982	1	4.99	1.8663	4.99	3.1237
16781	1	4.99	1.8663	4.99	3.1237
21918	1	4.99	1.8663	4.99	3.1237
16953	1	4.99	1.8663	4.99	3.1237
17506	1	4.99	1.8663	4.99	3.1237

Figure 28 Pressing <ENTER> commits the formula. Note the entire column fills down, and the column gets a generic name.

Notice the slightly darker color of the calculated column? This is a really nice feature that is new in v2, and helps you recognize columns that are calculated rather than imported.

Just like Excel Tables!

If that whole experience feels familiar, it is. The Tables feature in "normal" Excel has behaved just like that since Excel 2007. Here is an example:

	F	G	H	I	J	K	L
	Budgeted Sales	**AdjFactor**	**NewCol**				
	71510	40.7%	=[Budgeted Sales] * [				
	190248	40.7%			CalendarYear		
	4183	61.4%			MonthNumberOfYear		
	15429	34.2%			SalesTerritoryRegion		
	7916	62.4%			EnglishProductSubcategoryName		
	31825	35.7%			Budgeted Sales		
	4384	47.5%			AdjFactor		
	36068	1.7%			NewCol		

Figure 29 PowerPivot Autocomplete and column reference follows the precedent set by Excel Tables

OK, the Excel feature looks a bit snazzier – it can appear "in cell" and not just in the formula bar for instance – but otherwise it's the same sort of thing.

Rename the New Column

Notice how the new column was given a placeholder name? It's a good idea to immediately rename that to something more sensible, just like we do immediately after importing data. Right-click the column header of the new column, choose Rename:

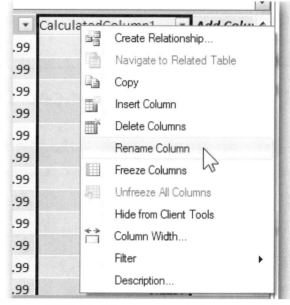

Figure 30 Right click column header to rename column

Reference the New Column in Another Calculation

Calculated columns are referenced precisely the same way as imported columns. Let's add another calculated column with the following formula:

```
=[Margin] / [SalesAmt]
```

And here is the result:

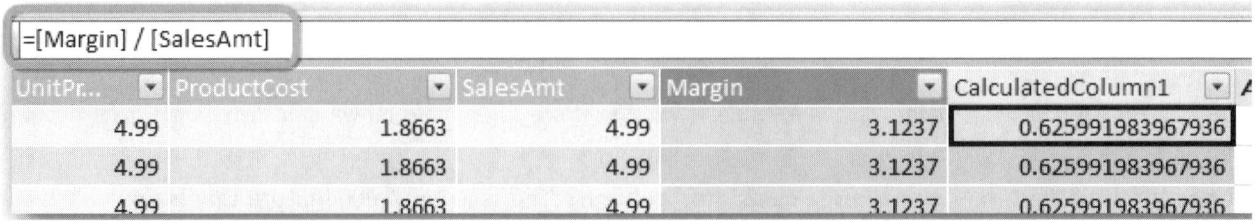

=[Margin] / [SalesAmt]					
UnitPr...	ProductCost	SalesAmt	Margin	CalculatedColumn1	
4.99	1.8663	4.99	3.1237	0.625991983967936	
4.99	1.8663	4.99	3.1237	0.625991983967936	
4.99	1.8663	4.99	3.1237	0.625991983967936	

Figure 31 A second calculated column, again using a simple Excel-style formula and [ColumnName]-style references

> (i) Notice how we referenced the [Margin] column using its new (post-rename) name, as opposed to its original name of [CalculatedColumn1]? In PowerPivot, the column names are not just labels. They also serve the role of named ranges. There isn't one name used for display and another for reference; they are one and the same. This is a good thing, because you don't have to spend any additional time maintaining separate named ranges.

Properties of Calculated Columns

No Exceptions!

Every row in a calculated column shares the same formula. Unlike Excel Tables, you cannot create exceptions to a calculated column. One formula for the whole column. So if you want a single row's formula to behave differently, you have to use an IF().

No "A1" Style Reference

PowerPivot *always* uses named references like [SalesAmt]. There is no A1-style reference in PowerPivot, ever. This is good news, as formulas are much more readable as a result.

Columns are referenced via [ColumnName]. And yes, that means column names can have spaces in them.

Columns can *also* be referenced via 'TableName'[ColumnName]. This becomes important later, but for simple calculated columns within a single table, it is fine to omit the table name.

Tables are referenced via 'TableName'. Single quotes are used around table names. But the single quotes can be omitted if there are no spaces in the table name (meaning that TableName[ColumnName] is also legal, without single quotes, in the event of a "spaceless" table name).

Slightly More Advanced Calculations

Let's try a few more things before moving on to measures.

Function Names Also Autocomplete

Let's write a third calc column, and this time start the formula off with "=SU"...

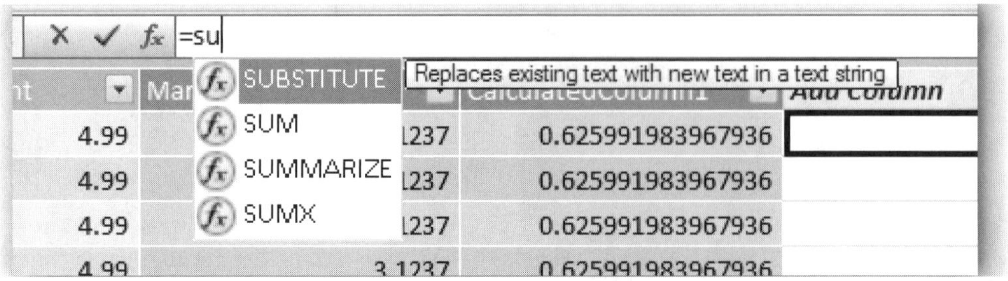

X ✓ fx	=su			
nt	Mar	*fx* SUBSTITUTE	Replaces existing text with new text in a text string	
			CalculatedColumn1	Add Column
4.99		*fx* SUM	.237	0.625991983967936
4.99		*fx* SUMMARIZE	.237	0.625991983967936
4.99		*fx* SUMX	.237	0.625991983967936
4.99			3.1237	0.625991983967936

Figure 32 The names of functions also autocomplete. Note the presence of two familiar functions – SUM() and SUBSTITUTE() – as well as two new ones – SUMMARIZE() and SUMX()

We'll get to SUMMARIZE() and SUMX() later in the book. For now, let's stick with functions we already know from Excel, and write a simple SUM:

=SUM([ProductCost])

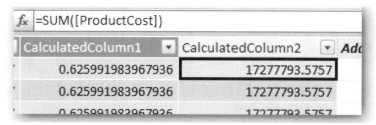

Figure 33 SUM formula summed the entire column

Aggregation Functions Implicitly Reference the Entire Column

Notice how SUM applied to the entire [ProductCost] column rather than just the current row? Get used to that – **aggregation functions like SUM(), AVERAGE(), COUNT(), etc. will *always* "expand" and apply to the entire column.**

Quite a Few "Traditional" Excel Functions are Available

Many familiar faces have made the jump from normal Excel into PowerPivot. Let's try a couple more.

=MONTH([OrderDate])

and

=YEAR([OrderDate])

To receive the following results:

MonthNum	Year	Add
8	2003	
8	2003	
8	2003	
8	2003	
8	2003	

Figure 34 MONTH() and YEAR() functions also work just like they do in Excel

If you'd like to take a quick tour through the function list in PowerPivot, you can do so by clicking the little "fx" button, just like in Excel:

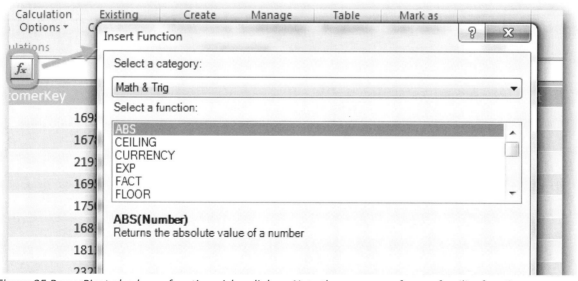

Figure 35 PowerPivot also has a function picker dialog. Note the presence of many familiar functions.

Excel functions are identical in PowerPivot

If you see a familiar function, one that you know from normal Excel, you already know how to use it. It will have the same parameters and behavior as the original function from Excel.

OK, before anyone calls me a liar, I'll qualify the above and say that it's true 99.9% of the time. The keen eye of Bill Jelen has found one or two places where things diverge in small ways, but PowerPivot has done a frankly amazing job of duplicating Excel's behavior, in no small part due to the Excel team helping them out. In most cases, PowerPivot uses exactly the same programming "under the hood" as Excel.

Enough Calculated Columns for Now

There is nothing inherently novel or game changing about calculated columns really. If that were the only calculation type offered by PowerPivot, it would definitely not be analogous to a "Biplane to jetplane" upgrade for Excel Pros.

We will come back to calculated columns a few more times during the course of the book, but first I want to introduce measures, the real game changer.

6- Introduction to DAX Measures

"The Best Thing to Happen to Excel in 20 Years"

That's a quote from Mr. Excel himself, Bill Jelen. He was talking about PowerPivot in general, but specifically measures. So what are measures?

On the surface, you can think of Measures as "formulas that you add to a pivot." But they offer you unprecedented power and flexibility, and their benefits extend *well* beyond the first impression. Several years after I started using PowerPivot professionally, I am still discovering new use cases all the time.

Aside: A Tale of Two Formula Engines

Some of you may already be saying, "hey, pivots have always had formulas."

Why yes, yes they have. Here's a glimpse of the formula dialog that has been in Excel for a long time:

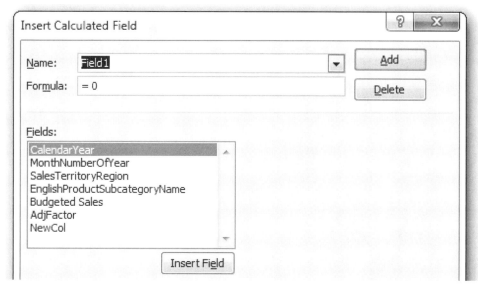

Figure 36 PowerPivot measures mean that you will NEVER use this "historical" pivot formula dialog again (if you ever used it at all)

This old feature has never been all that helpful, nor has it been widely used. (Oh and if you think it has been helpful, great! PowerPivot measures do all of this and much, much more).

It has not been very helpful or widely used because it never received much investment from the Excel team at Microsoft. The Excel pivot formula engine is completely separate from the primary formula engine (the one that is used on worksheets). Whenever it came time for us to plan a new version of Excel, we had to decide where to spend our engineering budget. The choice between investing development budget in features that everyone sees, like the worksheet formula engine, versus investing in a relatively obscure feature like this, was never one which required much debate. The pivot formula engine languished, and never really improved.

Remember the history of PowerPivot though? How I said it sprang from the longstanding SSAS product? Well, SSAS is essentially one big pivot formula engine. So now, all at once, we have a pivot formula engine that is the result of nearly 20 years of continuous development effort by an entire engineering team. Buckle up :-)

Adding Your First Measure

There are two places where you can add a measure:

1. **In the Excel window** (attached to a pivot)
2. **In the PowerPivot window** (in the measure grid). Note that this is called Calculation Area in the UI but I call it the measure grid since it only contains measures.

29

I highly recommend starting out with the first option – in the Excel window, attached to a pivot, because that gives you the right context for validating whether your formula is correct.

Create a Pivot

With that in mind, I use the pivot button on the ribbon in the PowerPivot window.

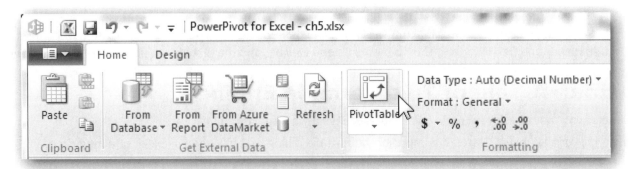

Figure 37 Creating a pivot

> (i) I could also use the similar button on the PowerPivot ribbon tab in the Excel window – they do exactly the same thing. I do NOT recommend using the pivot buttons on the Insert tab of the Excel window however, as that leads to a different experience.

This yields a blank pivot on a new worksheet:

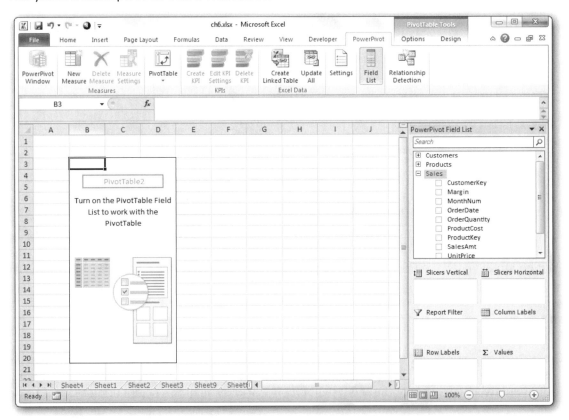

Figure 38 Blank pivot

Notice how the pivot field list contains all three tables from the PowerPivot window?

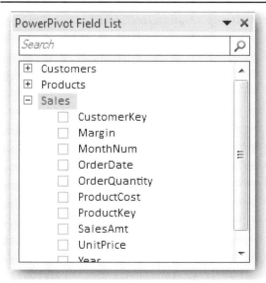

Figure 39 Every table from the PowerPivot window is available in the field list

For now, we are going to ignore the other tables and just focus on Sales. Exploring the advantages of multiple tables is covered later on.

Add a Measure!

I'm going to click the New Measure button on the PowerPivot ribbon tab in Excel:

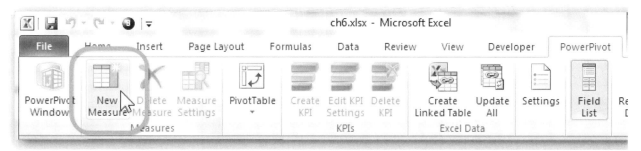

Figure 40 New Measure Button

This brings up the Measure Settings dialog, which I will often refer to as the measure editor, or often as just "the editor."

> (i) In Excel 2013, "Measures" are no longer called "Measures." They are now called "Calculated Fields," taking over the name of the old (and much more limited) feature that I made fun of at the beginning of this chapter. I'm pretty sure I will call them "measures" forever, and I will continue to use that word in this book. In the meantime though, here's the entry point on the Excel 2013 ribbon.

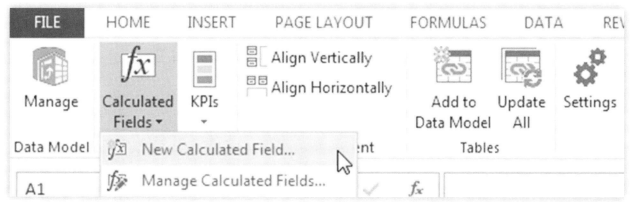

Figure 41 The equivalent entry point in Excel 2013, where Measures are now called Calculated Fields. This leads to the same editor (below) as the original "New Measure" button in PowerPivot V1 and V2.

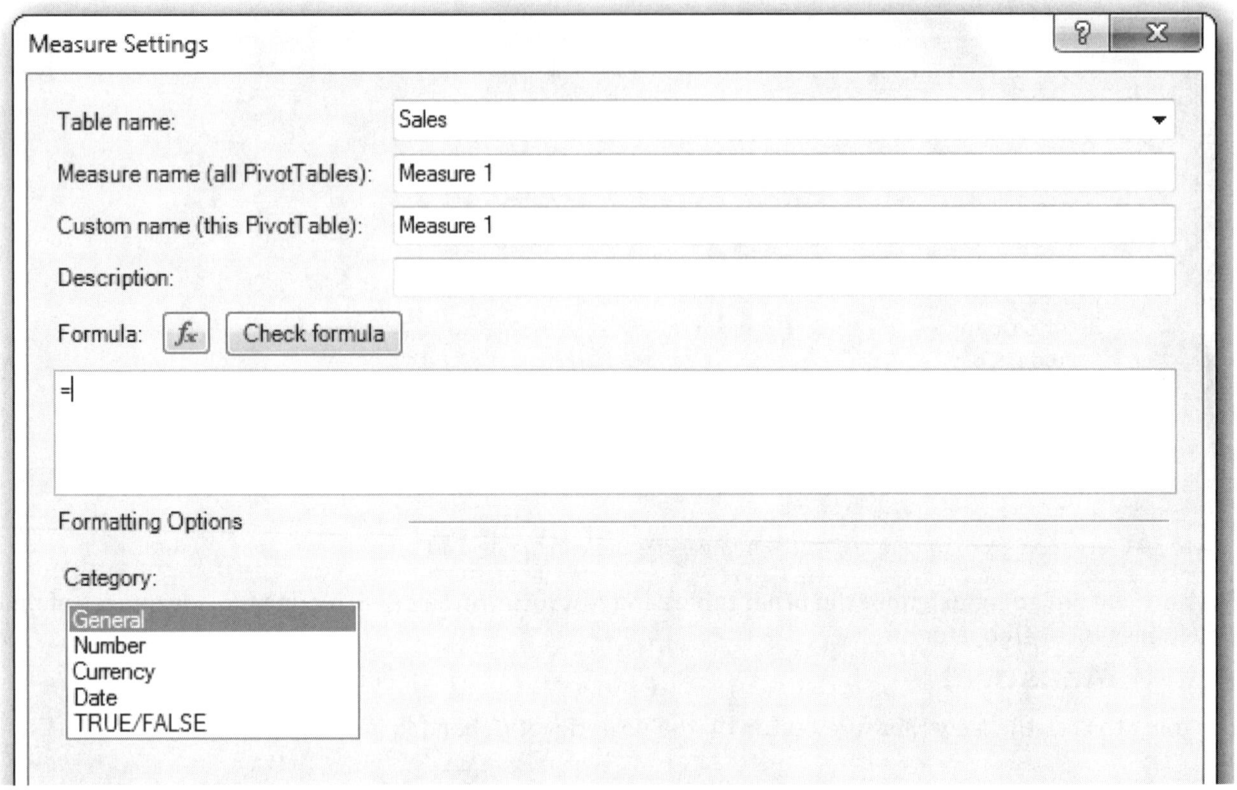

Figure 42 Measure Settings, also known as the Measure Editor, or The Editor :-)

There's a lot going on in this dialog, but for now let's ignore most of it and just write a simple formula:

```
=SUM(Sales[SalesAmt])
```

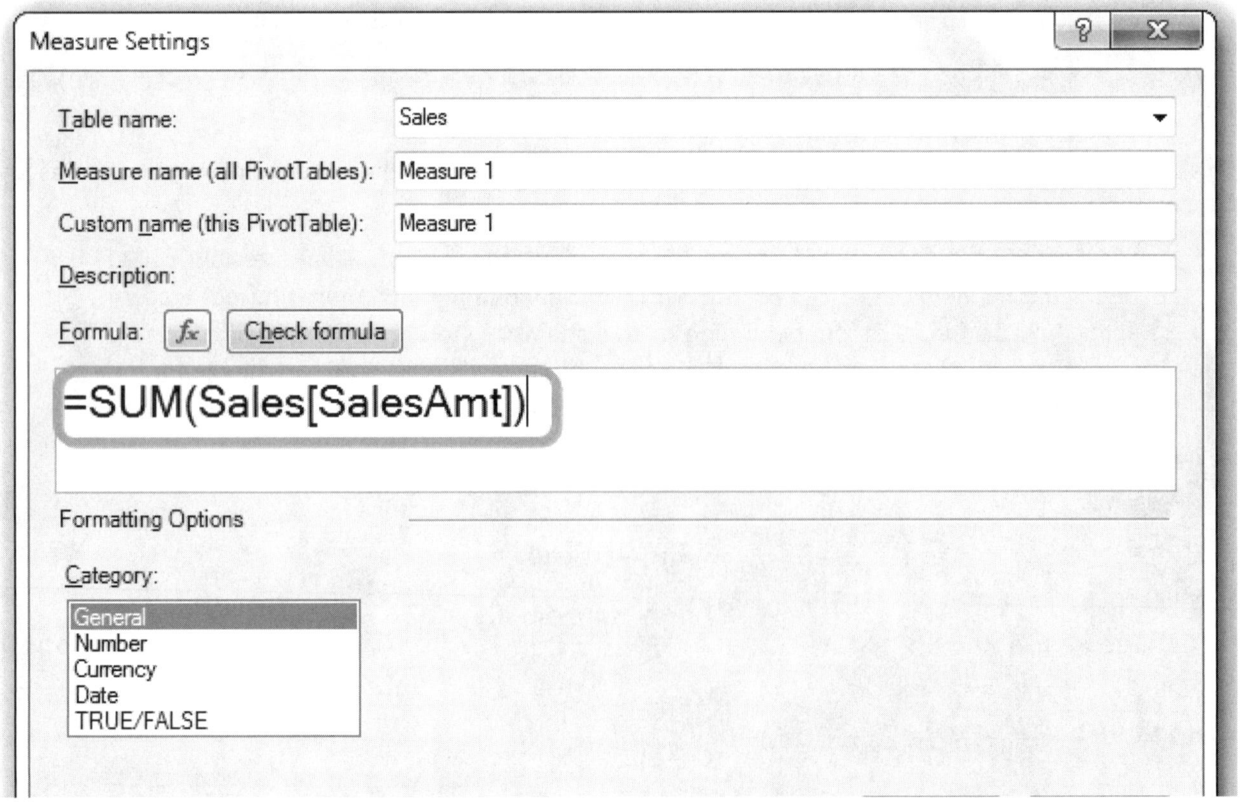

Figure 43 Entering a simple measure formula

Name the Measure

Before clicking OK, I will give the measure a name. This is just as important as giving sensible names to tables and columns.

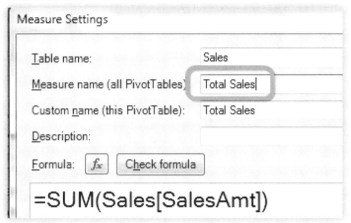

Figure 44 It is very important to give the measure a sensible name

 The "Measure name" box is the one you want to fill in. Ignore the "Custom name" box for now – that will automatically match what you enter in the "Measure name" box.

Results

Click OK, and I get:

Figure 45 The resulting pivot

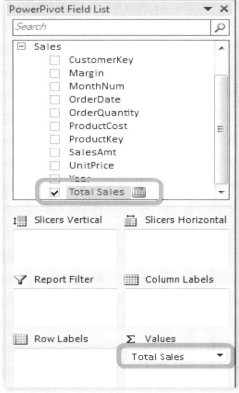

Figure 46 New checkbox added to the field list for the measure, and measure added to Values dropzone

Works As You Would Expect

Let's do some "normal pivot" stuff. I'll going to drag MonthNum to Rows and Year to Columns, yielding:

Total Sales	Column Labels				
Row Labels	2001	2002	2003	2004	Grand Total
1		596746.5568	438865.1718	1340244.95	2375856.679
2		550816.694	489090.3356	1462479.83	2502386.86
3		644135.2022	485574.7923	1480905.18	2610615.175
4		663692.2868	506399.2654	1608750.53	2778842.082
5		673556.1978	562772.5645	1878317.51	3114646.272
6		676763.6496	554799.2281	1949361.11	3180923.988
7	473388.163	500365.155	886668.84	50840.63	1911262.788
8	506191.6912	546001.4708	847413.51		1899606.672
9	473943.0312	350466.9912	1010258.13		1834668.152
10	513329.474	415390.2333	1080449.58		2009169.287
11	543993.4058	335095.0887	1196981.11		2076069.605
12	755527.8914	577314.0002	1731787.77		3064629.662
Grand Total	3266373.657	6530343.526	9791060.298	9770899.74	29358677.22

Figure 47 MonthNum field on Rows, Year on Columns, Total Sales Measure just "does the right thing"

OK, our first measure is working well. Let's take stock of where we stand before moving on.

"Implicit" versus "Explicit" Measures

We have done nothing special so far, we are just laying the groundwork. I mean, a simple SUM of the SalesAmt column is something I always could have done in normal pivots.

In fact, I can uncheck the [Total Sales] measure and then just click the [SalesAmt] checkbox, and get precisely the same results as before:

Figure 48 Unchecked the [Total Sales] measure, checked the [SalesAmt] checkbox

Total Sales	Column Labels ▼				
Row Labels ▼	2001	2002	2003	2004	Grand Total
1		596746.5568	438865.1718	1340244.95	2375856.679
2		550816.694	489090.3356	1462479.83	2502386.86
3		644135.2022	485574.7923	1480905.18	2610615.175
4		663692.2868	506399.2654	1608750.53	2778842.082
5		673556.1978	562772.5645	1878317.51	3114646.272
6		676763.6496	554799.2281	1949361.11	3180923.988
7	473388.163	500365.155	886668.84	50840.63	1911262.788
8	506191.6912	546001.4708	847413.51		1899606.672
9	473943.0312	350466.9912	1010258.13		1834668.152
10	513329.474	415390.2333	1080449.58		2009169.287
11	543993.4058	335095.0887	1196981.11		2076069.605
12	755527.8914	577314.0002	1731787.77		3064629.662
Grand Total	3266373.657	6530343.526	9791060.298	9770899.74	29358677.22

Figure 49 Yields the same exact pivot results

 Just like in normal pivots, if you check the checkbox for a numerical column, that will default to creating a SUM in the Values area of the field list. And checking a non-numeric field will place that field on Rows by default.

So we have two ways to "write" a SUM in PowerPivot – we can write a formula using the Measure Editor, or we can just check the checkbox for a numeric column.

I have my own terms for this:

1. **Explicit Measure** – a measure I create by writing a formula in the Editor
2. **Implicit Measure** – what I get when I just check a numeric column's checkbox

Turns out, I have a very strong opinion about which of these is better.

 I never, ever, EVER create implicit measures! Even if it's a simple SUM that I want, I *always* fire up the measure editor, write the formula, and give the measure a sensible name. I think it is important that checking a numeric checkbox does what it does, because that matches people's expectations from normal Excel. But that does not mean you should do it! Trust me on this one, you want to do things explicitly. There are too many benefits to the explicit approach. You will not see me create another implicit measure in this book. They are dead to me :-)

Referencing Measures in Other Measures

I'll show you one reason why I prefer explicit measures right now.

Another Simple Measure First

First, let me create another simple SUM measure, for Margin:

=SUM(Sales[Margin])

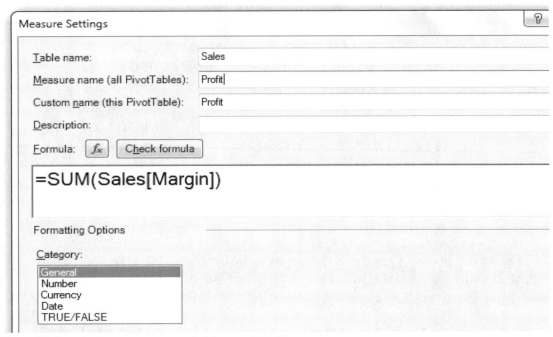

Figure 50 Creating a new measure, that I named Profit

Figure 51 Profit measure added to field list

Row Labels	2001 Total Sales	2001 Profit	2002 Total Sales	2002 Profit	2003 Total Sales	2003 Profit	2004 Total Sales	2004 Profit	Total Total Sales	Total Profit
1			596746.557	240320.91	438865.172	183728.206	1340245	554959.023	2375856.679	979008.139
2			550816.694	219507.52	489090.336	205186.474	1462479.8	604917.116	2502386.86	1029611.11
3			644135.202	259370.475	485574.792	203897.055	1480905.2	612934.286	2610615.175	1076201.82
4			663692.287	267392.109	506399.265	212618.101	1608750.5	662243.34	2778842.082	1142253.55
5			673556.198	271926.439	562772.565	238672.303	1878317.5	779974.147	3114646.272	1290572.89
6			676763.65	273032.243	554799.228	235050.708	1949361.1	806300.87	3180923.988	1314383.82
7	473388.163	190967.542	500365.155	202013.054	886668.84	362115.145	50840.63	28365.7176	1911262.788	783461.459
8	506191.6912	203872.516	546001.471	221445.745	847413.51	353404.118			1899606.672	778722.379
9	473943.0312	188489.502	350466.991	142096.9	1010258.13	420575.209			1834668.152	751161.611
10	513329.474	206121.74	415390.233	172136.184	1080449.58	449117.105			2009169.287	827375.029
11	543993.4058	218924.75	335095.089	136436.673	1196981.11	496559.426			2076069.605	851920.849
12	755527.8914	303229.82	577314	241171.901	1731787.77	711809.271			3064629.662	1256210.99
Grand Total	3266373.657	1311605.87	6530343.53	2646850.15	9791060.3	4072733.12	9770899.7	4049694.5	29358677.22	12080883.6

Figure 52 Profit measure added to pivot, along with Total Sales measure

Creating a Ratio Measure

OK, time for some fun. Here's a new measure:

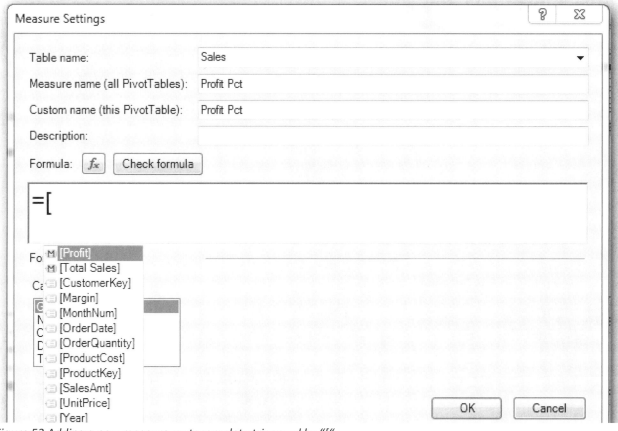

Figure 53 Adding a new measure, autocomplete triggered by "["

Do you see the first item in the autocomplete list? Zooming in:

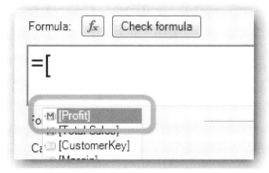

Figure 54 The [Profit] measure appears in autocomplete!

There's even a little "M" icon, for measure, next to [Profit] in the autocomplete.

[Total Sales] is also in there, so let's try:

```
=[Profit] / [Total Sales]
```

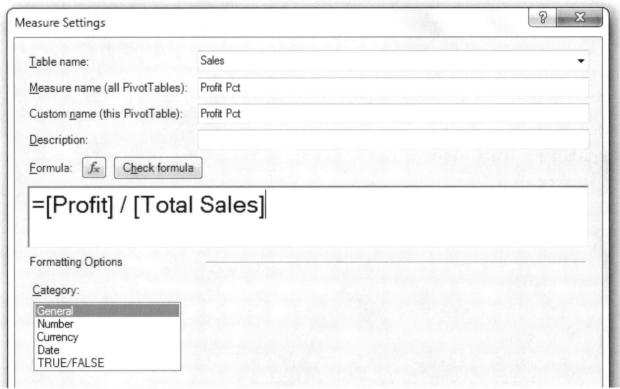

Figure 55 Measures can reference other measures, useful for creating things like ratios and percentages (and a million other things)

Original Measures do NOT Have to Remain on the Pivot

I'll click OK now and create this new [Profit Pct] measure, but then I'll uncheck the other two measures so we just see [Profit Pct] in the pivot:

Profit Pct	Column Labels				
Row Labels	2001	2002	2003	2004	Grand Total
1		0.402718553	0.418643851	0.414072833	0.412065318
2		0.398512831	0.41952674	0.413624246	0.411451613
3		0.402664648	0.41990865	0.413891648	0.412240696
4		0.402885666	0.419862579	0.411650736	0.411053783
5		0.403717522	0.424100815	0.415251491	0.414356167
6		0.403438103	0.423668052	0.413623143	0.413208183
7	0.403405824	0.403731259	0.408399539	0.55793403	0.40991823
8	0.402757532	0.405577196	0.417038569		0.409938747
9	0.397704976	0.405450167	0.416304701		0.409426419
10	0.401538877	0.414396319	0.415676135		0.41179956
11	0.40244008	0.407158079	0.41484316		0.410352739
12	0.40134828	0.417748228	0.411025694		0.409906295
Grand Total	**0.401548019**	**0.405315607**	**0.415964461**	**0.414464851**	**0.411492778**

Figure 56 [Profit Pct] measure displayed by itself – its two "ancestor" measures are not required on the pivot

Changes to "Ancestor" Measures Flow Through to Dependent Measures

Let's simplify the pivot a bit, and put the [Profit] measure back on:

Row Labels	Profit Pct	Profit
1	0.412065318	979008.1385
2	0.411451613	1029611.111
3	0.412240696	1076201.816
4	0.411053783	1142253.551
5	0.414356167	1290572.89
6	0.413208183	1314383.821
7	0.40991823	783461.4593
8	0.409938747	778722.3793
9	0.409426419	751161.6111
10	0.41179956	827375.029
11	0.410352739	851920.8486
12	0.409906295	1256210.991
Grand Total	**0.411492778**	**12080883.65**

Figure 57 Removed [Year] from Columns, added [Profit] measure back

Let's focus just on that first row for a moment:

Row Labels	Profit Pct	Profit
1	0.412065318	979008.1385

Figure 58 About 41% for [Profit Pct], and 979k for [Profit]

What happens if we modify the formula for the [Profit] measure? Let's find out.

Right click the [Profit] measure in the field list and choose Edit formula:

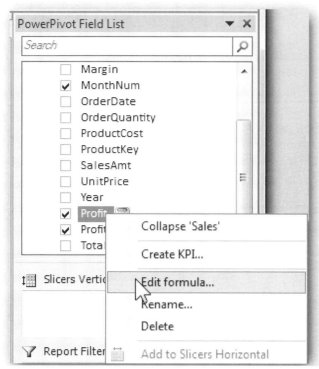

Figure 59 It is easy to open a measure to edit its formula

Now let's do something silly. Let's just arbitrarily boost our profits by 10%, by multiplying the original SUM formula by 1.1:

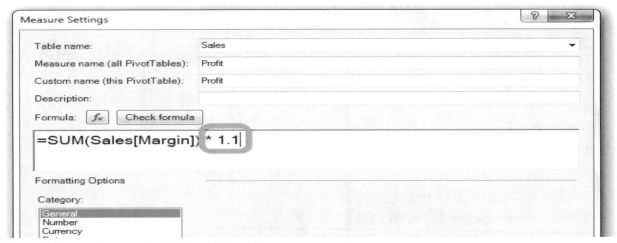

Figure 60 You would never do this in real life, unless you are, say, Enron

Click OK and let's look at the first row in the pivot again:

Figure 61 [Profit] is now 10% higher, as expected. But that ALSO impacted [Profit Pct], since [Profit Pct] is based in part on [Profit].

Cases Where This Makes Real Sense

The model we're working with here is pretty simple at the moment, and lacks things like Tax, Shipping, and Discount. It's not hard to imagine defining [Profit] or [Total Sales] in ways that include/exclude those other miscellaneous amounts, and sometime later (perhaps much later) realizing that you need to change that.

In fact, it might just be a change in the business that triggers you to change your definition of [Total Sales] – it is not necessary that you made a mistake!

You may ultimately find yourself with literally dozens of measures (if not hundreds) that all depend back to more fundamental measures. Those dependencies can even run many "layers" thick – [X] depends on [Y] which depends on [Z] etc.

When you realize that you have hundreds of impacted calculations, but you only need to change a single formula to fix EVERYTHING, it is a glorious moment indeed.

It's worth driving this point home, so I will restate it: Imagine having an entire suite of sophisticated Excel reports that all assume a certain calculation method for Profit and Sales. And then something fundamental changes, rendering that approach invalid. You could be performing spreadsheet surgery for days, perhaps weeks. If you use PowerPivot properly, that same situation might only take a few seconds to address.

 The first time you experience this "I fix one thing and everything is updated" moment, you will know that your life has changed. How often do you find statements like that in a book about *formulas*? I'm guessing never, but it's the truth :-)

Don't "Redefine" Measures!

In order to reap the benefit outlined above, it's important to use the names of measures in formulas rather than the formula that defined the original measure.

For instance, these two formulas for [Profit Pct] would return the same results:

```
=SUM(Sales[Margin]) / SUM(Sales[SalesAmt])
```

would yield the same results as:

```
=[Profit] / [Total Sales]
```

But only the second approach gives you the "fix once, benefit everywhere" payoff. So act accordingly.

 Instinctively, I expected that tying everything tightly together like this, building "trees" of measures that depend on other measures, sometimes in layers, would lead to inflexibility and problems later on. In practice, that has never been the case. It has been all benefit in my experience.

Related: if you discover places where you need, for example, a Sales measure that is calculated differently, the right approach is just to define a second Sales measure with an appropriate name, such as [Sales – No Tax] or [Sales Incl Commissions], etc. That works splendidly. Seriously, I am smiling as I type this.

Other Fundamental Benefits of Measures

There are a few more benefits that no chapter titled "Intro to Measures" would be complete without. Let's cover those quickly before continuing.

Use in Any Pivot

Up until now I have just been working with a single pivot. But if I create a brand-new pivot, guess what? All of the measures I created on that first pivot are still available in my new pivot!

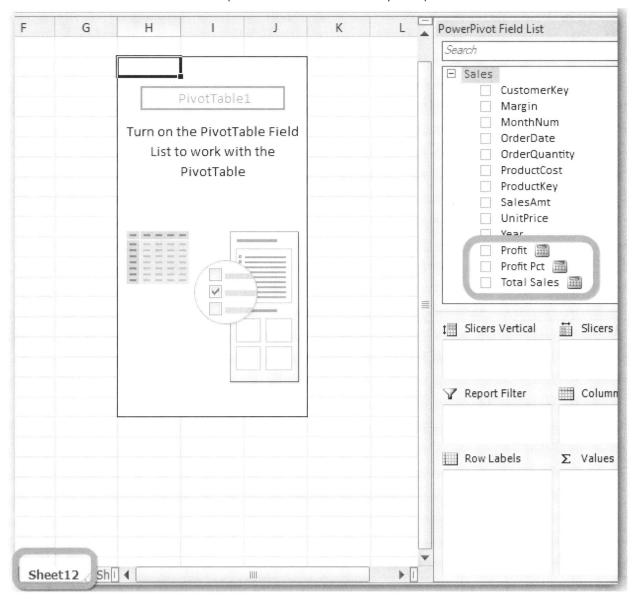

Figure 62 New pivot, new worksheet, but the measures are still available for re-use!

Centrally-defined Number Formatting

So far, I've been looking at ugly-formatted measures. Let's add all three measures to this new pivot to illustrate:

Profit	Total Sales	Profit Pct
13288972.01	29358677.22	0.452642056

Figure 63 Unformatted measures in my pivot

I can always use Format Cells, or even better, Number Format, to change this:

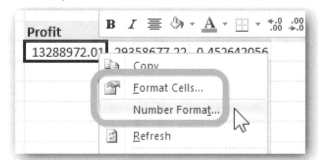

Figure 64 These two ways to format numbers in a pivot are SO antiquated! Be gone!

Instead, let's bring up the measure editor for one of these measures:

Figure 65 Setting [Profit] to be formatted as Currency, with 0 decimal places

The results are the same as if I had used Format Cells or Number Format:

Profit	Total Sales	Profit Pct
$13,288,972	29358677.22	0.452642056

Figure 66 [Profit] measure is now formatted nicely in the pivot, just as if I had used Format Cells or Number Format.

But that format now applies everywhere! Let's return to my previous pivot and Refresh it:

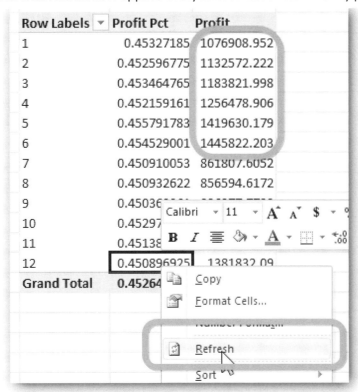

Figure 67 I return to the first pivot, where [Profit] is still formatted "ugly," and choose Refresh

The pivot picks up the new formatting!

Row Labels	Profit Pct	Profit
1	0.45327185	$1,076,909
2	0.452596775	$1,132,572
3	0.453464765	$1,183,822
4	0.452159161	$1,256,479
5	0.455791783	$1,419,630
6	0.454529001	$1,445,822
7	0.450910053	$801,808
8	0.450932622	$856,595
9	0.450369061	$826,278
10	0.452979516	$910,113
11	0.451388013	$937,113
12	0.450896925	$1,381,832
Grand Total	0.452642056	$13,288,972

Figure 68 Currency formatting on [Profit] now shows up on original pivot, too

> ⓘ A refresh is not strictly required. Any manipulation of the other pivot will cause the formatting to be "picked up." Reorder fields, click a slicer, click a "+" to drill down, etc. – all of these will cause the formatting to be picked up.

Now let's set a percentage format on the [Profit Pct] measure:

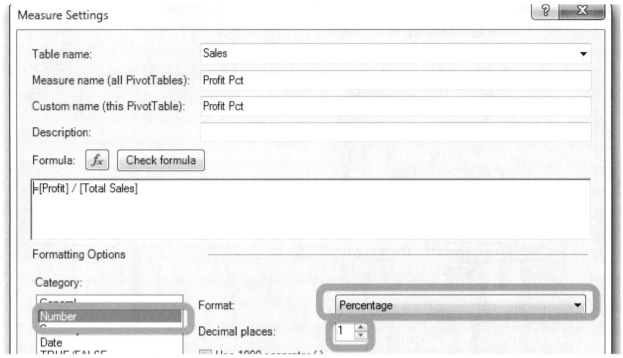

Figure 69 Formatting as Number, Percentage, 1 Decimal Place

The results are as expected:

Row Labels ▾	Profit Pct	Profit
1	45.3 %	$1,076,909
2	45.3 %	$1,132,572
3	45.3 %	$1,183,822
4	45.2 %	$1,256,479
5	45.6 %	$1,419,630
6	45.5 %	$1,445,822
7	45.1 %	$861,808
8	45.1 %	$856,595
9	45.0 %	$826,278
10	45.3 %	$910,113
11	45.1 %	$937,113
12	45.1 %	$1,381,832
Grand Total	**45.3 %**	**$13,288,972**

Figure 70 Percentage format? Check.

Whetting Your Appetite: COUNTROWS() and DISTINCTCOUNT()

This chapter is running a bit long, but hey, there's a lot of value to convey. And I still want to end with some "sizzle."

Let's use a couple of new functions to define two measures:

```
[Transactions] =
COUNTROWS(Sales)
```

and

```
[Days Selling] =
DISTINCTCOUNT(Sales[OrderDate])
```

When you see me use the syntax [Foo] = <formula>, that means I am creating a new measure named [Foo], with that formula. That way I don't have to show screenshots of the Measure Editor every time I add a measure.

Let's see what that looks like:

Row Labels ▼	Total Sales	Days Selling	Transactions
1	$2,375,857	93	5,017
2	$2,502,387	85	5,059
3	$2,610,615	93	5,178
4	$2,778,842	90	5,589
5	$3,114,646	93	6,064
6	$3,180,924	90	6,080
7	$1,911,263	124	4,019
8	$1,899,607	92	4,256
9	$1,834,668	89	4,229
10	$2,009,169	92	4,536
11	$2,076,070	90	4,536
12	$3,064,630	93	5,835
Grand Total	$29,358,677	1124	60,398

Figure 71 [Transactions] and [Days Selling] – introduction to COUNTROWS() and DISTINCTCOUNT()

COUNTROWS(Sales)

This function does exactly what it sounds like – it returns the number of rows in the table you specify. So for instance, in the figure above, there are 5,017 rows in the Sales table that have a MonthNum of 1.

 I named this measure [Transactions] only because I know that each row in my Sales table is a transaction. But if a single transaction were spread across multiple rows, I couldn't do that. I'd have to use COUNTDISTINCT() against a Transaction ID column, which I don't have in this example.

DISTINCTCOUNT(Sales[OrderDate])

Again, this function does what it sounds like it does. It returns the number of distinct (unique) values of the column you specify.

So while there are 5,017 rows for MonthNum 1, and all of them obviously have a value for the [OrderDate] column, there are only 93 different unique values for [OrderDate] in those 5k rows.

Deriving More Useful Measures From These Two

Now I define two more measures that depend on the two measures above.

```
[Sales per Transaction] =
[Total Sales] / [Transactions]
```

and

```
[Sales per Day] =
[Total Sales] / [Days Selling]
```

Results:

Row Labels ▾	Total Sales	Days Selling	Transactions	Sales per Transaction	Sales per Day
1	$2,375,857	93	5,017	$473.56	$25,547
2	$2,502,387	85	5,059	$494.64	$29,440
3	$2,610,615	93	5,118	$504.17	$28,071
4	$2,778,842	90	5,589	$497.20	$30,876
5	$3,114,646	93	6,064	$513.63	$33,491
6	$3,180,924	90	6,080	$523.18	$35,344
7	$1,911,263	124	4,019	$475.56	$15,413
8	$1,899,607	92	4,256	$446.34	$20,648
9	$1,834,668	89	4,229	$433.83	$20,614
10	$2,009,169	92	4,536	$442.94	$21,839
11	$2,076,070	90	4,536	$457.69	$23,067
12	$3,064,630	93	5,835	$525.22	$32,953
Grand Total	$29,358,677	1124	60,398	$486.09	$26,120

Figure 72 Two meaningful business measures – can't do these in normal pivots!

Rearrange Pivot, Measures Automatically Adjust!

I remove MonthNum from Rows, drag ProductKey on instead, then drag Year to slicers and select 2002:

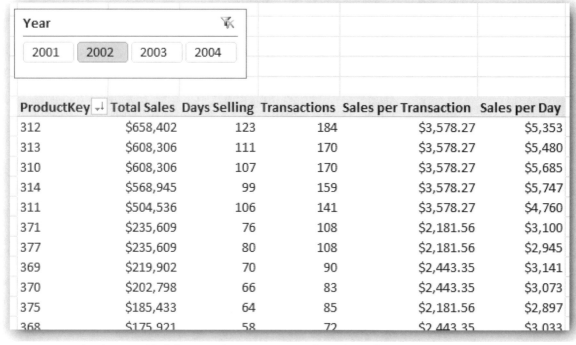

ProductKey ↓	Total Sales	Days Selling	Transactions	Sales per Transaction	Sales per Day
312	$658,402	123	184	$3,578.27	$5,353
313	$608,306	111	170	$3,578.27	$5,480
310	$608,306	107	170	$3,578.27	$5,685
314	$568,945	99	159	$3,578.27	$5,747
311	$504,536	106	141	$3,578.27	$4,760
371	$235,609	76	108	$2,181.56	$3,100
377	$235,609	80	108	$2,181.56	$2,945
369	$219,902	70	90	$2,443.35	$3,141
370	$202,798	66	83	$2,443.35	$3,073
375	$185,433	64	85	$2,181.56	$2,897
368	$175,921	58	72	$2,443.35	$3,033

Figure 73 Completely scrambled the pivot, but my measure formulas still work!

Measures Are "Portable Formulas"

Stop and think about that "rearrange the pivot and the formulas still work" point for a moment. Let's say your workgroup originally requested a report that displayed Sales per Day and Sales per Transaction, grouped by Month.

How would you build that report in normal Excel? You couldn't just write formulas in a pivot. You'd have to do some pretty serious formula alchemy to get it working.

And those formulas, in normal Excel, would be very much "hardwired" to the "I want to see it by month" requirement.

Then some executive sees the report, loves it, and says "Wow, if only I could see this grouped by Product instead!"

Switching the normal Excel report over to be grouped by Product rather than Month (and sliceable by Year) would *not* be a modification. That would be starting from scratch, in many ways, and rebuilding the entire report.

With PowerPivot, you just drag fields around in the field list.

 This is why I often describe measures as "portable formulas" – they can be used in many different contexts without needing to be rewritten. "Write once, use anywhere" is another way to say it. And even just the ability to re-use the same formula on another worksheet, in another pivot, by just clicking a checkbox, is a stunning example of portability. As your measure formulas become more sophisticated and powerful, this benefit becomes more and more impactful.

I even wrote a guest post for the official Excel blog on this topic, if you are interested:

http://ppvt.pro/PortableFormulas

But before we go any further, we need to talk about how measures actually *work*.

7- The "Golden Rules" of DAX Measures

How Does the DAX Engine Arrive at Those Numbers?

In the previous chapter I showed you a bunch of examples of measures, displayed in various-shaped pivots. And of course, the numbers displayed in all of those cases are accurate.

Since we're writing some pretty interesting formulas in pivots now, we need to take a quick step back and reflect, just a little bit, about how pivots work behind the scenes.

 On an instinctive level, I'm pretty sure you already understand everything I'm going to explain in this chapter, but your understanding is informal and "loose." What we need to do is take your informal understanding and make it crisper. We need to put it into words.

For instance, if I asked you what the highlighted cell in this pivot "means," I'm pretty sure you will immediately have an answer.

Row Labels	Profit	Total Sales	Profit Pct
2001	$287,087	$652,367	44.0 %
312	$236,794	$547,475	43.3 %
328	$2,831	$6,292	45.0 %
344	$47,462	$98,600	48.1 %
2002	$337,581	$768,886	43.9 %
312	$284,772	$658,402	43.3 %
328	$5,347	$11,885	45.0 %
344	$47,462	$98,600	48.1 %
Grand Total	$624,668	$1,421,253	44.0 %

Figure 74 Question: Can you explain what the $98,600 "means?"

Let's make this multiple choice. Choose Answer A or Answer B:

- **Answer A:** "$98,600 worth of product 344 was sold in the year 2001."

- **Answer B:** "When you filter the Sales table to just the rows where Year=2001 and ProductKey=344, then sum up the SalesAmt column over those remaining rows, you get $98,600."

I bet you chose A. Am I right? Yeah, I'm right. Don't lie to me. Unless you have actually merged with Excel over the years to form a cyborg calculator, you still think more like a person than a machine. And people think like Answer A.

But Answer B is *exactly* how the DAX engine arrived at the $98,600 number. So learning to think that way, just a little bit, is a goal of this chapter.

 It's important for you to get comfortable thinking about measures the way the DAX engine thinks about them - like Answer B. Thinking like a human (Answer A) is still important, too, and even when writing measures it's going to be ok most of the time. That's because most of the time, your measure formula just works the first time you write it. But when your measure formula doesn't do what you expect, you usually have to think "the DAX way" (Answer B) in order to fix it.

Teaching you to "think like DAX" is essentially the point of this chapter. Don't worry if you haven't grasped this yet, I'm going to break it down a few ways for you.

Stepping Through That Example

Let's step through that same "98,600" example from above, this time in the PowerPivot window so that we have a picture at each step.

Here's the Sales table:

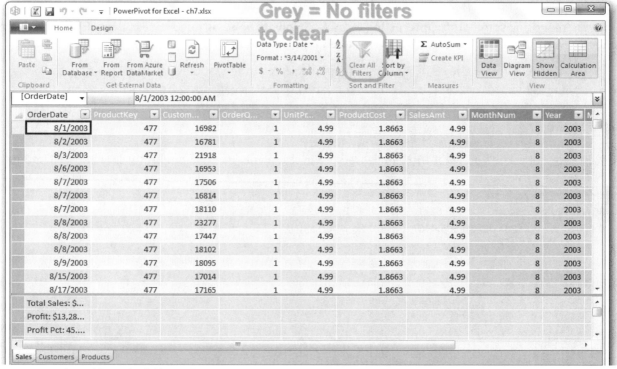

Figure 75 Sales table with all filters cleared

There are three elements of this window I'd like to call out.

1. **The "Clear All Filters" Button on the Ribbon.** Highlighted in the picture above. When this is greyed out like this, you know there are no filters applied on the current table.

2. **The row count readout.** Pictured here, it shows there are 60,398 rows in the Sales table when all filters are cleared.

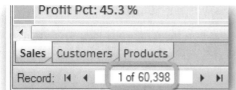

Figure 76 Row Count Readout: 60,398 rows are currently being displayed in the Sale table.

3. **The measure grid (the three cells at the bottom of the table).** Let's widen the first column so we can see what those were.

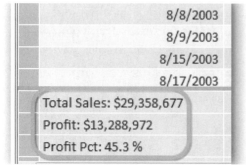

Figure 77 Our three measures from the pivot also appear here, in the Measure Grid.

This area at the bottom of the table is called the Measure Grid. This feature is new in v2, and I'm not sure I like it very much yet. But it's superb for demonstrating "the DAX way," so we're gonna use it here to great effect.

All right, let's filter Year to be 2001:

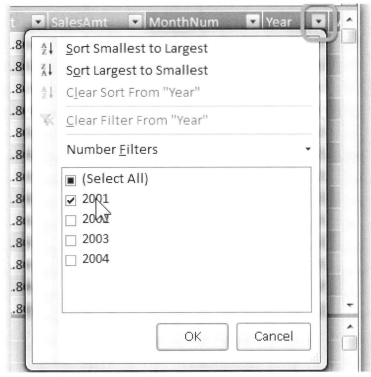

Figure 78 Filtering to Year=2001

After the filter is applied, let's check out the measure grid and row readout:

Figure 79 Sales have dropped from $27M to $3.2M, row count dropped from 60k to 1k

OK, now let's apply the ProductKey=344 filter and then check the same stuff:

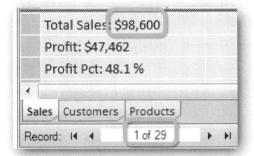

Figure 80 With both filters applied, we get the $98,600 number (the sum of SalesAmt from 29 rows)

Hey hey! It matches the pivot!

Notice that [Profit] is displaying as $47,462 and [Profit Pct] as 48.1%? Those were the numbers in the pivot as well:

Row Labels ⊤	Profit	Total Sales	Profit Pct
⊟ 2001	$287,087	$652,367	44.0 %
312	$236,794	$547,475	43.3 %
328	$2,831	$6,292	45.0 %
344	$47,462	$98,600	48.1 %
⊟ 2002	$337,581	$768,886	43.9 %
312	$284,772	$658,402	43.3 %
328	$5,347	$11,885	45.0 %
344	$47,462	$98,600	48.1 %
Grand Total	$624,668	$1,421,253	44.0 %

Figure 81 [Profit] and [Profit Pct] in the pivot also match up to what we see in the filtered Measure Grid.

Hey, where are our other measures? If we make the measure grid taller, we see that they are here too:

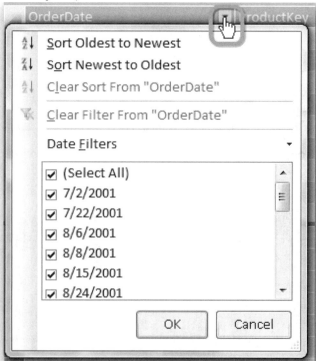

Figure 82 All of our measures are here. Note that [Transactions] = 29, which is also what the row readout tells us.

Do you think the [Days Selling] = 18 number is correct? Of course it is, but double checking it is a good excuse to show you another trick I use a lot. I dropdown the OrderDate filter:

Figure 83 Scroll through this list and count how many dates show up. (Hint: there are 18).

Dropping down the filters in the PowerPivot window is a very helpful trick. It will only show you the values that are "legal" in the context of the filters applied to all other columns at the moment, just like in normal Excel Autofilter. This trick is especially useful for seeing whether there are any Blank values in this column once the other column filters are respected. (Even when there are too many values in the column, and you see the "Not all items shown" warning, the Blanks checkbox will show up if there are blanks, and if it's missing, you know there are none).

Enough examples. I promised you some Golden Rules, and Golden Rules I will deliver.

Translating the Examples Into Three Golden Rules

I've been teaching these, that I call the Golden Rules of DAX measures, for a few years now. They serve as the foundation – once you understand these, most everything that follows will be simple and incremental.

 When you are reading these rules, I encourage you to reference back to the examples above to help clarify what the rules mean.

Rule A: DAX Measures Are Evaluated Against the Source Tables, NOT the Pivot

It is very tempting to think that the Grand Total cell at the bottom of a pivot is the sum of the cells above it, but that is NOT the way it is calculated. As far as DAX is concerned, the fact that the Grand Total matches the sum of the numbers above it borders on *coincidence*.

So when you are thinking about how to construct a measure formula, or are debugging one that isn't quite working, **visualize the underlying table in the PowerPivot window, because the DAX engine is doing its work in that context.**

For an example of this, we need look no further than the age-old problem of "the average of averages is meaningless."

Row Labels	Profit	Total Sales	Profit Pct
⊟ 2001	$287,087	$652,367	44.0 %
312	$236,794	$547,475	43.3 %
328	$2,831	$6,292	45.0 %
344	$47,462	$98,600	48.1 %
⊟ 2002	$337,581	$768,886	43.9 %
312	$284,772	$658,402	43.3 %
328	$5,347	$11,885	45.0 %
344	$47,462	$98,600	48.1 %
Grand Total	$624,668	$1,421,253	44.0 %

Does NOT Match

Average: 45.5 % Count: 6 Sum: 272.8 %

Figure 84 The six selected cells' Average is 45.5% but the pivot Grand Total is 44.0% - only a calculation against the individual rows in the Sales table will yield the right result.

Rule B: Each Measure Cell is Calculated Independently

When thinking about how your measure is calculated, it is best to think "one cell at a time."

Month	Profit
1	$1,076,909
2	$1,132,572
3	$1,183,822
4	$1,256,479
5	$1,419,630
6	$1,445,822
7	$861,808
8	$856,595
9	$826,278
10	$910,113
11	$937,113
12	$1,381,832
Grand Total	**$13,288,972**

Figure 85 The DAX engine may not calculate in precisely this 1-4 order, but you should think that it does

So, pick a cell and visualize how it was calculated, as if it were an island.

 The value in one measure cell NEVER impacts the value in another measure cell. The measures are calculated independently, and calculated against the source table(s). See Rule 1 :-)

Rule C: DAX Measures Are Evaluated in Three Phases
Phase One: Detect Filters.

Before the DAX engine even *looks* at your formula, it detects the "coordinates" of the current measure cell in the pivot.

To illustrate this, let's use a slightly "richer" pivot:

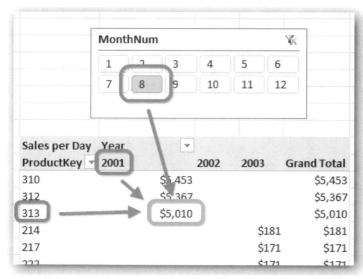

Figure 86 The selected measure cell has three "coordinates" – MonthNum=8, Year=2001, and ProductKey=313.

A measure cell's set of filter coordinates is often referred to as its **Filter Context**

Phase Two: Apply Those Filter Coordinates to the Underlying Tables

Those coordinates (the filters in the filter context) are then applied to the underlying tables. (You never see this filtering of course- because it happens behind the scenes).

Phase Three: Evaluate the Arithmetic

Once the filter context of a measure cell (determined by its coordinates in the pivot) has been used to filter the underlying table(s), ONLY THEN is the arithmetic in your formula evaluated.

In other words, your SUM() or COUNTROWS() function doesn't run until the filter context has been applied to the source table(s).

 To summarize Rule C, each measure cell in the pivot is evaluated in three phases: Detect Filters, apply those filters, *then* run the arithmetic.

The Three Phases of Rule C "Visualized"

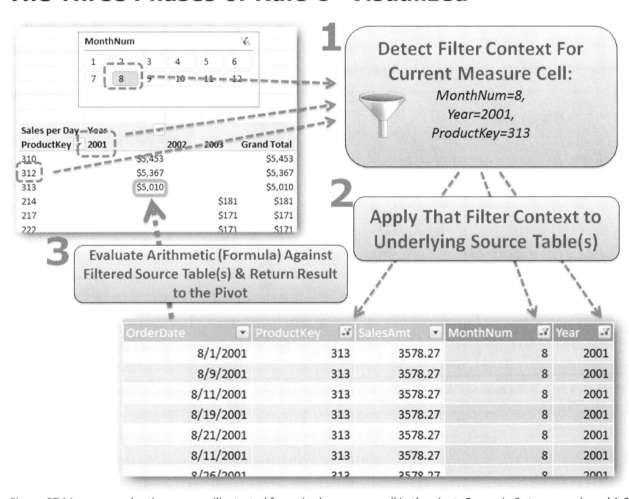

Figure 87 Measure evaluation process illustrated for a single measure cell in the pivot: Occurs in 3 steps, numbered 1-3.

A Few More Tips

No "Naked Columns" in Measure Formulas

When you reference a column in a measure formula, it always has to be "wrapped" in some sort of function. A "naked" reference to a column will yield an error in a measure. Let's take a look at an example:

```
[My New Measure] =

Sales[Margin]
```

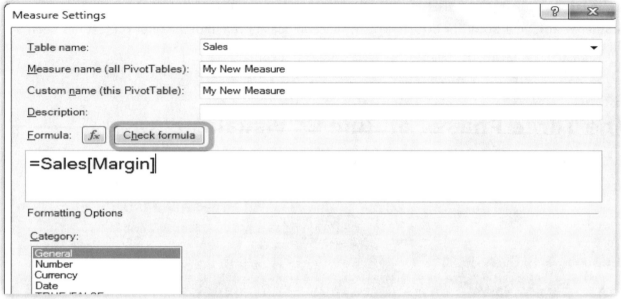

Figure 88 I enter a "naked" column reference into the measure editor, then click Check Formula...

Figure 89 ...leading to a relatively cryptic error message.

Let's look at that error message:

"Calculation error in measure 'Sales'[My New Measure]: The value for column 'Margin' in table 'Sales' cannot be determined in the current context. Check that all columns referenced in the calculation expression exist, and that there are no circular dependencies."

Not a great error message. It really should be more helpful. But when you see this error, in your head you should translate this to be "I have a naked column reference somewhere."

 "Cannot be determined in the current context" should become a trigger phrase for you to think "I have a naked column reference somewhere in my measure formula."

But all of the following would be valid:

```
=SUM(Sales[Margin])

=AVERAGE(Sales[Margin])

=MIN(Sales[Margin])

=MAX(Sales[Margin])

...
```

Any aggregation function will do. Think of it this way: pivots are, by their nature, aggregation devices. They take sets of rows and turn them into more compact numerical results. Referencing "naked columns" is what calculated column formulas do. **Measure are aggregations, and they don't accept naked column references on their own.**

 Remember, naked column references are OK in calculated columns. This rule only applies to *measures*.

Best Practice: Reference Columns and Measures Differently

Whenever I am writing a measure formula,

- **To reference a column, I *include* the table name:** TableName[ColumnName]
- **To reference a measure, I *omit* the table name:** [MeasureName]

I do this so that my formulas are more readable. If I see a reference with a table name preceding it, I know immediately that it's a column, and if I see a reference that lacks a table name, I know it's a measure.

Additionally, there are many situations in which omitting the table name on a column reference will return an error. Following this best practice avoids that issue as well.

Best Practice: Assign Measures to the Right Tables

The "Table name" box in the measure editor controls which table the measure will be assigned to in the field list.

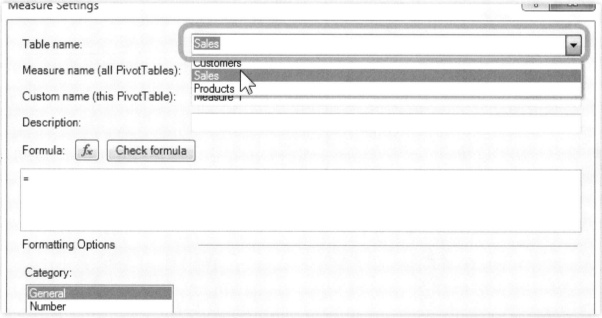

Figure 90 If you set this dropdown to the Sales table...

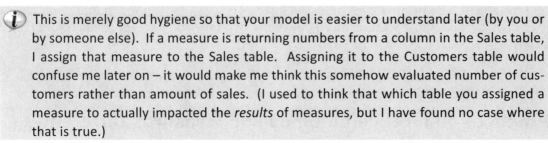

Figure 91 ...the measure will be "parented" to the Sales table in the field list.

Simple Rule: I assign my measures to the tables that contain the numeric columns used in the formula.

>  This is merely good hygiene so that your model is easier to understand later (by you or by someone else). If a measure is returning numbers from a column in the Sales table, I assign that measure to the Sales table. Assigning it to the Customers table would confuse me later on – it would make me think this somehow evaluated number of customers rather than amount of sales. (I used to think that which table you assigned a measure to actually impacted the *results* of measures, but I have found no case where that is true.)

8- CALCULATE() – Your New Favorite Function

A Supercharged SUMIF()

Have you ever used the Excel function SUMIF(), or perhaps its newer cousin, SUMIFS()?

I describe CALCULATE() as "the SUMIF/SUMIFS you always wish you'd had." You are going to love this function, because it works wonders.

In case you are one of the pivot pros who managed to skip SUMIF() and SUMIFS() in normal Excel, they are both very useful functions: they sum up a column you specify, but filter out rows that don't fit the filter criteria you specify in the formula. So for instance, you can use SUMIF to sum up a column of Sales figures, but only for rows in the table where the Year column contains 2012.

Does that sound familiar? It sounds a lot like the Golden Rules from the prior chapter – "filter, then arithmetic." An interesting similarity, and CALCULATE() continues in that same tradition.

Anyway, CALCULATE() is superior to SUMIF() and SUMIFS() in three fundamental ways:

1. **It has cleaner syntax.** This is the smallest of the three advantages, but it *feels* good. And a *happier* formula writer is a *better* formula writer.

2. **It is an "anything" IF, and not limited to SUM/COUNT/AVERAGE.** There is no MAXIF() function in Excel for instance. That always bugged me. Nor is there a MINIF(), and there is definitely no STDEV-IF(). CALCULATE() is literally unlimited – it allows you to take *any* aggregation function (or even a complex multi-function expression!) and quickly produce an IF version of it.

3. **It can be used in pivots** (as part of a measure), which normal SUMIF() cannot.

CALCULATE() Syntax

 CALCULATE(<measure expression>, <filter1>, <filter2>, ...)

Ex: CALCULATE(SUM(Sales[Margin]), Sales[Year]=2001)

Ex: CALCULATE([Sales per Day], Sales[Year]=2002, Sales[ProductKey]=313)

CALCULATE() In Action – A Few Quick Examples

Let's start with a simple pivot. Year on rows, [Total Sales] measure on values:

Year	Total Sales
2001	$3,266,374
2002	$6,530,344
2003	$9,791,060
2004	$9,770,900
Grand Total	**$29,358,677**

Figure 92 Simple pivot – the basis for our first foray into CALCULATE()

OK, let's add a new measure, one that is always filtered to Year=2002:

```
[2002 Sales] =
    CALCULATE([Total Sales], Sales[Year]=2002)
```

Three things to note in this formula:

1) I used the name of a measure for the <measure expression> argument of CALCU-LATE. Any expression that is legal for a measure is ok there – that includes the name of a pre-defined measure, or any formula expression that could be used to define a measure.

2) In the <filter> argument, 2002 is *not* in quotes. That's because the Year column is numeric. If it were a text column, I would have needed to use ="2002" instead.

3) I only used one <filter> argument this time, but I could use as many as I want in a single CALCULATE formula.

And the results:

Year	Total Sales	2002 Sales
2001	$3,266,374	$6,530,344
2002	$6,530,344	$6,530,344
2003	$9,791,060	$6,530,344
2004	$9,770,900	$6,530,344
Grand Total	$29,358,677	$6,530,344

Figure 93 Our new measure matches the original measure's 2002 value in every situation!

Do those results surprise you? I bet they are *close* to what you expected, but maybe not exactly. You might have expected years 2001 and 2003 to display zeroes for our new measure, and you might be scratching your head a bit about the grand total cell, but otherwise, having the new measure always return the 2002 value from the original measure is probably pretty instinctive.

It's not very often that I write a CALCULATE measure that filters against a column that is also on the pivot (Sales[Year] in this case). That seldom makes any real-world sense. I just started out like this so you can see that the $6,530,344 number matches up.

So to make this a bit more realistic, let's take Year off of the pivot and put MonthNum on there instead:

MonthNum	Total Sales	2002 Sales
1	$2,375,857	$596,747
2	$2,502,387	$550,817
3	$2,610,615	$644,135
4	$2,778,842	$663,692
5	$3,114,646	$673,556
6	$3,180,924	$676,764
7	$1,911,263	$500,365
8	$1,899,607	$546,001
9	$1,834,668	$350,467
10	$2,009,169	$415,390
11	$2,076,070	$335,095
12	$3,064,630	$577,314
Grand Total	$29,358,677	$6,530,344

Figure 94 A more sensible example pivot in which to use that same CALCULATE measure

This probably makes even more sense than the prior pivot. The grand total is still that $6.5M number, but every other cell returns a distinct number – the sales from 2002 matching the MonthNum from the pivot.

This is the sales for month 2 (Feb) of 2002

All 12 cells selected sum to our "magic" $6.5M number, and matches grand total

Year	▼	Total Sales	2002 Sales
1		$2,375,857	$596,747
2		$2,502,387	$550,817
3		$2,610,615	$644,135
4		$2,778,842	$663,692
5		$3,114,646	$673,556
6		$3,180,924	$676,764
7		$1,911,263	$500,365
8		$1,899,607	$546,001
9		$1,834,668	$350,467
10		$2,009,169	$415,390
11		$2,076,070	$335,095
12		$3,064,630	$577,314
Grand Total		$29,358,477	$6,530,344

et7 / Sheet6 / Sheet12 / Sheet11

Average: $544,195   Count: 12   Sum: $6,530,344

Figure 95 Previous results examined: each month of 2002 is returned separately, and the grand total matches all of 2002. Exactly what we want and expect!

How CALCULATE() Works

Now that we've looked at a couple of examples, let's examine how CALCULATE() truly works, because that will clear up the handful of somewhat unexpected results in that first example.

There are three key points to know about CALCULATE(), specifically about the <filter> arguments:

1. **The <filter> arguments operate during the "filter" phase of measure calculation.** They modify the filter context provided by the pivot – this happens before the filters are applied to the source tables, and therefore also before the arithmetic phase.

2. **If a <filter> argument acts on a column that IS already on the pivot, it will *override* the pivot context for that column.** So in our first example above, the pivot is "saying" that Sales[Year]=2001, but I have Sales[Year]=2002 in my CALCULATE(), so the pivot's "opinion" of 2001 is completely overridden by CALCULATE(), and becomes 2002. That is why even the 2001 and 2003 cells (and the grand total cell) in the first example returned the 2002 sales number.

3. **If a <filter> argument acts on a column that is NOT already on the pivot, that <filter> will purely *add* to the filter context.** In our second example, where we had Sales[MonthNum] on the pivot but not Sales[Year], the Sales[Year]=2002 filter was applied on top of the Month context coming in from the pivot, and so we received the intersection – 2002 sales for month 1, 2002 sales for month 2, etc.

So it might be time to revise that diagram from last chapter, to add step 1a:

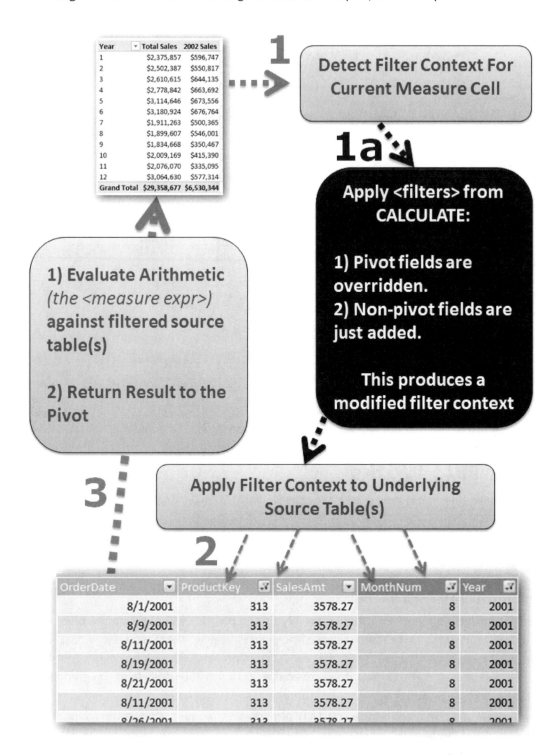

Figure 96 The DAX Golden Rules Diagram from last chapter: revised to include CALCULATE()'s impact on filter context

Two Useful Examples of CALCULATE( )

The [2002 Sales] measure that I have been using as an example so far is a good way to show you how CAL-CLATE() works, but it might not seem terribly useful. So let me show you two quick examples that are much more broadly applicable.

Example 1: Transactions of a Certain Type

Here is one that I see all the time in the retail sales business: not all transactions are normal sales. Some businesses record many different transaction types including "Normal Transaction," "Refund," and "Promotional Sales Transaction."

My database has a column for that, so I went ahead and imported it into my Sales table (using Table Properties). Here, we see that it has three values:

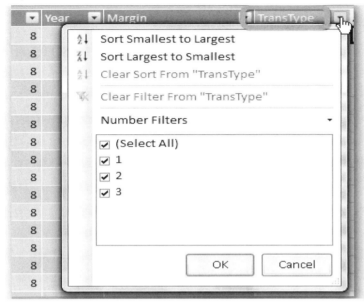

Figure 97 My newly-imported TransType column

I now want to write four new measures, defined here in English:

- **"Regular" Sales** – Just transactions of type 1

- **"Promotional" Sales** – Just transaction of type 3

- **"Refunds"** – transactions of type 2, expressed as a negative number

- **"Net Sales"** – Regular plus Promotional sales, less Refunds

Now, here are the formulas for each:

```
[Regular Sales] =
  CALCULATE([Total Sales], Sales[TransType]=1)


[Promotional Sales] =
  CALCULATE([Total Sales], Sales[TransType]=3)


[Refunds] =
  CALCULATE([Total Sales], Sales[TransType]=2) * -1


[Net Sales] =
  [Regular Sales] + [Promotional Sales] + [Refunds]
```

> (i) Note that my treatment of [Refunds] assumes that refunds are recorded as positive values in my Sales table. If they were recorded as negative values, I would remove the multiplication by -1 from the [Refunds] measure.

Results:

Row Labels	Normal Sales	Promo Sales	Refunds	Net Sales
2001	$2,235,112	$505,235	($526,027)	$2,214,320
2002	$4,677,472	$915,346	($937,525)	$4,655,293
2003	$6,965,623	$1,441,621	($1,383,817)	$7,023,427
2004	$6,906,155	$1,480,472	($1,384,273)	$7,002,355
Grand Total	$20,784,362	$4,342,674	($4,231,642)	$20,895,394

Figure 98 All four measures added to pivot, with Year on rows

Neat huh?

And then continuing down Practical Road, let's see what percentage of our sales are due to us running promotional campaigns:

```
[Pct Sales on Promo] =

 [Promotional Sales] / ([Regular Sales] + [Promotional Sales])
```

Results:

Row Labels	Normal Sales	Promo Sales	Refunds	Net Sales	Pct Sales on Promo
2001	$2,235,112	$505,235	($526,027)	$2,214,320	18.4 %
2002	$4,677,472	$915,346	($937,525)	$4,655,293	16.4 %
2003	$6,965,623	$1,441,621	($1,383,817)	$7,023,427	17.1 %
2004	$6,906,155	$1,480,472	($1,384,273)	$7,002,355	17.7 %
Grand Total	$20,784,362	$4,342,674	($4,231,642)	$20,895,394	17.3 %

Figure 99 Highlighted measure tells us what percentage of our sales dollars come from promotional campaigns

Example 2: Growth Since Inception

I'm going to define a new "base" measure that tracks how many customers were active in a given timeframe:

```
[Active Customers] =

DISTINCTCOUNT(Sales[CustomerKey])
```

 "Base measure" is how I refer to measures that do not refer to other measures, and are pure arithmetic like the one above.

And now a measure that always tells me how many customers were active in 2001 (my first year in business):

```
[2001 Customers] =

CALCULATE([Active Customers], Sales[Year]=2001)
```

Results:

Year	Active Customers	2001 Customers
2001	1013	1013
2002	2677	1013
2003	9309	1013
2004	11377	1013
Grand Total	18484	1013

Figure 100 Active customers by year, and active customers for 2001 specifically

And then a measure that tells me percentage growth in customer base since 2001:

```
[Customer Growth Since 2001] =

([Active Customers]-[2001 Customers]) / [2001 Customers]
```

Results:

Year	Active Customers	2001 Customers	Customer Growth Since 2001
2001	1013	1013	0.0 %
2002	2677	1013	164.3 %
2003	9309	1013	819.0 %
2004	11377	1013	1023.1 %
Grand Total	**18484**	**1013**	**1724.7 %**

Figure 101 Percentage growth in customer base since 2001

Alternatives to the "=" Operator in <filters>

In a <filter> argument to CALCULATE(), you are not limited to the "=" operator. You can also use:

- < (Less than)
- > (Greater than)
- <= (Less than or equal to)
- >= (Greater than or equal to)
- <> (Not equal to)

Evaluation of Multiple <filters> in a Single CALCULATE()

All of the <filter> arguments in a single CALCULATE() behave as if they are wrapped in an AND() function. In other words, a row must match every <filter> argument in order to be included in the calculation.

If you need an "OR()" style of operation, you can use the "||" operator. For instance:

```
CALCULATE([Total Sales], Sales[TransType]=1 ||
                         Sales[TransType]=3)
```

 When you use the || operator like this, it can only be used between comparisons on a single column – TransType in this case. You cannot use || between comparisons that operate on different columns, such as TransType and Year.

The "ALL" (aka "Unfiltered") Filter Context

That [Active Customers] measure provides an opportunity to explain how the Grand Total cell works in the pivot.

Let's look at the pivot again:

Figure 102 Sum of all years is MUCH higher than the Grand Total cell

A perfect example of why it's important to think about the measures evaluating against the source table(s) rather than in the pivot itself. Also, we've talked a lot about filter context to this point, but so far, we have not discussed the filter context of the grand total cell.

It's pretty simple actually: the grand total cell represents the *absence* of a filter. In the context of that cell, it's as if the Year field is not even *on* the pivot.

To drive this home, let's remove Year from the pivot:

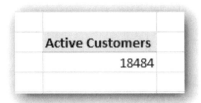

Figure 103 Remove Year from the pivot, and the result matches the Grand Total cell from when Year IS on the pivot. This is not an accident!

It makes sense: some of our customers from 2001 stuck around and bought things in 2002 (and later), and some 2002 customers similarly persisted into 2003. If we summed the individual totals for each year, we'd count those "carryover" customers more than once (and end up with 24,376). But when we clear the Year filter, the DISTINCTCOUNT(Sales[CustomerKey]) arithmetic runs against an unfiltered table, and only counts each customer once! We end up with 18,484, which is the correct answer.

 Don't skip the paragraph above. The world won't end if you *do* skip it, but it's worth more attention than the average un-bolded text :-)

Not all Totals Are Completely (or Even Partially) Grand

To clarify, let's drag Year to Columns, and add MonthNum to rows:

Active Customers	Year				
MonthNum	2001	2002	2003	2004	Grand Total
1		188	244	1777	2132
2		171	272	1794	2167
3		199	272	1879	2260
4		207	294	1981	2418
5		214	335	2145	2621
6		214	321	2135	2596
7	146	253	511	931	1817
8	156	281	1509		1926
9	146	198	1553		1885
10	161	229	1624		1991
11	169	193	1634		1971
12	235	330	2037		2532
Grand Total	1013	2677	9309	11377	18484

Year=ALL, MonthNum=1

Year=2001, MonthNum=ALL

Year=ALL, MonthNum=ALL

Figure 104 Filter context for three different kinds of grand totals – total across Years, total across MonthNums, and total across both.

Every total in a pivot is really just the *absence* of one or more filters – a place where one or more of the pivot fields does not apply, as if the field were completely absent from the pivot.

As you add more fields to rows and columns, you get many different variations of totals. For instance, nothing really changes when you nest one field under another. Let's nest MonthNum under Year on Rows as an example:

Figure 105 Nesting does not really change anything. Note the subtotal for 2002 (2677) was a grand total cell when Year was on Columns (in the previous pivot).

 The physical location of a measure cell in the pivot is *not* important. Only its "coordinates" are important. A filter context of Year=2002, Month=ALL is exactly the same to the DAX engine, no matter where the Year and MonthNum fields were located – rows, columns, report filters, or slicers.

9- ALL() – The "Remove a Filter" Function

Given where the last chapter left off, this sure seems like a great time to introduce the ALL() function.

In fact, given last chapter's section on the "ALL" filter context, and the title of this chapter, you can probably already guess most everything you need to know about the ALL() function. So I won't bore you with long-winded explanations of the basics. I will keep it crisp and practical.

The Crisp Basics

The ALL() function is used within a CALCULATE(), as one of the <filter> arguments, to remove a filter from the filter context.

Let's jump straight to an example. Consider the following pivot: [Net Sales] displayed by MonthNum, with Year on a slicer:

Month	Net Sales
1	$325,923
2	$384,359
3	$332,465
4	$364,024
5	$458,236
6	$346,219
7	$675,507
8	$570,071
9	$783,861
10	$756,351
11	$807,463
12	$1,218,949
Grand Total	$7,023,427

Year slicer: 2001, 2002, 2003 (selected), 2004

Figure 106 We will use this pivot to demonstrate the usage of ALL().

OK, time for a new measure:

```
[All Month Net Sales] =
    CALCULATE([Net Sales], ALL(Sales[MonthNum]))
```

And the results:

Month	Net Sales	All Month Net Sales
1	$325,923	$7,023,427
2	$384,359	$7,023,427
3	$332,465	$7,023,427
4	$364,024	$7,023,427
5	$458,236	$7,023,427
6	$346,219	$7,023,427
7	$675,507	$7,023,427
8	$570,071	$7,023,427
9	$783,861	$7,023,427
10	$756,351	$7,023,427
11	$807,463	$7,023,427
12	$1,218,949	$7,023,427
Grand Total	$7,023,427	$7,023,427

Year slicer: 2001, 2002, 2003 (selected), 2004

Figure 107 Because ALL() removed the filter from MonthNum, every measure cell in the right column has precisely the same filter context (coordinates) as the grand total in the left column

 I suppose you can also think of ALL() as a means by which to "reference" one of the total cells in a pivot, as long as you also understand that fundamentally, what you are doing is clearing/removing a filter from the filter context.

The Practical Basics – Two Examples

Time for a couple of examples of where ALL() is useful.

Example 1 – Percentage of Parent

Let's do a simple ratio of the two measures already on the pivot:

```
[Pct of All Month Net Sales] =

    [Net Sales] / [All Month Net Sales]
```

Results:

Month	Net Sales	All Month Net Sales	Pct of All Month Net Sales
1	$325,923	$7,023,427	4.6 %
2	$384,359	$7,023,427	5.5 %
3	$332,465	$7,023,427	4.7 %
4	$364,024	$7,023,427	5.2 %
5	$458,236	$7,023,427	6.5 %
6	$346,219	$7,023,427	4.9 %
7	$675,507	$7,023,427	9.6 %
8	$570,071	$7,023,427	8.1 %
9	$783,861	$7,023,427	11.2 %
10	$756,351	$7,023,427	10.8 %
11	$807,463	$7,023,427	11.5 %
12	$1,218,949	$7,023,427	17.4 %
Grand Total	$7,023,427	$7,023,427	100.0 %

Year: 2001 2002 **2003** 2004

Figure 108 New measure returns each month's contribution to the "all month" total

We can remove the original ALL measure from the pivot and the new "pct of total" measure still works:

Month	Net Sales	Pct of All Month Net Sales
1	$325,923	4.6 %
2	$384,359	5.5 %
3	$332,465	4.7 %
4	$364,024	5.2 %
5	$458,236	6.5 %
6	$346,219	4.9 %
7	$675,507	9.6 %
8	$570,071	8.1 %
9	$783,861	11.2 %
10	$756,351	10.8 %
11	$807,463	11.5 %
12	$1,218,949	17.4 %
Grand Total	$7,023,427	100.0 %

Year: 2001 2002 **2003** 2004

Figure 109 Pct of total measure still works without the ALL() measure on the pivot

> ⓘ Yes, you can do this in Excel pivots without the use of ALL(). You can use the Show Values As feature and achieve the same visual result. But that conversion (from raw value to % of total) happens after the DAX engine has done its work, meaning that the DAX engine only has the raw value. In other words, if you ever want to use a "Pct of total" value in a DAX calculation, Show Values As is useless – you absolutely need to use ALL() as illustrated above.

Example 2 – Negating a Slicer

This one is useful, but also a lot of fun. Let's start with the following pivot (we just added ProductKey as a slicer, and made a few selections).

Figure 110 Pivot with product slicer

Now add a measure that ignores any filters on ProductKey:

```
[Net Sales – All Products] =

   CALCULATE([Net Sales], ALL(Sales[ProductKey]))
```

And a measure that is the ratio of that to the original [Net Sales]:

```
[Selected Products Pct] =

   [Net Sales] / [Net Sales – All Products]
```

Results:

Figure 111 The seven selected products account for 4.3% of all Net Sales in April 2003, but only 0.1% of all sales in July 2003.

> ⓘ I'm a big believer in conditional formatting. I apply conditional formatting to my pivots almost instinctively at this point.

Now I change the selection of products on the slicer:

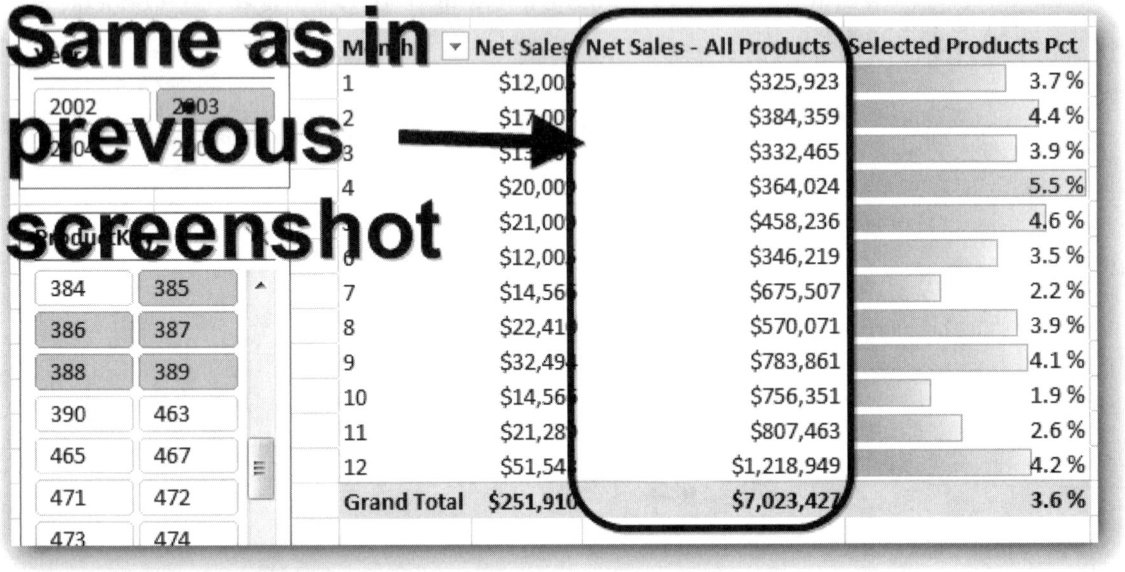

Month	▼	Net Sales	Net Sales - All Products	Selected Products Pct
1		$12,00	$325,923	3.7 %
2		$17,00	$384,359	4.4 %
3		$1...	$332,465	3.9 %
4		$20,00	$364,024	5.5 %
		$21,00	$458,236	4.6 %
		$12,00	$346,219	3.5 %
7		$14,56	$675,507	2.2 %
8		$22,41	$570,071	3.9 %
9		$32,49	$783,861	4.1 %
10		$14,56	$756,351	1.9 %
11		$21,28	$807,463	2.6 %
12		$51,54	$1,218,949	4.2 %
Grand Total		$251,910	$7,023,427	3.6 %

Figure 112 These five products account for a lot larger share of Net Sales than the previous seven. Note that the high-lighted middle column (the ALL measure) is unchanged from the previous screenshot.

> (i) You cannot achieve these results using Show Values As. ALL() is the only way.

Variations

ALL() can be used with arguments other than a single column. Both of these variations are also valid:

- ALL(<Col1>, <Col2>, ...) – You can list more than one column. *EX: ALL(Sales[ProductKey], Sales[Year])*

- ALL(<TableName>) – shortcut for applying ALL() to every column in the named table. *EX: ALL(Sales)*

ALLEXCEPT()

- Let's say you have 12 columns in a table, and you want to apply ALL() to 11 of the 12, but leave one of them alone.

- You can then use ALLEXCEPT(<Table>, <col1 to leave alone>, <col2 to leave alone>...)

- Example:

```
ALLEXCEPT(Sales, Sales[ProductKey])
```

Is the same as listing out *every* column in the Sales table *except* ProductKey:

```
ALL (

    Sales[OrderQuantity],  Sales[UnitPrice],
    Sales[ProductCost],   Sales[CustomerKey],
    Sales[OrderDate], Sales[MonthNum],...

    <every other column except ProductKey>

)
```

So ALLEXCEPT() is a lot more convenient in cases like this.

> (i) The other difference, besides convenience, is that if you subsequently add a new column to the Sales table, ALLEXCEPT() will "pick it up" and apply ALL() behavior to it, without requiring you to change your measure formula. The ALL(<list every column>) approach obviously will not apply to the new column until you edit the formula.

ALLSELECTED()

This is a new one in PowerPivot v2, and it's something I have needed a few times in v1. I don't expect to use it super frequently, but when you need it, I have found there is no workaround – when you need this function, you *really* need it.

First, let me show you a trick that has nothing to do with DAX.

Did you know that a field on rows or columns or report filter can also be dragged to Slicers and be two places at once?

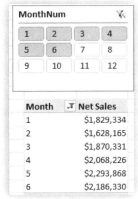

Figure 113 MonthNum field on both Rows and Slicer – makes for quick filtering of the Row area without having to use the Row Filters dropdown

 Remember the people who consume the work of Excel Pros? The people who don't enjoy working with data as much as we do? They do not like using the Row Filters dropdown, at all. Nor do they like using Report Filters. Most of them do enjoy working with slicers though, so this "duplicate a field on Rows and on a Slicer" trick is something we do on their behalf. Actually, it's better for us, too.

Now let's just find the [All Month Net Sales] measure that we defined using ALL() and put that on the pivot:

Month	Net Sales	All Month Net Sales
1	$1,829,33	$20,895,394
2	$1,628,16	$20,895,394
3	$1,870,33	$20,895,394
4	$2,068,22	$20,895,394
5	$2,293,86	$20,895,394
6	$2,186,33	$20,895,394
Grand Total	$11,876,254	$20,895,39

Figure 114 The selected measure is defined with ALL(-Sales[MonthNum])

Now let's clear the filter on the slicer and see what we get:

Month	Net Sales	All Month Net Sales
1	$1,829,334	$20,895,394
2	$1,628,165	$20,895,394
3	$1,870,331	$20,895,394
4	$2,068,226	$20,895,394
5	$2,293,868	$20,895,394
6	$2,186,330	$20,895,394
7	$1,369,088	$20,895,394
8	$1,335,607	$20,895,394
9	$1,238,364	$20,895,394
10	$1,474,433	$20,895,394
11	$1,462,976	$20,895,394
12	$2,138,673	$20,895,394
Grand Total	$20,895,394	$20,895,39

Figure 115 The selected measure is defined with ALL(-Sales[MonthNum])

But my goal here is to create a "percent of everything I *SEE*" measure. If I select six months on the slicer, I want a measure that returns *just the total of those six months*.

So let's define a new measure, and this time use ALLSELECTED() instead:

```
[Net Sales for All Selected Months] =
CALCULATE([Net Sales], ALLSELECTED(Sales[MonthNum]))
```

And then a ratio measure:

```
[Pct of All Selected Months Net Sales] =
[Net Sales] / [Net Sales for All Selected Months]
```

Results:

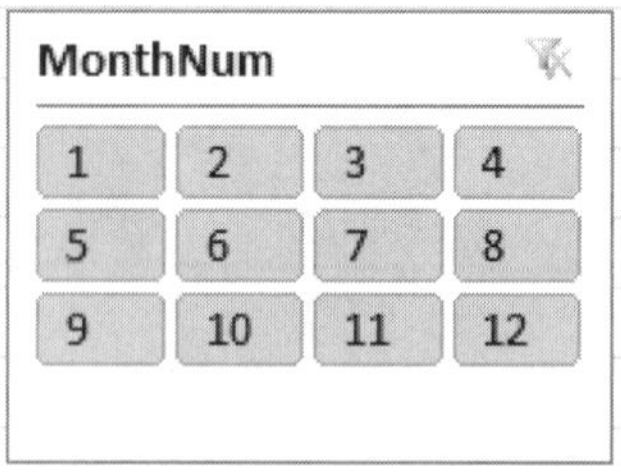

Month	Net Sales	Net Sales for All Selected Months	Pct of All Selected Months Net Sales
1	$1,829,334	$20,895,394	8.8 %
2	$1,628,165	$20,895,394	7.8 %
3	$1,870,331	$20,895,394	9.0 %
4	$2,068,226	$20,895,394	9.9 %
5	$2,293,868	$20,895,394	11.0 %
6	$2,186,330	$20,895,394	10.5 %
7	$1,369,088	$20,895,394	6.6 %
8	$1,335,607	$20,895,394	6.4 %
9	$1,238,364	$20,895,394	5.9 %
10	$1,474,433	$20,895,394	7.1 %
11	$1,462,976	$20,895,394	7.0 %
12	$2,138,673	$20,895,394	10.2 %
Grand Total	$20,895,394	$20,895,394	100.0 %

Figure 116 Looks the same as the ALL() measure, so far…

But now let's select a subset of the months on the slicer:

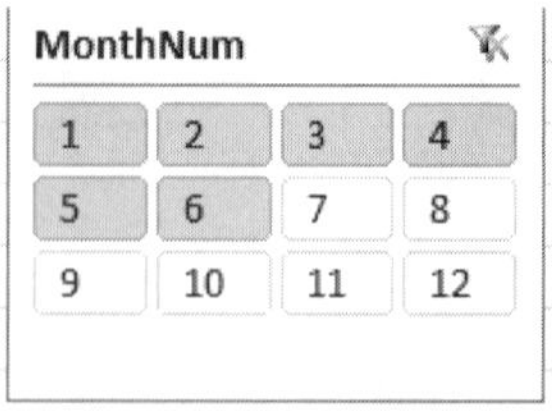

Month	Net Sales	Net Sales for All Selected Months	Pct of All Selected Months Net Sales
1	$1,829,334	$11,876,254	15.4 %
2	$1,628,165	$11,876,254	13.7 %
3	$1,870,331	$11,876,254	15.7 %
4	$2,068,226	$11,876,254	17.4 %
5	$2,293,868	$11,876,254	19.3 %
6	$2,186,330	$11,876,254	18.4 %
Grand Total	$11,876,254	$11,876,254	100.0 %

Figure 117 NOW we see a difference. Middle column is no longer over $20M. Also note the highlighted grand total is 100% - if we were using ALL(), that number would be lower (closer to 50% since 6 months are selected).

That's enough about ALL() and its variants for now.

10- Thinking in Multiple Tables

A Simple and Welcome Change

In the opening chapters, I mentioned that PowerPivot offers a lot of benefits when you are working with multiple tables of data. But so far, I have shown none of those - I have only worked with the Sales table. Why have I waited?

Working with multiple tables is not complicated – it actually requires you to *unlearn old habits* more than it requires you to learn new ones. This is not going to be a difficult adjustment for you, just a little different.

The reason I waited until now to cover "multi table" is this: **All of the concepts covered so far work the same way with multiple tables as they do with one table.** I didn't want to risk confusing you by teaching the CALCULATE() function at the same time as multi-table.

So this chapter really just extends what I have already covered, and shows how the same rules apply *across* **tables as they do** *within* **tables.**

Unlearning the "Thou Shalt Flatten" Commandment

Normal Excel literally *requires* **that all of your data resides in a single table** before you can build a pivot or chart against it. Since your data often arrives in multi-table format, Excel Pros have also become part-time Professional Data Flatteners.

- **That usually means flattening via VLOOKUP().** Sometimes it means *lots* of VLOOKUP().

- **Sometimes it involves database queries.** Some Excel Pros who know their way around a database also write queries that flatten the data into one table before it's ever imported.

You do *not* **need to do either of these anymore. In fact, you** *should* **not.**

> In PowerPivot there are many *advantages* to leaving tables separate. It may be tempting to pull columns from Table B into Table A, especially using the new RELATED() function. You should resist this temptation. I sometimes use RELATED() to partially combine tables but only when debugging or inspecting my data. I delete that column when I am done with my investigation.

Got it? Just leave those tables alone. And if you already have flattened versions of your tables in your data-base, I actually recommend not using those versions – import the tables "raw" (separately).

Relationships Are Your Friends

This *won't* **be a step-by-step tutorial on the creation of relationships.** I think that is well-covered in Bill's book if you aren't yet familiar with them.

But let's create one very quickly. Take a look at my Products table:

ProductK...	EnglishProductNa...	StandardC...	FinishedGoodsF...	Color	Weight	SafetyStockLe...	ReorderPo...	ListPc...
422	LL Road Rear Wheel	49.9789	TRUE	Black	1050	500	375	112.565
423	ML Road Rear Wheel	122.2709	TRUE	Black	1000	500	375	275.385
413	LL Road Front Wheel	37.9909	TRUE	Black	900	500	375	85.565
424	HL Road Rear Wheel	158.5346	TRUE	Black	890	500	375	357.06
414	ML Road Front Wheel	110.2829	TRUE	Black	850	500	375	248.385
415	HL Road Front Wheel	146.5466	TRUE	Black	650	500	375	330.06
557	ML Crankset	113.8816	TRUE	Black	635	500	375	256.49
556	LL Crankset	77.9176	TRUE	Black	600	500	375	175.49
558	HL Crankset	179.8156	TRUE	Black	575	500	375	404.99
555	Front Brakes	47.286	TRUE	Silver	317	500	375	106.5
514	Rear Brakes	47.286	TRUE	Silver	317	500	375	106.5
601	LL Bottom Bracket	23.9716	TRUE	NA	223	500	375	53.99
542	LL Mountain Pedal	17.9776	TRUE	Silver/Bla...	218	500	375	40.49
543	ML Mountain Pedal	27.568	TRUE	Silver/Bla...	215	500	375	62.09
501	Rear Derailleur	53.9282	TRUE	Silver	215	500	375	121.46
545	LL Road Pedal	17.9776	TRUE	Silver/Bla...	189	500	375	40.49
544	HL Mountain Pedal	35.9596	TRUE	Silver/Bla...	185	500	375	80.99
603	HL Bottom Bracket	53.9416	TRUE	NA	170	500	375	121.49

Figure 118 I have not yet used the Products table, but it contains a lot of useful columns!

I'm going to create a relationship between Products and Sales, using the ProductKey column:

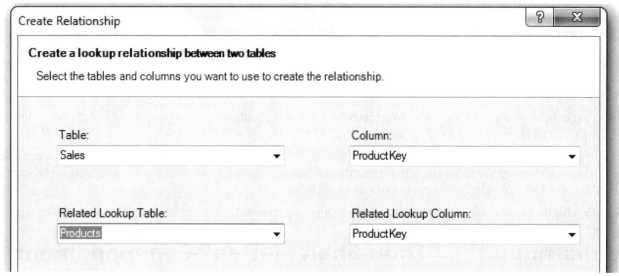

Figure 119 Relating Sales to Products

"Lookup" Tables

Note how I selected Products to be the Lookup table? That's important. So important, in fact, that Power-Pivot will not let me get it wrong. Let's try reversing the two and see what happens:

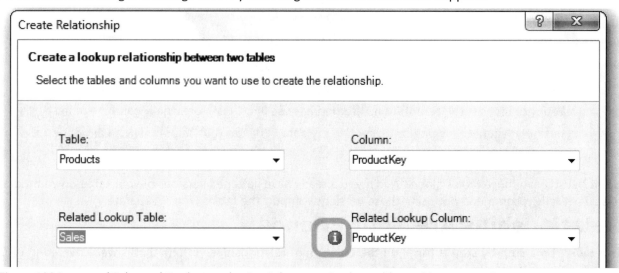

Figure 120 I reversed Sales and Products, selecting Sales as my Lookup table, and I get a warning

Hover over the warning icon and I get an explanation:

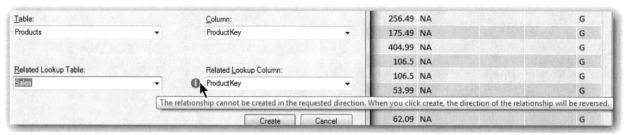

Figure 121 PowerPivot detects that I got the order wrong, and when I click OK, Products will be correctly used as the Lookup table!

The use of the word "Lookup" was deliberate. Back at Microsoft, we chose that word so that it would "rhyme" with Excel Pros' familiarity with VLOOKUP.

Think of Lookup tables as the tables from which you would have "fetched" values when writing a VLOOKUP. Lookup tables tend to be the places where friendly labels are stored for instance.

From here on, I will refer to the two tables' roles in a relationship as the "lookup table" and the "data table."

The Diagram View

This feature is new in PowerPivot v2, and it becomes very helpful as your models grow more sophisticated. But in smaller models, Diagram View is a fabulous gift to the authors of PowerPivot books, because we don't have to spend long hours making graphical representations of tables and relationships :-)

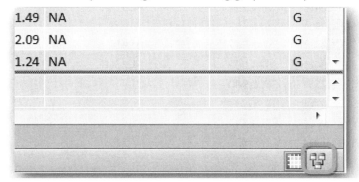

Figure 122 The button for Diagram View is on the bottom-right corner of the PowerPivot window.

Clicking that button gives me:

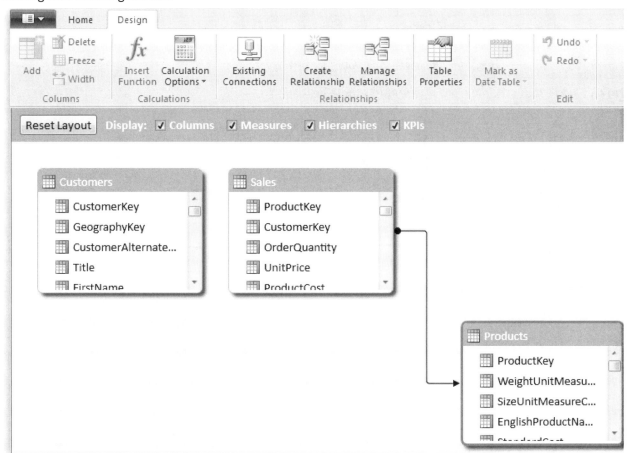

Figure 123 Diagram View! All three tables displayed, with two of them linked by the relationship I just created.

 Notice the direction of the arrow. The arrow always points to the Lookup table.

Using Related Tables in a Pivot

Now let's revisit a pivot that uses ProductKey on Rows, and enhance it with some of the columns from this Products table.

ProductKey ▼	Normal Sales	Promo Sales	Refunds	Net Sales	Pct Sales on Promo
214	$54,934	$11,932	($11,162)	$55,704	17.8 %
217	$52,170	$10,742	($10,042)	$52,870	17.1 %
222	$52,205	$11,547	($10,602)	$53,150	18.1 %
225	$13,854	$3,012	($2,823)	$14,042	17.9 %
228	$14,897	$2,899	($3,649)	$14,147	16.3 %
231	$16,247	$2,200	($3,649)	$14,797	11.9 %
234	$16,047	$2,500	($4,049)	$14,497	13.5 %
237	$14,197	$3,399	($3,049)	$14,547	19.3 %
310	$862,363	$150,287	($189,648)	$823,002	14.8 %
311	$669,136	$164,600	($171,757)	$661,980	19.7 %
312	$837,315	$182,492	($186,070)	$833,737	17.9 %
313	$722,811	$196,805	($161,022)	$758,593	21.4 %
314	$755,015	$157,444	($143,131)	$769,328	17.3 %
320	$9,088	$2,097	($2,097)	$9,088	18.8 %

Figure 124 ProductKey pivot – but of course, ProductKey is meaningless to me.

OK, let's remove ProductKey:

Normal Sales	Promo Sales	Refunds	Net Sales	Pct Sales on Promo
$20,784,362	$4,342,674	($4,231,642)	$20,895,394	17.3 %

Figure 125 Be gone, ProductKey! And never show your face on a pivot again.

Now I'll add ProductName from the Products table instead:

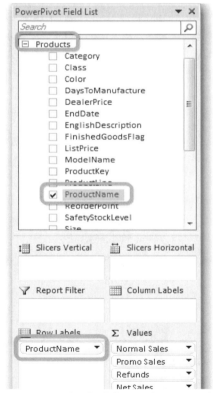

Figure 126 Checked the ProductName field in the field list, adding it to Rows

ProductName	Normal Sales	Promo Sales	Refunds	Net Sales	Pct Sales on Promo
Road-650 Black, 58	$34,312	$16,191	($7,494)	$43,009	32.1 %
Touring-1000 Blue, 54	$226,487	$104,899	($50,065)	$281,320	31.7 %
Touring-3000 Yellow, 54	$23,013	$8,166	($4,454)	$26,725	26.2 %
Mountain-100 Black, 38	$108,000	$37,125	($20,250)	$124,875	25.6 %
Mountain-400-W Silver, 46	$68,485	$23,085	($14,620)	$76,949	25.2 %
Touring-2000 Blue, 60	$64,387	$20,652	($13,363)	$71,676	24.3 %
Touring-1000 Yellow, 54	$252,711	$73,906	($50,065)	$276,552	22.6 %
Touring-3000 Yellow, 62	$25,982	$7,424	($3,712)	$29,694	22.2 %
Hitch Rack - 4-Bike	$26,880	$7,560	($4,920)	$29,520	22.0 %
Mountain-500 Silver, 44	$14,125	$3,955	($3,955)	$14,125	21.9 %
Road-650 Red, 44	$36,073	$9,927	($8,529)	$37,472	21.6 %
Road-150 Red, 52	$722,811	$196,805	($161,022)	$758,593	21.4 %
Road-650 Black, 62	$33,976	$9,228	($5,844)	$37,360	21.4 %
Road-750 Black, 52	$140,937	$37,799	($29,699)	$149,037	21.1 %
Touring-3000 Blue, 58	$28,209	$7,424	($6,681)	$28,952	20.8 %
Road-550-W Yellow, 48	$196,046	$49,982	($37,777)	$208,251	20.3 %
Classic Vest, L	$8,255	$2,096	($2,032)	$8,319	20.2 %
Touring-1000 Blue, 60	$236,023	$59,602	($54,834)	$240,791	20.2 %

Figure 127 ProductName replaced ProductKey: much more readable

But I'm not limited to using any one field from Products – all of them can be used now that I have a relationship established. Let's try a few different ones:

Category	Normal Sales	Promo Sales	Refunds	Net Sales	Pct Sales on Promo
Accessories	$495,995	$107,804	($96,961)	$506,838	17.9 %
Bikes	$20,047,702	$4,188,222	($4,082,220)	$20,153,704	17.3 %
Clothing	$240,664	$46,649	($52,460)	$234,852	16.2 %
Grand Total	**$20,784,362**	**$4,342,674**	**($4,231,642)**	**$20,895,394**	**17.3 %**

Figure 128 Category (from Products table) on Rows

Category-SubCat	Normal Sales	Promo Sales	Refunds	Net Sales	Pct Sales on Promo
Accessories	**$495,995**	**$107,804**	**($96,961)**	**$506,838**	**17.9 %**
Bike Racks	$26,880	$7,560	($4,920)	$29,520	22.0 %
Bike Stands	$28,779	$5,565	($5,247)	$29,097	16.2 %
Bottles and Cages	$40,697	$8,151	($7,951)	$40,897	16.7 %
Cleaners	$5,032	$1,185	($1,002)	$5,215	19.1 %
Fenders	$33,454	$6,616	($6,550)	$33,520	16.5 %
Helmets	$159,309	$34,220	($31,806)	$161,724	17.7 %
Hydration Packs	$27,825	$6,654	($5,829)	$28,650	19.3 %
Tires and Tubes	$174,019	$37,853	($33,657)	$178,216	17.9 %
Bikes	**$20,047,702**	**$4,188,222**	**($4,082,220)**	**$20,153,704**	**17.3 %**
Mountain Bikes	$7,199,563	$1,360,830	($1,392,367)	$7,168,026	15.9 %
Road Bikes	$10,217,336	$2,190,321	($2,112,927)	$10,294,730	17.7 %
Touring Bikes	$2,630,803	$637,071	($576,927)	$2,690,947	19.5 %
Clothing	**$240,664**	**$46,649**	**($52,460)**	**$234,852**	**16.2 %**
Caps	$13,854	$3,012	($2,823)	$14,042	17.9 %
Gloves	$24,514	$5,486	($5,020)	$24,980	18.3 %
Jerseys	$122,990	$22,606	($27,355)	$118,241	15.5 %
Shorts	$50,883	$9,519	($10,918)	$49,483	15.8 %
Socks	$3,785	$629	($692)	$3,722	14.3 %
Vests	$24,638	$5,398	($5,652)	$24,384	18.0 %
Grand Total	**$20,784,362**	**$4,342,674**	**($4,231,642)**	**$20,895,394**	**17.3 %**

Figure 129 SubCategory (also from Products table) nested under Category

Color	Normal Sales	Promo Sales	Refunds	Net Sales	Pct Sales on Promo
Black	$6,272,549	$1,267,427	($1,298,436)	$6,241,540	16.8 %
Blue	$1,531,913	$400,061	($347,121)	$1,584,854	20.7 %
Multi	$75,241	$14,009	($17,220)	$72,031	15.7 %
NA	$308,861	$66,930	($59,326)	$316,465	17.8 %
Red	$5,417,765	$1,153,707	($1,152,859)	$5,418,613	17.6 %
Silver	$3,721,517	$713,957	($677,916)	$3,757,557	16.1 %
White	$3,785	$629	($692)	$3,722	14.3 %
Yellow	$3,452,730	$725,954	($678,071)	$3,500,614	17.4 %
Grand Total	$20,784,362	$4,342,674	($4,231,642)	$20,895,394	17.3 %

Figure 130 Even Color can be used! (Another column from Products table)

Why That Works: Filter Context "Travels" Across Relationships

Let's examine a single measure cell and walk through the filter context "flow":

Color	Normal Sales
Black	$6,272,549
Blue	$1,531,913
Multi	$75,241
NA	$308,861
Red	$5,417,765
Silver	$3,721,517
White	$3,785
Yellow	$3,452,730
Grand Total	$20,784,362

Figure 131 Let's examine how filter context flows for the highlighted measure cell

First, the Color="Red" filter is applied to the Products table:

Produ...	StandardC...	FinishedGoodsF...	Color
325	486.7066	TRUE	Red
324	413.1463	TRUE	Red
323	486.7066	TRUE	Red
322	413.1463	TRUE	Red
321	486.7066	TRUE	Red
320	413.1463	TRUE	Red
331	486.7066	TRUE	Red
330	413.1463	TRUE	Red
329	486.7066	TRUE	Red
328	413.1463	TRUE	Red
327	486.7066	TRUE	Red
326	413.1463	TRUE	Red
316	884.7083	TRUE	Red
315	884.7083	TRUE	Red
319	884.7083	TRUE	Red
318	884.7083	TRUE	Red
317	884.7083	TRUE	Red
372	1554.9479	TRUE	Red
371	1320.6838	TRUE	Red

Figure 132 Products table filtered to Color="Red" as result of filter context

The ProductKey column is not filtered directly, but it obviously *has* been reduced to a subset of its overall values, thanks to the Color="Red" filter on the table.

Active Values for the Products[ProductKey] column:
{325; 324; 323; 322; 321; 320; 331; 330; 329; 328;
... 245; 244; 243; 242; 241; 214; 213; 212}

Figure 133 Only those ProductKeys that correspond to Red products are left "active" at this point (63 ProductKey values out of a total of 397).

That filtered set of 63 ProductKeys then flows across the relationship and filters the Sales table to that same set of ProductKeys:

OrderQ...	ProductKey	UnitPr...	ProductCost	Custom...	OrderDate
1	324	699.0982	413.1463	26620	7/30
1	324	699.0982	413.1463	20165	10/5
1	324	699.0982	413.1463	19415	12/15
1	324	699.0982	413.1463	20558	1/7
1	324	699.0982	413.1463	18010	2/6
1	324	699.0982	413.1463	25718	2/16
1	324	699.0982	413.1463	14737	2/24
1	324	699.0982	413.1463	18039	3/7
1	324	699.0982	413.1463	14746	3/9
1	324	699.0982	413.1463	25920	4/20
1	324	699.0982	413.1463	14755	4/25
1	324	699.0982	413.1463	19472	4/25
1	324	699.0982	413.1463	14756	4/28
1	324	699.0982	413.1463	25928	5/6
1	324	699.0982	413.1463	14896	5/19
1	324	699.0982	413.1463	25947	6/10
1	325	782.99	486.7066	20577	7/2
1	325	782.99	486.7066	19924	7/11
1	325	782.99	486.7066	15155	7/18
1	325	782.99	486.7066	26021	7/26

| 2002 Sales: $... | Pct of All Month N... | Normal Sal... | Refunds: ($19,... | Pct Sales on... | Total Sales: $13... |

Sales | Customers | Products

Figure 134 Sales table gets filtered (via relationship) to that same set of ProductKey values: {325; 324;...}

And then the arithmetic runs against the filtered Sales table. So it's the same Golden Rules as before. Those rules just extend across relationships.

 During the filter phase of measure evaluation, filters applied to a Lookup table (Products in this case) flow through to the Data table(s) related to that Lookup table.

This does NOT, however, apply in reverse: filters applied to Data tables don't flow back "up" to Lookup tables.

Visualizing Filters Flowing "Downhill" – One of My Mental Tricks

In my head, I always see Lookup tables floating above the Data tables. That way the filters flowing "downhill" into the Data tables.

I'll drag tables around in the Diagram View in order to represent that:

Figure 135 Products table dragged to be "above" Sales table

I also resized the tables so that the Data table (Sales) is bigger than the Lookup table (Products) – another mental trick.

I'll now create a relationship from Customers to Sales. Here's the updated diagram:

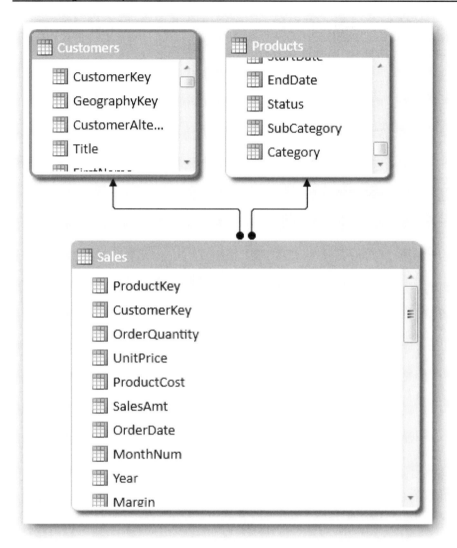

Figure 136 Two Lookup tables, both "above" the Data table that they filter

> (i) It's a shame, in my opinion, that the relationship arrows flow toward the Lookup tables.
> Arrows point from Data to Lookup in the database world, but in PowerPivot I'd prefer
> that they point in the direction of filter flow. Yes, it's the little things that bug me :-)

Filters from All Related Lookup Tables Are Applied

Let's put columns from both Customers and Products on the same pivot:

| Total Sales | Marital Status ▾ | | |
SubCategory ↴	M	S	Grand Total
Road Bikes	$7,419,057	$7,101,527	$14,520,584
Mountain Bikes	$5,208,539	$4,744,220	$9,952,760
Touring Bikes	$1,974,918	$1,869,883	$3,844,801
Tires and Tubes	$140,253	$105,276	$245,529
Helmets	$123,830	$101,506	$225,336
Jerseys	$93,590	$79,361	$172,951
Shorts	$43,604	$27,716	$71,320
Bottles and Cages	$32,122	$24,676	$56,798
Fenders	$27,079	$19,540	$46,620
Hydration Packs	$22,821	$17,487	$40,308
Bike Stands	$21,783	$17,808	$39,591
Bike Racks	$22,920	$16,440	$39,360
Vests	$19,558	$16,129	$35,687
Gloves	$19,470	$15,551	$35,021
Caps	$10,662	$9,026	$19,688
Cleaners	$4,158	$3,061	$7,219
Socks	$3,012	$2,095	$5,106
Grand Total	**$15,187,376**	**$14,171,301**	**$29,358,677**

Figure 137 Products[SubCategory] and [Customers[MaritalStatus] on the same pivot: they each impact measures, as expected

This isn't worth belaboring really – I just wanted to point out that you can use more than one Lookup table on a single pivot with no issue.

CALCULATE() <Filters> *Also* Flow Across Relationships

Until now, all of our <filter> arguments in CALCULATE have been filtering columns in the Sales table. But <filter> arguments are completely legal against Lookup tables (in fact, encouraged!), so let's define a CALCULATE measure using a column in a Lookup table:

```
[Sales to Parents] =

  CALCULATE([Total Sales], Customers[NumberChildrenAtHome]>0)
```

And compare that to its base measure, [Total Sales]:

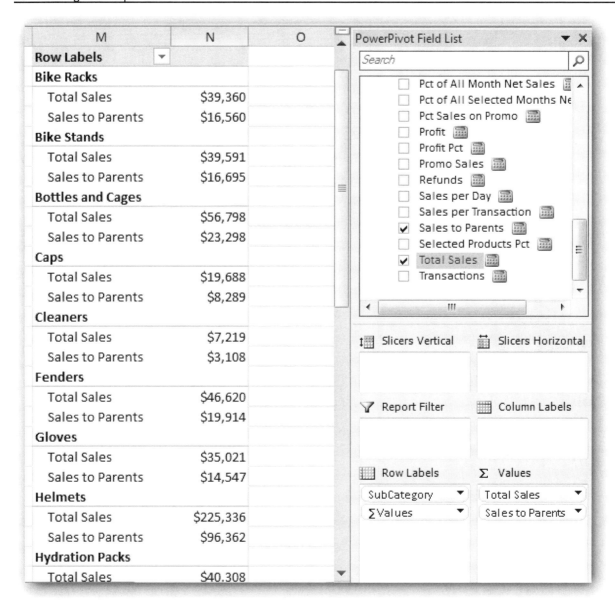

Figure 138 Proof that CALCULATE <filters> also flow across relationships: [Sales to Parents] returns smaller numbers than its base measure [Total Sales]

 I think that's probably sufficient to explain the concept, but to be super precise, I should also say that <filters> in CALCULATE() are applied *before* filters flow across relationships.

Taking that precision one step further, here's an updated version of the Filter Context Flow diagram:

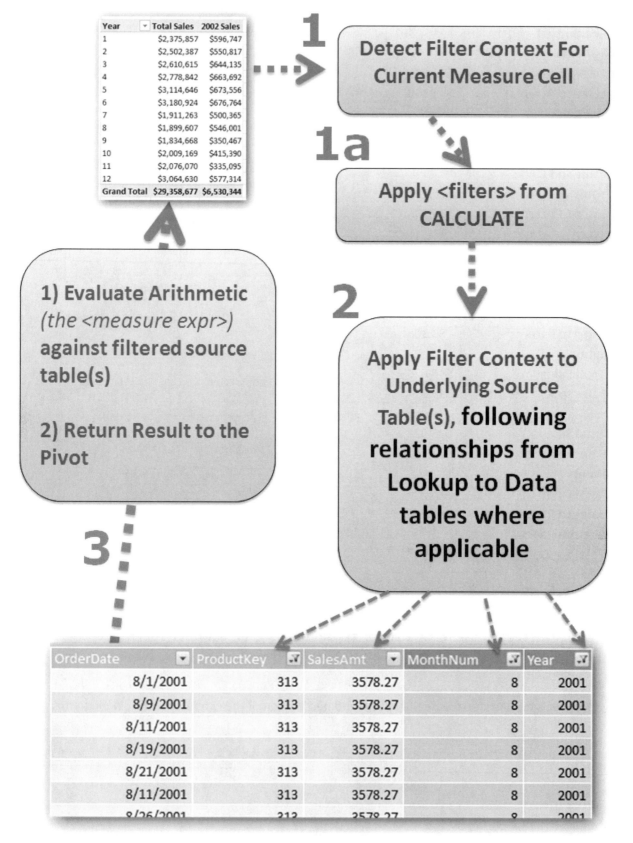

Figure 139 Updated Filter Context flow diagram to highlight that relationship traversal happens after CALCULATE() <filters> are applied

11- "Intermission" – Taking Stock of Your New Powers

If you've followed everything up until this point in the book, I want you to know three things:

1. You understand about as much about PowerPivot formulas (DAX) as I did after several months of experimenting on my own.

(And "experimenting" is the right word – I had moved away from Redmond before DAX was ready to be used, even by members of the PowerPivot team. So I learned as an "outsider.")

2. What you've read so far covers about the same amount of material as a full day of intensive training in one of my onsite, personalized courses.

3. If PowerPivot *only* contained the functionality covered so far, it would still be a *massive* enhancement to your capabilities as an Excel Pro.

In other words, if you wanted, you could stop right now, close the book and file it away. You'd still improve the quantity and quality of the insights you can deliver by 4-5x, without needing to know anything covered hereafter.

But there's no reason to do that. What follows is no more difficult than what's been covered so far. Actually I think it's easier, because it just builds on the fundamentals established in the previous chapters. **And there is some *serious* magic awaiting you :-)**

My point in this brief "intermission" was just to let you know that you're already VERY competent at PowerPivot. Take a bow. Now let's go cover some seriously amazing stuff :-)

12- Disconnected Tables

A disconnected table is one that you add to your PowerPivot model but *intentionally* do not relate it to any other tables. At first that may seem a little strange – if there is no relationship between it and any other tables, filter context can never flow into it or out of it, so a disconnected table would never contribute anything meaningful to a pivot involving other tables.

But once you learn a simple new trick, it will make sense. It helps to have an example.

A Parameterized Report

Let's work backwards this time: I will show you the result, and then explain how I did it.

Take a look at this pivot:

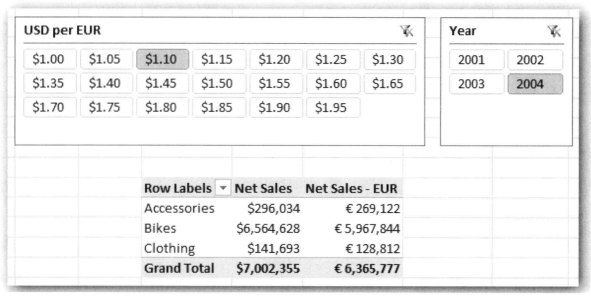

Figure 140 Just a simple little pivot with two slicers, right?

Nothing exciting on the surface. But let's change that "USD per EUR" from $1.10 to $1.80 and see what happens:

Figure 141 Net Sales in Euros dropped sharply while the original Net Sales (in Dollars) remained unchanged

Are you seeing what I'm seeing? **This is a pivot where the user/consumer can dynamically input parameters (via slicers) and have those parameters reflected in calculations!**

This is absolutely real, and it's simple to build.

Adding a "Parameter Harvesting" Measure

I'm going to ignore one of my own recommendations here and create a table via copy/paste. I feel ok about doing so, because this is a table that isn't going to change frequently (if at all), and I'm not going to write a bunch of formulas on this table (so if I needed to recreate it later, it would not be difficult to do).

I create a single column table in Excel. This is going to be the basis for my "USD per EUR" (dollars per euro) slicer:

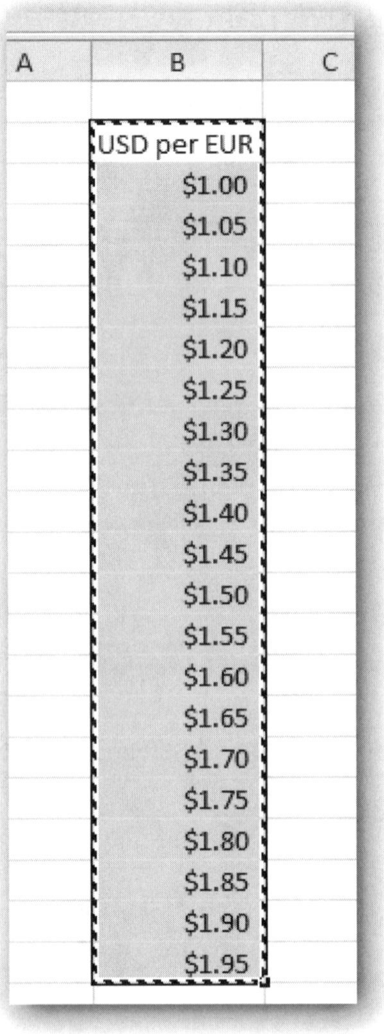

And then paste as new table in PowerPivot, yielding:

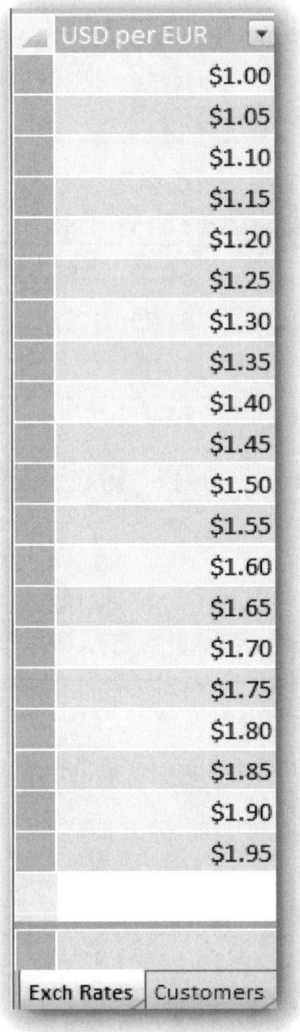

Figure 142 Copying a simple table of data from Excel and Pasted as Exch Rates table in PowerPivot

Now we can create a new pivot, and put that column on a slicer:

Figure 143 New pivot, Category on Rows and the newly-pasted table/column on a slicer

 Because I most often use Disconnected Tables as parameters, and those parameters are usually exposed as slicers, you may also think of them as "Slicer Tables" or "Parameter Tables."

Adding a "parameter harvesting" measure

Now we're going to do something interesting: we're going to add a measure on the Exch Rates table. This will be the first (but not last!) time that we create a measure on a non-data table.

The measure is:

```
[EURUSD] =
    MAX('Exch Rates'[USD per EUR])
```

And the result:

Figure 144 Measure that returns $1.95 all the time? Why would I want such a thing?

The "punchline" here is that when I make a selection on the slicer, something neat happens:

Figure 145 The measure returns whatever is selected on the slicer!

Cool! But this is just regular old filter context doing its thing. Before the arithmetic (MAX) runs, the Exch Rates table gets filtered by the pivot, and the pivot is saying "[USD per EUR]=$1.45."

> *(i)* Because only a single row is selected when the user picks a single slicer value, I could also have used MIN() or AVERAGE() or even SUM() as the aggregation function in my [ExchangeRateEURUSD] measure – they all return the same result when a single value is selected. Your choice of function in cases like this is partly a matter of personal preference and partly a question of how you want to handle cases where the user picks more than one value. You can even decide to return an error – which we will cover in a later chapter.

The Field List is Grumpy About This

At this point, the field list is giving me a warning:

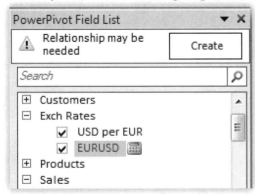

Figure 146 Yes, there is no relationship between my Products table (where the Category field comes from) and my Exch Rates table (where this new measure comes from)

This warning, alas, merely goes with the territory of using Disconnected tables. And I don't like sacrificing real estate in my field list to a warning that tells me nothing. So I tend to turn this warning off using the PowerPivot ribbon in Excel:

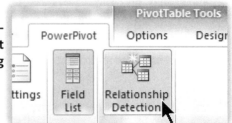

Figure 147 Toggle this button to disable that warning

Using the Parameter Measure for Something...Useful

OK, the [ExchangeRateEURUSD] measure is neat and all, but having a measure that tells the user what they've selected is of course pretty useless :-)

But now we can use that measure in other measures:

```
[Net Sales - EUR Equivalent] =

[Net Sales] / [EURUSD]
```

USD per EUR							🍸
$1.00	$1.05	$1.10	$1.15	$1.20	$1.25	$1.30	
$1.35	$1.40	$1.45	$1.50	$1.55	$1.60	$1.65	
$1.70	$1.75	$1.80	$1.85	$1.90	$1.95		

Row Labels ▾	EURUSD	Net Sales - EUR
Accessories	$1.45	€ 349,544
Bikes	$1.45	€ 13,899,106
Clothing	$1.45	€ 161,967
Components	$1.45	
Grand Total	**$1.45**	**€ 14,410,617**

Figure 148 New measure tells me what my sales would look like in Euros at the selected exchange rate!

 I even used the formatting options in the measure editor to format the new measure in Euros. Oddly satisfying.

And I don't need the parameter measure displayed in order for it to work, so now I remove it to clean up the pivot:

USD per EUR							🍸
$1.00	$1.05	$1.10	$1.15	$1.20	$1.25	$1.30	
$1.35	$1.40	$1.45	$1.50	$1.55	$1.60	$1.65	
$1.70	$1.75	$1.80	$1.85	$1.90	$1.95		

Row Labels ▾	Net Sales - EUR
Accessories	€ 349,544
Bikes	€ 13,899,106
Clothing	€ 161,967
Grand Total	**€ 14,410,617**

Figure 149 Remove the parameter measure to produce a cleaner report

Add the Year column from the Sales table as a second slicer:

Figure 150 Year slicer works like it always has

Parameter Table Can Be Used on Rows and Columns too!

For grins, clear the slicer selection so that all exchange rates are selected, then drag that column to Rows instead:

Figure 151 Disconnected "slicer" field works on Rows too!

Are you surprised this works on Rows too? It felt weird to me the first time I did this, but it shouldn't have. Each measure cell corresponds to a single value of the Exch Rate column. *This is no different from using a normal column (one that IS connected to the Sales table via relationship, or is IN the Sales table) on Slicers versus Rows.*

OK the result above is a little hard to see, let's rearrange a bit:

Year		Category		
2003	**2004**	Accessories	Bikes	
2001	2002	Clothing	Components	

Row Labels	Net Sales - EUR
$1.00	€ 296,034
$1.05	€ 281,937
$1.10	€ 269,122
$1.15	€ 257,421
$1.20	€ 246,695
$1.25	€ 236,827
$1.30	€ 227,718
$1.35	€ 219,284
$1.40	€ 211,453
$1.45	€ 204,161
$1.50	€ 197,356
$1.55	€ 190,990
$1.60	€ 185,021

Figure 152 Easier to see now with Category on slicer – EUR EquivalentSales go down as Exchange Rate goes up

That may seem counterintuitive but it is accurate: if your country's currency is worth a lot relative to other countries' currencies, you make less money selling your products overseas than when your currency is worth less. So in some sense it's "better" for a country's currency to be worth less (and worse in other ways), but that's not exactly a DAX topic now is it? I just didn't want you thinking that I messed this one up :-)

Why is it Important That They Be Disconnected?

What would happen if our Exch Rates table *were* related to, say, the Sales table?

Short answer: nothing good. What column would we use to form the relationship? There isn't a column in the Sales table that matches the values in the Exch Rates table. We could *invent* one I suppose, but then we'd have to arbitrarily assign transaction rows to individual exchange rate values, which would be nonsense.

And then when the user selected an exchange rate on the slicer, not only would that impact the [ExchangeRateEURUSD] measure (as desired) but it would *also* filter out rows from the Sales table (not desired). We'd undercount our sales figures, and in completely random fashion.

In real life, something like exchange rate is completely separate from Sales, so it shouldn't surprise us really that we can't create a meaningful relationship between them.

A Very Powerful Concept

There are *many* variations on disconnected tables. In fact this concept borders on infinitely flexible. We will return to this topic and cover a few more variations as the book progresses. Let's look at one right now in fact.

Disconnected Table Variation: Thresholds

In the previous example, we used a disconnected table to inject a numerical parameter into certain calculations, and give the report consumer/user control over that parameter.

Now let's try another example: giving the user control over "cutoffs," or thresholds, in terms of, say, which products should be included and which shouldn't.

Again, let's work backwards by showing you the desired result first:

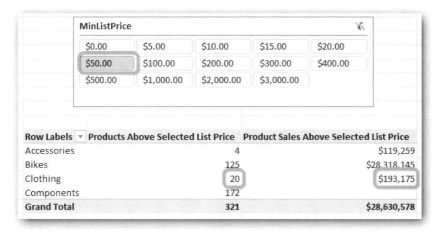

Figure 153 This pivot shows us, for instance, that there are 20 different products under the Clothing category that list for $50 or higher, and they accounted for $193k in sales.

Nifty huh? The "how to" starts out just like the last example:

Create a Disconnected Table to Populate the Slicer:

Figure 154 Another disconnected table

Write a Measure to "Harvest" the User's Selection:

```
[MinListThreshold] =

MAX(MinListPrice[MinListPrice])
```

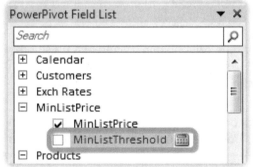

Figure 155 "Harvester" measure [MinListThreshold] created on the disconnected table

Diverging From the Prior Example: We Need to Filter, Not Perform Math

Hmm, now what? Last time, at this point we just divided an existing measure by our parameter measure to create something new. This time though, math isn't going to do it.

Since we need to filter out Products unless they fit our criteria, we need to use our friend, CALCULATE().

And hey, CALCULATE() supports the ">=" operator, so let's go ahead and do:

```
[Products Sales Above Selected List Price] =

CALCULATE([Total Sales], Products[ListPrice]>=
[MinListThreshold])
```

Enter it into the measure editor:

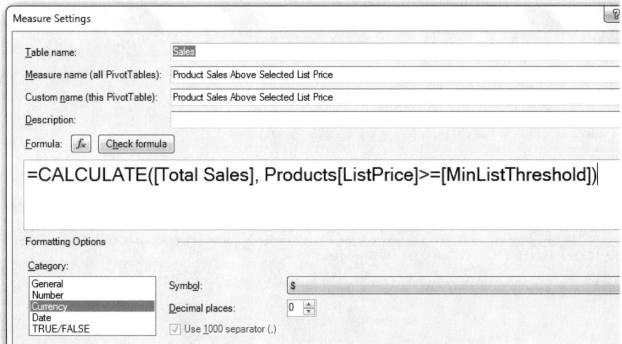

Figure 156 [Products Sales Above Selected List Price] entered into measure editor

And click Check Formula:

Figure 157 Error: A function 'CALCULATE' has been used in a True/False expression that is used as a table filter expression. This is not allowed.

 That's a terribly-worded error message. In my opinion, here is what that error message *should* say:

'An expression was provided on the right side of a <filter> argument to CALCULATE. Only static values like 6 or "Red" are allowed in that location.'

CALCULATE() requires that you provide a static value on the right side of a <filter> expression.

CALCULATE() Has a Limitation? Not really.

Hard to believe isn't it? CALCULATE *never* fails us!

Well it's not failing us now either. It's actually protecting us, and there *is* a version of this formula that works:

```
[Products Sales Above Selected List Price] =

CALCULATE([TotalSales],
          FILTER(Products,
                 Products[ListPrice]>=[MinListThreshold]
                 )
          )
```

What is the FILTER() function, and what is it doing occupying one of our <filter> arguments to CALCULATE?

FILTER() is the next function on your PowerPivot journey. And while it's pretty straightforward, I don't want to "hide" it in this chapter. It deserves its own. So we will come back to this threshold example, but we will do it in the context of the FILTER() chapter.

MinListPrice
$0.00
$5.00
$10.00
$15.00
$20.00
$50.00
$100.00
$200.00
$300.00
$400.00
$500.00
$1,000.00
$2,000.00
$3,000.00

MinListPrice | Exch Rates

13- Introducing the FILTER() Function, and Disconnected Tables Continued

When to Use FILTER()

Simple rule: use FILTER() when, in a <filter> argument to CALCULATE(), you need to perform a more complex test than "<column> equals <fixed value>" or "<column> greater than <fixed value>," etc.

Examples of <filter> tests that *require* you to use FILTER():

- <column> = <measure>
- <column> = <formula>
- <column> = <column>
- <measure> = <measure>
- <measure> = <formula>
- <measure> = <fixed value>

I used "=" in all of the above, but the other comparison operators (<, >, <=, >=, <>) are all implied.

 You can also use FILTER() as the <table> argument to functions like COUNTROWS() and SUMX() in order to have those functions operate on a subset of the table rather than all rows in the current filter context. This chapter will focus on its primary usage however, which is as a <filter> argument to CALCULATE().

FILTER() Syntax

 FILTER(<table>, <single "rich" filter>)

Why is FILTER() Necessary?

I mean, why can't we just slap any old complex test expression into the <filter> argument of CALCULATE()? Why the extra hassle?

I have made my peace with having to use FILTER(). I quite like it. Here's why.

It's All About Performance (Speed of Formula Evaluation)

Short answer:

1. **Formulas written using just CALCULATE() are *always* going to be fast**, because CALCULATE() has built-in "safeties" that prevent you from writing a slow formula. "Raw" CALCULATE() refuses richer <filter> tests because those *can* be slow if used carelessly.

2. **FILTER() *removes* those safeties** and therefore gives you a mental trigger to be more careful – you can still write fast formulas using FILTER(), but if you are careless you can write something that is slow.

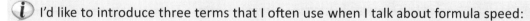 I'd like to introduce three terms that I often use when I talk about formula speed:

Performance: the practice of keeping your reports fast for your users. For instance, if someone clicks a slicer and it takes 30 seconds for the pivot to update, I would refer to that as "poor performance." If it responds instantly, I might call that "excellent performance," or I might say that the pivot "performs well."

Response time: the amount of time it takes a report to respond to a user action and display the updated results. In the example above, I described a "response time" of 30 seconds as poor. Generally we try to keep response times to 3 seconds or less.

Expensive: an operation is said to be "expensive" if it consumes a lot of time and therefore impacts performance/response time. For instance, above I could have described <column> = <static value> tests as "inexpensive" for the DAX engine, and richer comparisons like <column> = <measure> as "potentially expensive."

I will say more about these concepts in a subsequent chapter dedicated to Performance. For now this is enough.

Anyway, the important thing to understand is that FILTER() removes the safeties and lets you perform an incredible variety of filter tests, but you have to be careful when you use it.

How to Use FILTER() Carefully

You are going to love this, because the vast majority of "being careful" comes down to two simple rules:

1. **When you use FILTER(), use it against Lookup tables, *never* against Data tables.**
2. **Never use FILTER() when a "raw" CALCULATE() will get the job done.**

Pretty simple. For those of you who want to know more about the "why" behind that first rule, I am saving that for the chapter on Performance.

Applying FILTER() in the "Thresholds" Example
Revisiting the Successful Formula

Let's return to our "thresholds" example from the previous chapter, where we wanted to only include products whose Products[ListPrice] column was >= our [MinListThreshold] measure:

MinListPrice

$0.00	$5.00	$10.00	$15.00	$20.00
$50.00	$100.00	$200.00	$300.00	$400.00
$500.00	$1,000.00	$2,000.00	$3,000.00	

Row Labels ▼	Products Above Selected List Price	Product Sales Above Selected List Price
Accessories	4	$119,259
Bikes	125	$28,318,145
Clothing	20	$193,175
Components	172	
Grand Total	**321**	**$28,630,578**

Figure 158 Back to the "threshold" example: only including products whose ListPrice is >= the selection on the slicer.

The formula I ended up using for the measure on the right was:

```
[Product Sales Above Selected List Price] =
CALCULATE([Total Sales],
        FILTER(Products,
            Products[ListPrice]>=[MinListThreshold]
            )
    )
```

Am I following the rules for using FILTER() carefully? Let's check.

1. **Products is a Lookup table**, not a Data table (like Sales). **YES on rule #1.**

2. **I am comparing Products[ListPrice] to a measure**, which cannot be done in raw CALCULATE(). **YES on rule #2.**

OK, so now the [Products Above Selected List Price] measure – that gives me a count of products that pass the [MinListThreshold] test, and it's executed the same way as the measure above.

First though, I need a base measure that just counts products:

```
[Product Count] =
COUNTROWS(Products)
```

Note how I assigned that measure to the Products table, since it counts rows in that table:

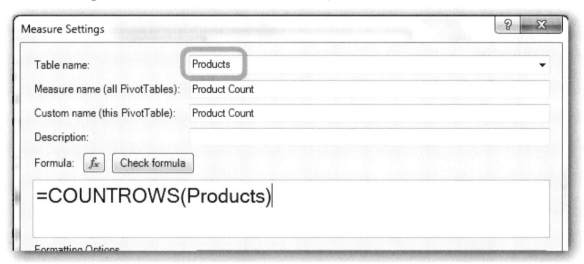

Figure 159 [Product Count] measure is assigned to the Products table since its arithmetic operates on the Product table (best practice)

Now I can create [Products Above Selected List Price] using that new base measure:

```
[Products Above Selected List Price] =
CALCULATE([Product Count],
        FILTER(Products,
            Products[ListPrice]>=[MinListThreshold]
            )
    )
```

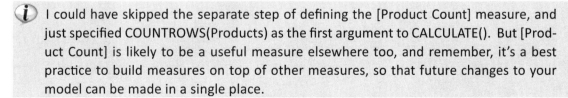

I could have skipped the separate step of defining the [Product Count] measure, and just specified COUNTROWS(Products) as the first argument to CALCULATE(). But [Product Count] is likely to be a useful measure elsewhere too, and remember, it's a best practice to build measures on top of other measures, so that future changes to your model can be made in a single place.

Verifying That the Measures Work

Well the measures are returning some numbers, but are they the right numbers? Let's investigate a little bit (I won't do this for every measure but I think it's good to show a few validation approaches).

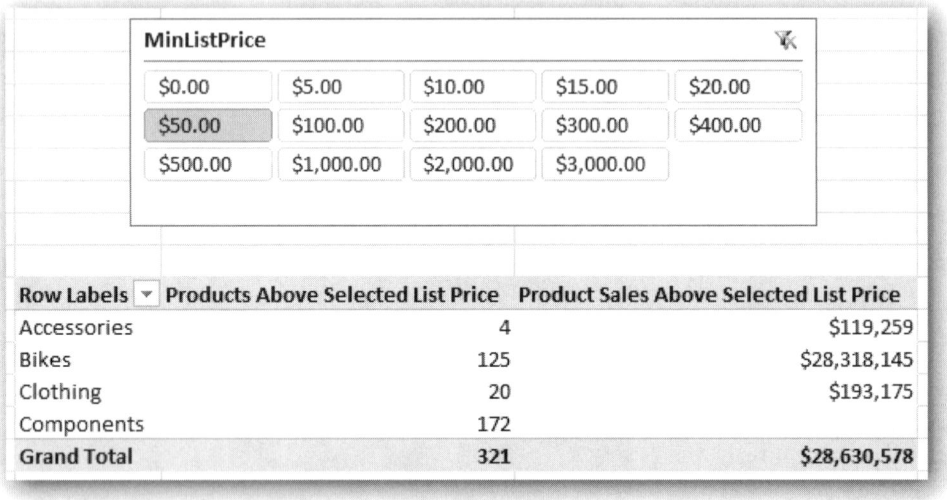

MinListPrice				
$0.00	$5.00	$10.00	$15.00	$20.00
$50.00	$100.00	$200.00	$300.00	$400.00
$500.00	$1,000.00	$2,000.00	$3,000.00	

Row Labels	Products Above Selected List Price	Product Sales Above Selected List Price
Accessories	4	$119,259
Bikes	125	$28,318,145
Clothing	20	$193,175
Components	172	
Grand Total	321	$28,630,578

Figure 160 How do we know the measures are correct?

The first thing to do is just change slicer selection and make sure that it has an impact. Let's try $20 as our minimum list price:

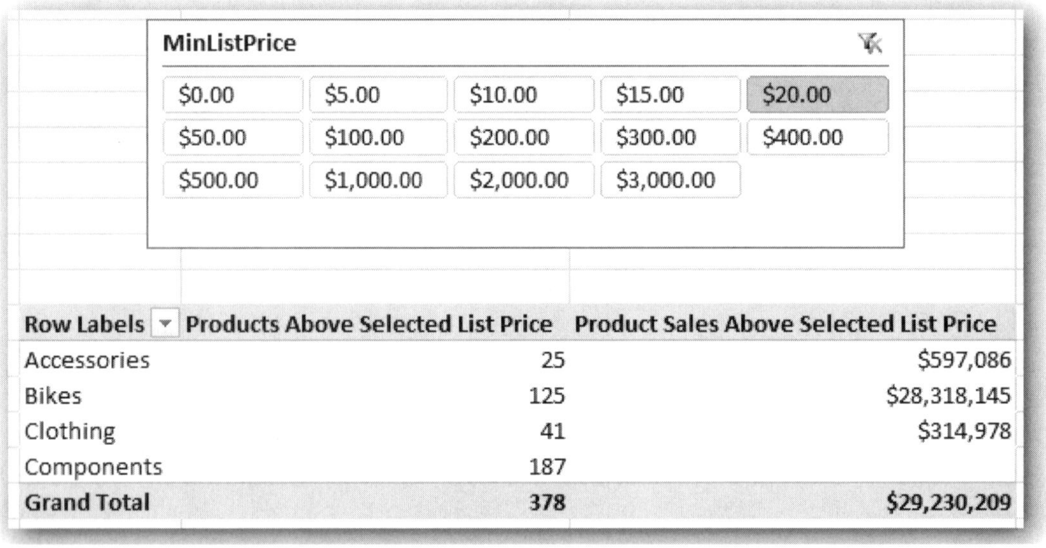

MinListPrice				
$0.00	$5.00	$10.00	$15.00	$20.00
$50.00	$100.00	$200.00	$300.00	$400.00
$500.00	$1,000.00	$2,000.00	$3,000.00	

Row Labels	Products Above Selected List Price	Product Sales Above Selected List Price
Accessories	25	$597,086
Bikes	125	$28,318,145
Clothing	41	$314,978
Components	187	
Grand Total	378	$29,230,209

Figure 161 We would expect both measures to return larger numbers with $20 as the selected threshold, and they both do

A good sign. But let's make sure that the measures are truly counting the right products. Let's put Products[ProductKey] on Rows, and set the slicer to $3,000 since that should only show us a small number of products:

MinListPrice

$0.00	$5.00	$10.00	$15.00	$20.00
$50.00	$100.00	$200.00	$300.00	$400.00
$500.00	$1,000.00	$2,000.00	**$3,000.00**	

Row Labels ▾	Products Above Selected List Price	Product Sales Above Selected List Price
310	1	$1,202,299
311	1	$1,005,494
312	1	$1,205,877
313	1	$1,080,638
314	1	$1,055,590
344	1	$197,199
345	1	$142,800
346	1	$166,600
347	1	$122,400
348	1	$165,375
349	1	$151,875
350	1	$202,499
351	1	$192,374
Grand Total	**13**	**$6,891,018**

Figure 162 Only 13 products show up – another good sign

But we really need to see the ListPrice. Let's put that on Rows too:

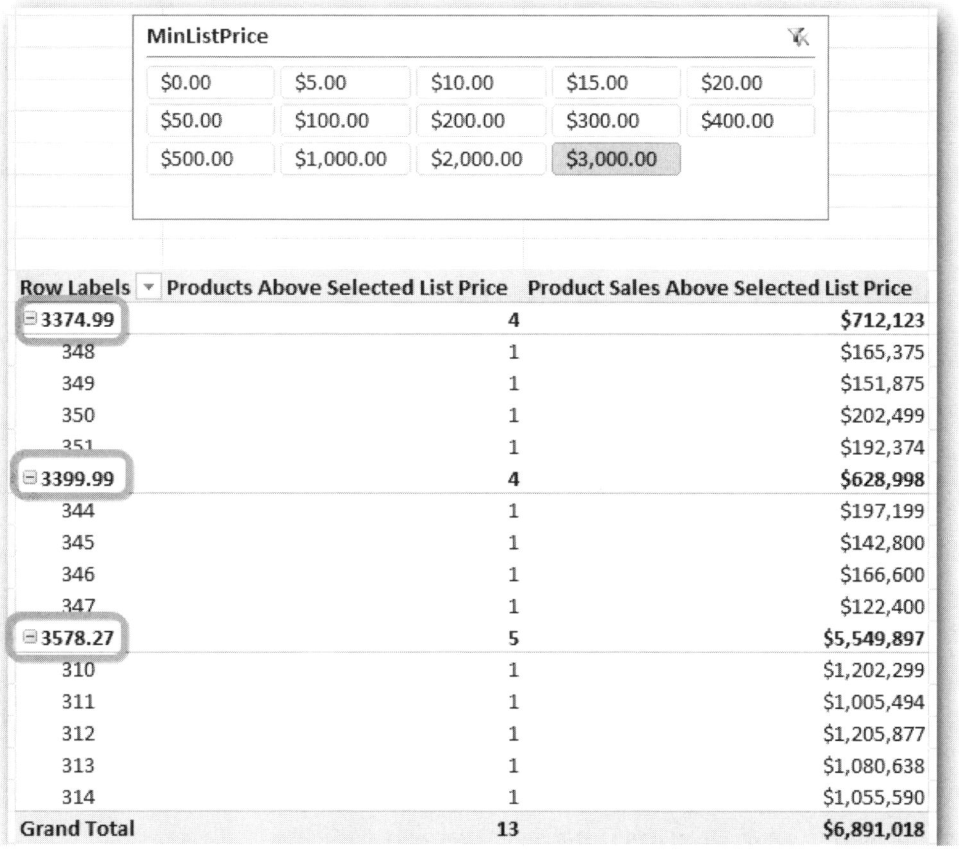

MinListPrice

$0.00	$5.00	$10.00	$15.00	$20.00
$50.00	$100.00	$200.00	$300.00	$400.00
$500.00	$1,000.00	$2,000.00	**$3,000.00**	

Row Labels ▾	Products Above Selected List Price	Product Sales Above Selected List Price
⊟ 3374.99	4	$712,123
348	1	$165,375
349	1	$151,875
350	1	$202,499
351	1	$192,374
⊟ 3399.99	4	$628,998
344	1	$197,199
345	1	$142,800
346	1	$166,600
347	1	$122,400
⊟ 3578.27	5	$5,549,897
310	1	$1,202,299
311	1	$1,005,494
312	1	$1,205,877
313	1	$1,080,638
314	1	$1,055,590
Grand Total	**13**	**$6,891,018**

Figure 163 OK, all of the products showing up are indeed priced over $3k

Lastly, over in the PowerPivot window, let's filter the Products table to ListPrice>=3000:

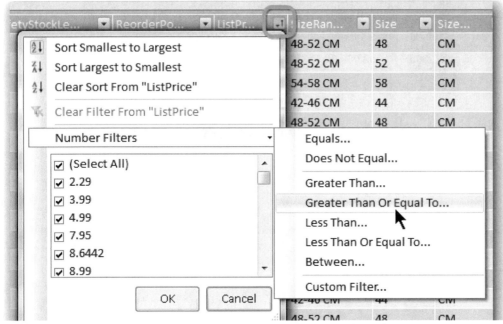

Figure 164 This should result in 13 rows, matching the grand total from the pivot...

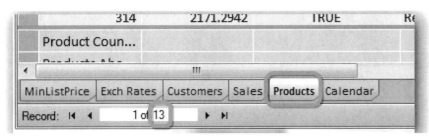

Figure 165 ...and it does

OK, this last step probably would be the first thing I would check. But I wanted to show that both the PowerPivot window and the pivot itself are important tools for validating/debugging. I use both.

Since both measures use the same FILTER() logic, once we validate this one, we can be pretty confident that the other is working too.

So there you have it: a simple threshold example driven by slicer, and it works.

This Could Not Be Done with Relationships

Just to reinforce: the disconnected table approach was absolutely necessary for this threshold example. A given product, like a $75 shirt, belongs to many different price ranges – it is included in the $0, $5, 10, $15, $20, and $50 price ranges. (In other words, the price ranges overlap with each other).

To see what I mean, imagine creating a column, in the Products table, to form the basis of the relationship. What would that column look like? If you committed to going down this road, you'd ultimately end up with multiple rows for each product (one for each price range that product "belongs to"). That would therefore require a "many to many" relationship with the slicer table (and with the Sales table), which PowerPivot does not support.

Tip: Measures Based on a Shared Pattern – Create via Copy/Paste

Notice how the two FILTER() measures above are identical except for their base measure? One uses [Total Sales] as the first argument to CALCULATE() and the other uses [Product Count], but otherwise the formulas are the same.

You will do this all the time. And there's a quick way to do it:

1. You write the first measure. In this case, the [Total Sales] version.

2. Then you right click that measure in the field list (or in the Values dropzone) and choose edit:

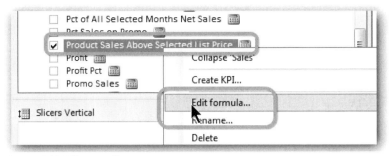

Figure 166 Edit your first measure

3. Copy the existing formula:

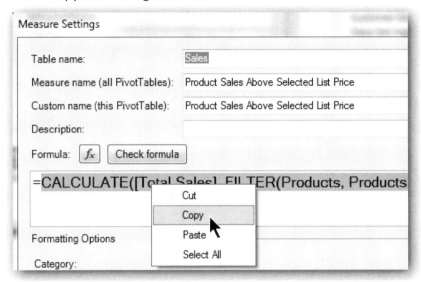

Figure 167 Copy the existing formula, which is conveniently selected already when you edit an existing measure

4. Cancel out of the editor, create a new measure, and then paste the formula:

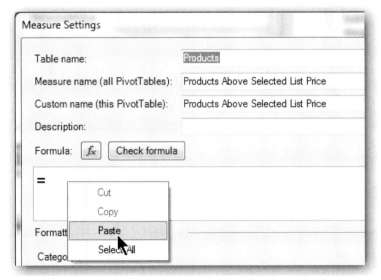

Figure 168 Paste the original measure's formula

5. Lastly, just replace the base measure reference ([Total Sales]) with the different desired measure ([Product Count]):

Figure 169 The whole process takes just a few seconds

You would discover this "trick" on your own pretty quickly (if you haven't already), but I do it so often that I wanted to make absolutely sure you are aware of it.

More Variations on Disconnected Tables

Upper and Lower Bound Thresholds

Let's take that Product[ListPrice] threshold example and extend it. Here's a new table:

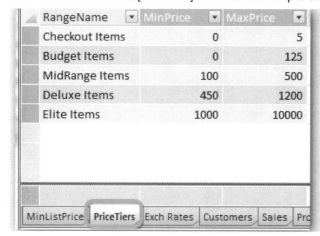

Figure 170 A new disconnected table, but this time with min and max price columns

> (i) Note again that the price tiers overlap, meaning a given product can belong to more than one, thus making a relationship impossible.

Now I'm going to define two "harvester" measures on that table:

            [PriceTierMin] =
            MIN(PriceTiers[MinPrice])

and

            [PriceTierMax] =
            MAX(PriceTiers[MaxPrice])

Now I'm going to use RangeName column as my slicer:

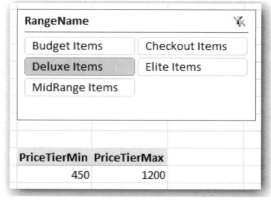

Figure 171 You can use a label column from a disconnected table on your pivot. Both "harvester" measures again capture the user's selection, but this time based on columns that the user does not see.

Fixing the Sort Order on the Slicer: The "Sort By Column" Feature

In our first threshold example, we used a numerical field on the slicer, which naturally sorted from smallest to largest. In this label example however, "Budget" alphabetically precedes "Counter," and out sort order is misleading as a result.

In PowerPivot v1, we had to "fix" this by prepending strings for correct sorting, yielding slicers with values like "1 – Counter" and "2 – Budget" on them. Yuck.

In PowerPivot v2 however, we have a much better fix: the Sort By Column feature.

First we need a single numerical (or text) column that sorts the table in the proper order.

Doesn't matter how you go about creating this column – as long as you create one (or already have one), it works.

In this case I will use a new calculated column:

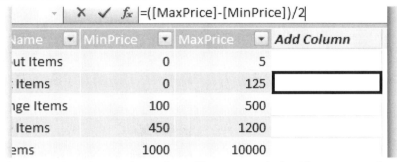

Figure 172 Creating a column that will sort properly (in this case, my column will be the midpoint of each price tier)

Now I select the RangeName column and click the Sort by Column button on the ribbon:

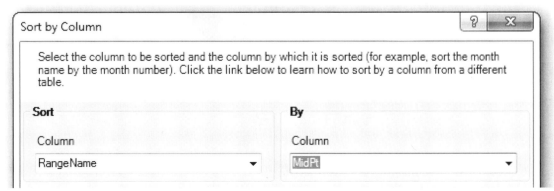

RangeName	MinPrice	MaxPrice	MidPt	Add Column
Checkout Items	0	5	2.5	
Budget Items	0	125	62.5	
MidRange Items	100	500	200	
Deluxe Items	450	1200	375	
Elite Items	1000	10000	4500	

Figure 173 Select label column, click Sort by Column

In the dialog, set it to sort by the new MidPt column:

Figure 174 Set the "sort by" column to the MidPt column

Flip back over to Excel:

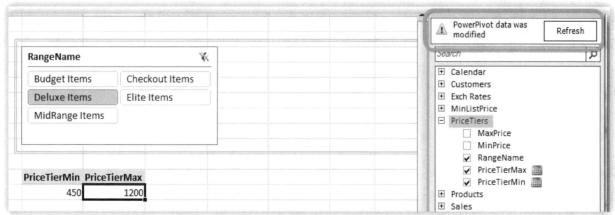

Figure 175 Changing the Sort By Column triggers the "refresh" prompt

Click the refresh button and the slicer sort order is fixed:

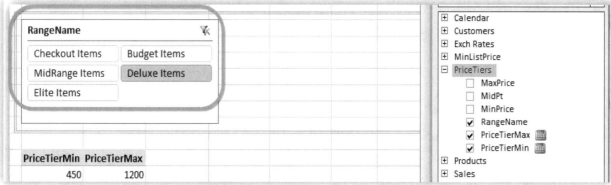

Figure 176 Refresh, and the Sort By Column feature "kicks in" – the slicer is now properly sorted

Completing the Min/Max Threshold

Now, just like in the simple threshold example, we need versions of [Product Count] and [Total Sales] measures that respect the user's selection on the slicer:

```
[ProductCount MinMaxTier] =
CALCULATE([Product Count],
          FILTER(
          Products, Products[ListPrice]>=[PriceTierMin] &&
          Products[ListPrice]<=[PriceTierMax]
          )
     )
```

> ⓘ Since FILTER() only supports a single <rich filter> expression, I use the && operator – a row of Products table needs to meet both of those comparison tests in order to be included.
>
> But since CALCULATE() itself *does* support multiple <filter> arguments, I could have done this without the && operator by using two FILTER() functions:
>
> CALCULATE(<measure>, FILTER(…), FILTER(…))
>
> That would yield the same results. I use the && approach whenever I can though, because it is less expensive (in terms of performance) to do so. More on this later.

And then the [Total Sales] version, again employing the "copy/paste/change base measure" trick:

```
[Total Sales MinMaxTier] =
CALCULATE([Total Sales],
          FILTER(
          Products, Products[ListPrice]>=[PriceTierMin] &&
          Products[ListPrice]<=[PriceTierMax]
          )
     )
```

Now I'll put both measures on the pivot, and remove the harvester measures:

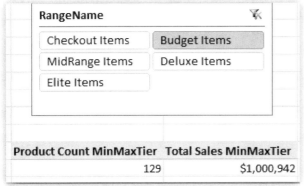

Figure 177 It's alive! :-)

A Way to Visualize Disconnected Tables

Disconnected tables, by definition, have no relationships to other tables in the model. If we look at diagram view, we see that the PriceTiers table, for instance, is an island like we expect:

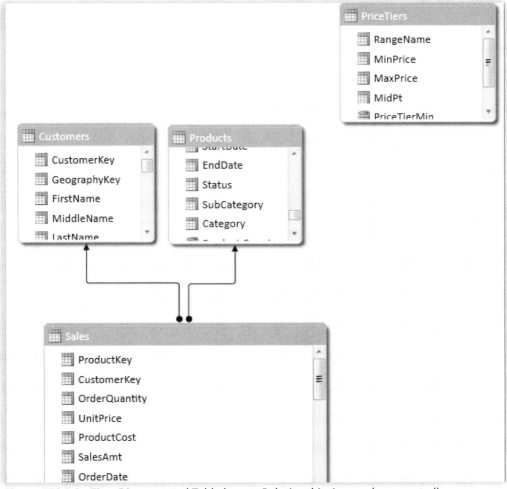

Figure 178 PriceTiers Disconnected Table has no Relationship Arrows (as expected)

But when we use the "MinMaxTier" measures that we wrote above, the PriceTiers table *does* act a lot *like* a Lookup table, since the PriceTiers filter context (such as user selections on the slicer) very much impacts the measure calculations and results.

So I often like to say that disconnected tables have a "dotted line" relationship with the tables that contain the corresponding FILTER() measures. In your head, you might think of it like this:

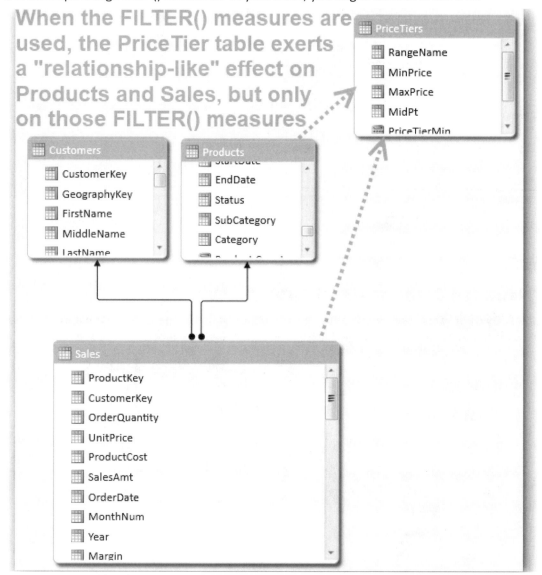

Figure 179 In your head, you can imagine "dotted line" relationships

> (i) Disconnected tables only impact the measures that are specifically written to "pay attention" to them – so the PriceTiers table impacts [ProductCount MinMaxTier] and [Total Sales MinMaxTier], but no other measures in the Products and Sales tables.

Putting This Chapter in Perspective

A couple things I want to emphasize before moving on:

- **We are not done with FILTER().** There's more to learn about FILTER() than what I have covered here, but I want to come back to those points later. It is not essential to learn the rest yet, and I am sticking to my philosophy of introducing things to you in the most learnable/useful order.

- **You will *not* use disconnected tables most of the time.** 90% of the pivots I create do *not* use disconnected tables. The other 10% of the time, they are very, *very* useful. I introduced disconnected tables in these last two chapters in large part because they are a great introduction to the FILTER() function (and *also* because they are a useful technique).

14- Introduction to Time Intelligence

At Last, It is Time!

(Get it? *Time?* There is no extra charge for humor of this quality).

I've been eagerly awaiting this chapter. PowerPivot measures really shine when you use them to perform intelligent calculations against the calendar.

It is a simple matter to perform calculations that answer questions like the following:

- How is our business performing relative to the same time last year?

- What were our Year to Date (YTD) sales as of June 1st?

- What was our best quarter over the past two years?

That is merely scratching the surface though. Good stuff. But before we dig in, a quick note about different types of calendars.

"Standard Calendar" versus "Custom Calendar"

Standard Calendars: The focus of This Chapter

Right up front, I want to let you know that this chapter will be written strictly from the perspective of the standard calendar.

What do I mean by "standard calendar?" It's the calendar with the following properties:

- February has 28 days (29 in leap years) in it, and all other months have 30 or 31 days in them

- Quarters consist of three consecutive months – months whose lengths are described above

- Years have 365 days in them (366 in leap years)

- A given month this year might have more/less Saturdays (or any other day) in it than the same month last year

In other words, a standard calendar is the calendar that you have hanging on your wall.

PowerPivot's time intelligence functions operate under the assumption that you use a standard calendar. So they represent a natural place to start the topic of time intelligence.

Custom Calendars: Perhaps Even More Important than Standard (Covered Later)

But many businesses do *not* measure themselves via the standard calendar. The standard calendar poses many problems that are often unacceptable:

- **Comparing this month to last month is often not "fair"** when last month had 31 days and this one has 30, for instance. Did we really perform 3% worse this month or is that just due to the different number of days?

- **Even two months of the same length are often not fair** comparisons since they contain different numbers of weekend days versus weekdays.

- **Sometimes the unit of time measured doesn't even *resemble* the wall calendar** – "Semesters" in the academic world and "Seasons" in the sports world for example

- **Going further, sometimes (such as in science), we want to literally compare *time* periods** instead of calendar periods – such as "the first five minutes after an event" compared to the following fifteen minutes etc.

In my experience, at least half of all organizations measure themselves by custom calendars. Retail businesses in particular are very sensitive to those first two problems.

So have no fear, we will address custom calendars too. We are only going to *start* with the standard calendar. Stay tuned, in later chapters, for the custom calendar treatment.

Calendar: A Very Special Lookup Table

Everything in time intelligence requires that you have a separate Calendar table. (It does not have to be named "Calendar," but I usually use that name, or "Dates.")

Where to Get a Calendar Table

There are many ways to create a calendar table. Here are a few options:

- **Import one from a database.** This is my favorite, for several reasons. But it's not an option for everyone.

- **Create one in Excel.** Pretty much available to everyone, but it does pose problems such as the need to adjust it every day.

- **Import one from Azure DataMarket (or elsewhere on the internet).** There's at least one calendar table available for free download on the internet, produced by the amazing Boyan Penev. See http://ppvt.pro/UltDate for more on this.

Properties of a Calendar Table

A calendar table must:

- **Contain at least one column of "date" data type.**

- **Contain exactly one row per day.**

- **Contain completely consecutive dates, no gaps** – even if your business is never open on weekends, those days must be in the calendar

- **Be related to all of your Data tables (Sales, etc.)**

- **Contain columns for all of your desired grouping and labels** – things like MonthName, DayOfWeek-Name, IsWknd, IsHoliday, etc. (strictly, you *can* have a Calendar table with just the one date column, but the Calendar table is the place to put all of these other columns if you *do* have them).

- ***Ideally* only "spans" the relevant date ranges for your purposes.** If your business opened in 2001, it doesn't make sense for your Calendar table to start in 2000. And if today is June 20, 2012, it doesn't make sense for June 21, 2012 to be in the Calendar yet. This is one of the trickier requirements – it's the primary reason why I like to source my Calendar from a database. It really is optional, but you will find it very useful over time. Don't worry about it much for now.

My Calendar table: imported and related

Date	DayNumberOfWeek	EnglishDayNameOfWeek	DayNumberOfMonth	Da
7/3/2003	5	Thursday	3	
7/4/2003	6	Friday	4	
7/5/2003	7	Saturday	5	
7/6/2003	1	Sunday	6	
7/7/2003	2	Monday	7	
7/8/2003	3	Tuesday	8	
7/9/2003	4	Wednesday	9	
7/10/2003	5	Thursday	10	
7/11/2003	6	Friday	11	
7/12/2003	7	Saturday	12	
7/13/2003	1	Sunday	13	
7/14/2003	2	Monday	14	
7/15/2003	3	Tuesday	15	
7/16/2003	4	Wednesday	16	
7/17/2003	5	Thursday	17	
7/18/2003	6	Friday	18	
7/19/2003	7	Saturday	19	
7/20/2003	1	Sunday	20	
7/21/2003	2	Monday	21	
7/22/2003	3	Tuesday	22	
7/23/2003	4	Wednesday	23	

stomers | Sales | Products | Calendar | Exch Rates | MinListPrice | PriceTiers

Figure 180 Calendar table – now we can get started!

Now I relate it to my Sales table, using the Date columns:

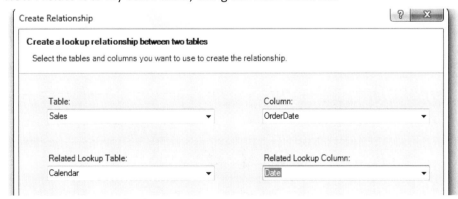

Figure 181 Relating Calendar to Sales

 In PowerPivot v1, the column used to relate Calendar to other tables *had* to be of data type Date. In v2, you can now relate using a column of a different data type, such as an integer, so you do *not* need a column of Type Date in your *Sales* table anymore, but you *do* still need a column of type Date in your *Calendar* table.

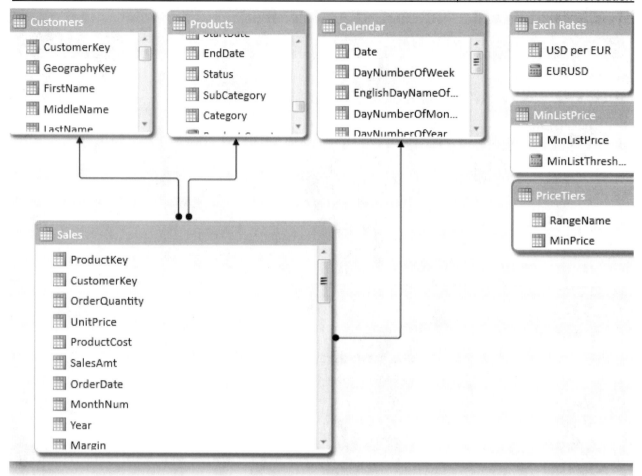

Figure 182 Updated diagram view: Calendar becomes the third lookup table

Operates Like a Normal Lookup Table

DayNameOfWeek ▼	Total Sales
Friday	$4,235,386
Monday	$4,154,920
Saturday	$4,342,674
Sunday	$4,231,642
Thursday	$4,113,749
Tuesday	$4,153,093
Wednesday	$4,127,215
Grand Total	**$29,358,677**

Figure 183 [Total Sales] with Calendar[DayNameOfWeek] on Rows

And the Sort By Column feature works here too of course:

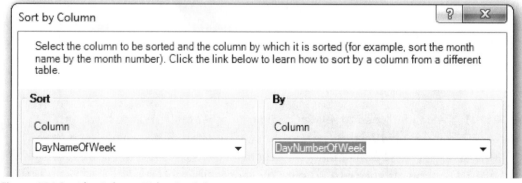

Figure 184 Sort by Column Rides Again!

DayNameOfWeek ▾	Total Sales
Sunday	$4,231,642
Monday	$4,154,920
Tuesday	$4,153,093
Wednesday	$4,127,215
Thursday	$4,113,749
Friday	$4,235,386
Saturday	$4,342,674
Grand Total	**$29,358,677**

Figure 185 Days sorting in proper order (if you want Monday to be first, just create a calculated column in Calendar that starts with 1 for Monday and ends on 7 for Sunday, and use that as your sort by column instead)

And we can repeat the same process for MonthName – every column can have its own separate sort by column:

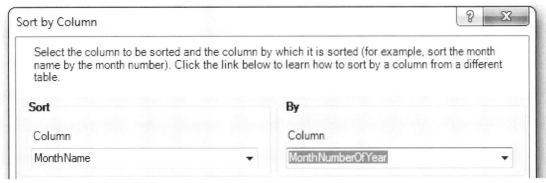

Figure 186 Setting sort order for MonthName

MonthName ▾	Total Sales
January	$2,375,857
February	$2,502,387
March	$2,610,615
April	$2,778,842
May	$3,114,646
June	$3,180,924
July	$1,911,263
August	$1,899,607
September	$1,834,668
October	$2,009,169
November	$2,076,070
December	$3,064,630
Grand Total	**$29,358,677**

Figure 187 Properly sorted month names!

First Special Feature: Enable Date Filtering via Mark as Date Table

With your Calendar table active, go to the Design tab of the ribbon and select Mark as Date Table:

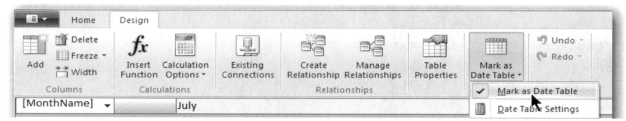

Figure 188 Make this a habit for your Calendar/Date table

Then, in the pivot, you get the special date filtering options:

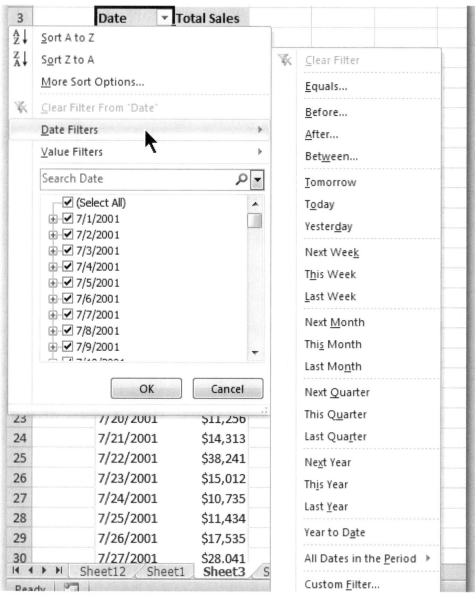

Figure 189 PowerPivot "tells" Excel that this is a Date table, so Excel enables these filter options for you (most of which are useless with my sample data since the dates are ancient, but more useful in the real world)

 If you are going to use a column of non-Date data type to relate your Calendar table to your Data tables, you MUST "mark it as date" in the PowerPivot window, or many other of the smart calculation features covered after this will not function properly.

Second Special Feature: Time Intelligence Functions!

PowerPivot includes many new functions relating to time:

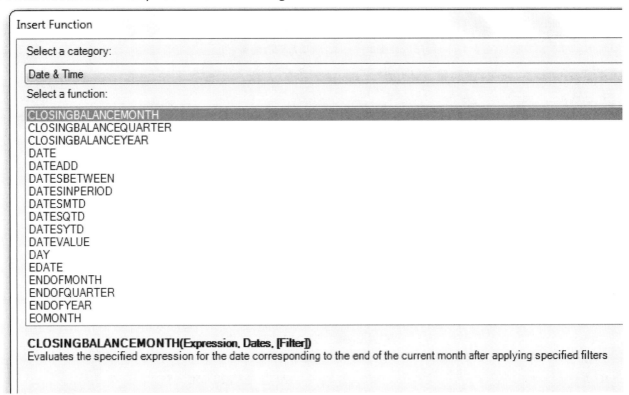

Figure 190 A subset of the DAX functions relating to time – a few are carryovers from normal Excel, but most are new.

Diving in with DATESYTD()

There are so many functions that it was hard for me to choose which one to cover first. I picked DATESYTD() not because it's somehow special relative to the others, but just because it makes for a good example.

Let's start with a simple pivot:

Figure 191 Our "testbed" for DATESYTD()

Now let's add a new measure, one that tracks Year to Date (YTD) sales:

```
[Total Sales YTD] =

=CALCULATE([Total Sales], DATESYTD(Calendar[Date]))
```

And...

CalendarYear	▼
2001	2002
2003	2004

Month ▼	Total Sales	Total Sales YTD
January	$1,340,245	$1,340,245
February	$1,462,480	$2,802,725
March	$1,480,905	$4,283,630
April	$1,608,751	$5,892,380
May	$1,878,318	$7,770,698
June	$1,949,361	$9,720,059
July	$50,841	$9,770,900
August		$9,770,900
Grand Total	$9,770,900	$9,770,900

Figure 192 New measure shows us a running total of YTD sales for each month!

And like all good PowerPivot measures, this formula is "portable" into basically any report shape you desire, just by rearranging the pivot – no formula surgery required! Remove [Total Sales] and drag Year to Columns...

Total Sales YTD	Year ▼				
Month ▼	2001	2002	2003	2004	Grand Total
January		$596,747	$438,865	$1,340,245	$1,340,245
February		$1,147,563	$927,956	$2,802,725	$2,802,725
March		$1,791,698	$1,413,530	$4,283,630	$4,283,630
April		$2,455,391	$1,919,930	$5,892,380	$5,892,380
May		$3,128,947	$2,482,702	$7,770,698	$7,770,698
June		$3,805,711	$3,037,501	$9,720,059	$9,720,059
July	$473,388	$4,306,076	$3,924,170	$9,770,900	$9,770,900
August	$979,580	$4,852,077	$4,771,584	$9,770,900	$9,770,900
September	$1,453,523	$5,202,544	$5,781,842		$5,781,842
October	$1,966,852	$5,617,934	$6,862,291		$6,862,291
November	$2,510,846	$5,953,030	$8,059,273		$8,059,273
December	$3,266,374	$6,530,344	$9,791,060		$9,791,060

Figure 193 Our new [Total Sales YTD] measure, like all good DAX measures, automatically adjusts to any new pivot shape – just rearrange using the field list, and the measure does the hard work!

Anatomy of DATESYTD()
Function Definition

ⓘ DATESYTD(<date column in calendar table>, <optional year end date>)

That first argument, <date column in calendar table>, is common to nearly all of the time intelligence functions. In PowerPivot itself, the function help just refers to it as Dates:

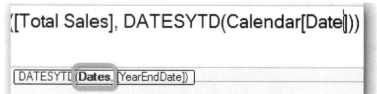

```
([Total Sales], DATESYTD(Calendar[Date]))

DATESYTD(Dates, [YearEndDate])
```

Figure 194 What I call "<date column in calendar table>, PowerPivot calls "Dates" – whenever you see that, remember my version of it, because that's what "Dates" means in the time intelligence function definitions.

DATESYTD() is used as a <filter> argument to CALCULATE(), much like ALL() and FILTER().

How Does it Work?

Like almost everything else "magical" in PowerPivot, DATESYTD() operates by manipulating filter context.

Let's return to a simple pivot layout, and highlight a particular measure cell:

CalendarYear		Month ▼	Total Sales YTD
2001	2002	January	$1,340,245
2003	**2004**	February	$2,802,725
		March	$4,283,630
		April	$5,892,380
		May	$7,770,698
		June	$9,720,059
		July	$9,770,900
		August	$9,770,900
		Grand Total	**$9,770,900**

Figure 195 For the highlighted measure cell...

DATESYTD() essentially identifies the latest date in the current filter context, and then "expands" the filter context backward from that date to the first date of the year (more specifically, to the first date in the year of that previously-identified latest date, which is 2004 in this case).

OK, then DATESYTD() modifies that filter context. Here's how.

Again, visualizing the Calendar table in calendar form:

Resulting in a new filter context:

Figure 196 If we imagine the Calendar table as a calendar rather than a table, where each row in Calendar is a single date, these are the active dates (rows) in the filter context for the measure cell highlighted in the prior figure.

Figure 197 DATESYTD() starts at the last date in the existing filter context, and then "expands" the filter context back to the first date of the year (the first date in the year of the current filter context)

Figure 198 New filter context highlighted (again visualizing the Calendar table as a calendar)

Changing the Year End Date

That last argument to DATESYTD(), which is an optional argument that I left blank in the first example, allows you to customize your calendar just a little bit. That allows you to treat June 30 as the last day of the year, for instance, which is common in Fiscal Calendars.

Here's a measure that does just that:

```
[Total Sales Fiscal YTD] =

CALCULATE([Total Sales], DATESYTD(Calendar[Date],"6/30/2004"))
```

Now let's compare that to the original YTD measure, side by side. I've added Calendar[WeekNumOfYear] to Rows, nested under Month:

CalendarYear		Month		Total Sales YTD	Total Sales Fiscal YTD
2001	2002	⊟ January			
2003	2004	1		$64,297	$2,788,930
		2		$160,190	$2,884,823
		3		$266,720	$2,991,353
		4		$361,655	$3,086,288
		5		$438,865	$3,163,498
		⊟ February			
		5		$457,003	$3,181,636
		6		$591,370	$3,316,003
		7		$711,294	$3,435,927
		8		$847,144	$3,571,777
		9		$927,956	$3,652,588
		⊟ March			
		9		$937,992	$3,662,625
		10		$1,061,270	$3,785,903
		11		$1,168,840	$3,893,473
		12		$1,284,089	$4,008,722
		13		$1,371,790	$4,096,423
		14		$1,413,530	$4,138,163
		⊟ April			
		14		$1,502,836	$4,227,469
		15		$1,621,929	$4,346,562

Figure 199 Original YTD measure starts from 0 in January, but Fiscal YTD version already is approaching $3M.

 Note how I have sliced the pivot to 2003 even though I specified 6/30/2004 in the measure. The year itself does not matter in that last argument – the DATESYTD() function only looks at month and day and ignores the year (in that particular argument.)

Now let's scroll down and see what happens at the end of June:

June			
23		$2,603,264	$5,327,897
24		$2,750,811	$5,475,444
25		$2,882,988	$5,607,621
26		$3,004,735	$5,729,367
27		$3,037,501	$5,762,134
July			
27		$3,194,171	$156,670
28		$3,387,544	$350,043
29		$3,563,304	$525,802
30		$3,782,105	$744,604
31		$3,924,170	$886,669
August			
31		$3,964,160	$926,658
32		$4,182,052	$1,144,551
33		$4,336,885	$1,299,384

Figure 200 Fiscal YTD measure resets at the end of June, just as desired

> (i) So the built-in time intelligence functions *are* capable of adapting to different year end dates. This still falls under what I call the Standard Calendar however, because the months are all still the same as the months on the wall calendar – June still has 30 days, July has 31, etc. Only when we start redefining our notions of Month/Quarter/Year to be a different from the wall calendar do we start to "break" functions like DATESYTD(). You will see what I mean when we get to that chapter.

DATESMTD() and DATESQTD() – "Cousins" of DATESYTD()

These functions are the "month to date" and "quarter to date" versions of DATESYTD(), so I won't walk you through them – their usage is just like what I've illustrated for DATESYTD(). The only difference is that neither of them offer that optional second argument for YearEnd Date.

TOTALYTD() – Another Cousin of DATESYTD()

TOTALYTD() is actually a replacement for CALCULATE(), one that "bakes in" a DATESYTD().

For example, our original YTD measure:

```
[Total Sales YTD] =

=CALCULATE([Total Sales], DATESYTD(Calendar[Date]))
```

Can be rewritten as:

```
[Total Sales YTD] =

=TOTALYTD([Total Sales], Calendar[Date])
```

I suppose that's a bit more readable – shorter for sure. But I don't see this as particularly necessary, we'd be fine without this function. Whether you choose to use it is really just a matter of personal preference.

The Remaining (Many) Time Intelligence Functions – Grouped Into "Families"

As I said previously, there are *many* time intelligence functions. But it's pretty easy to group them into "families" (to continue the "cousin" metaphor). If I cover an example from each family, that will give you a foundation – the ability to quickly adopt whatever function you need – without me boring us both to death covering every single function.

We've already covered the DATESYTD() family. Let's press forward, and take a tour of each remaining family.

FIRSTDATE() and LASTDATE()

This is a simple family, and it only contains these two.

Quite simply, these are the date versions of MIN() and MAX()

Briefly, let's define two measures:

```
[FIRSTDATE Example] =
  FIRSTDATE(Calendar[Date])
```

And:

```
[LASTDATE Example] =
  LASTDATE(Calendar[Date])
```

And look at them on our Month/Weeknum pivot:

CalendarYear		Month - WeekNumOfYear	FIRSTDATE Example	LASTDATE Example
2001	2002	⊟January	**1/1/2003**	**1/31/2003**
2003	2004	1	1/1/2003	1/4/2003
		2	1/5/2003	1/11/2003
		3	1/12/2003	1/18/2003
		4	1/19/2003	1/25/2003
		5	1/26/2003	1/31/2003
		⊟February	**2/1/2003**	**2/28/2003**
		5	2/1/2003	2/1/2003
		6	2/2/2003	2/8/2003
		7	2/9/2003	2/15/2003
		8	2/16/2003	2/22/2003
		9	2/23/2003	2/28/2003
		⊟March	**3/1/2003**	**3/31/2003**
		9	3/1/2003	3/1/2003

Figure 201 FIRSTDATE() and LASTDATE() in action

 In the field list I placed both of these measures on the Calendar table since their "arithmetic" operates on the Calendar itself – they return dates rather than sales data or product counts, etc.

ENDOFMONTH(), STARTOFYEAR(), etc.

These return single dates, and have special handling for different "size" periods of time.

Again, let's illustrate by example:

```
[ENDOFMONTH Measure] =
  ENDOFMONTH(Calendar[Date])
```

ENDOFMONTH Measure	Column Labels ▾				
Row Labels ▾	2001	2002	2003	2004	Grand Total
January		1/31/2002	1/31/2003	1/31/2004	1/31/2004
February		2/28/2002	2/28/2003	2/29/2004	2/29/2004
March		3/31/2002	3/31/2003	3/31/2004	3/31/2004
April		4/30/2002	4/30/2003	4/30/2004	4/30/2004
May		5/31/2002	5/31/2003	5/31/2004	5/31/2004
June		6/30/2002	6/30/2003	6/30/2004	6/30/2004
July	7/31/2001	7/31/2002	7/31/2003	7/31/2004	7/31/2004
August	8/31/2001	8/31/2002	8/31/2003	8/31/2004	8/31/2004
September	9/30/2001	9/30/2002	9/30/2003		9/30/2003
October	10/31/2001	10/31/2002	10/31/2003		10/31/2003
November	11/30/2001	11/30/2002	11/30/2003		11/30/2003
December	12/31/2001	12/31/2002	12/31/2003		12/31/2003
Grand Total	12/31/2001	12/31/2002	12/31/2003	8/31/2004	8/31/2004

Figure 202 Does about what you expect right?

Now let's swap out Month for Quarter on Rows:

ENDOFMONTH Measure	Column Labels ▾				
Quarter ▾	2001	2002	2003	2004	Grand Total
1		3/31/2002	3/31/2003	3/31/2004	3/31/2004
2		6/30/2002	6/30/2003	6/30/2004	6/30/2004
3	9/30/2001	9/30/2002	9/30/2003	8/31/2004	8/31/2004
4	12/31/2001	12/31/2002	12/31/2003		12/31/2003
Grand Total	12/31/2001	12/31/2002	12/31/2003	8/31/2004	8/31/2004

Figure 203 9/30/2001 is the last date in the last month of Q3 2001

Make sense? If you feed more than a single month to ENDOFMONTH(), it will find the last date in the last month.

But when you feed it a filter context of "size" *less* than a month, we get something different:

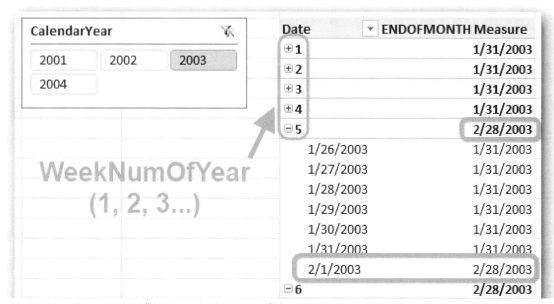

Figure 204 ENDOFMONTH() returns the last day of the month even if that day is NOT part of the current filter context.

The rest of this family behaves in much the same way.

CLOSINGBALANCEMONTH(),CLOSINGBALANCE-YEAR(), ETC.

These functions are CALCULATE() replacements that have "hardwired" date logic equivalent to END-OFMONTH(), STARTOFYEAR(), etc.

 CLOSINGBALANCEMONTH(<measure expression>,<Date Column>,<optional filter>)

Example measure:

```
[Total Sales CLOSINGBALANCEMONTH]=

CLOSINGBALANCEMONTH([Total Sales], Calendar[Date])
```

CalendarYear		Row Labels	Total Sales	Total Sales CLOSINGBALANCEMONTH
2001	2002	⊟ January	$97,267	$17,469
2003	2004	1/24/2003	$13,759	$17,469
		1/25/2003	$6,298	$17,469
		1/26/2003	$20,301	$17,469
		1/27/2003	$5,275	$17,469
		1/28/2003	$11,451	$17,469
		1/29/2003	$13,474	$17,469
		1/30/2003	$9,240	$17,469
		1/31/2003	$17,469	$17,469
		⊟ February	$489,090	$12,772
		2/1/2003	$18,138	$12,772
		2/2/2003	$19,624	$12,772
		2/3/2003	$11,302	$12,772

Figure 205 CLOSINGBALANCEMONTH() always returns the value of its base measure on the last day of the month in the current filter context (I have used a Sales measure here to demonstrate, but in reality, these functions are more useful with things like Inventory or Cash Balance.)

DATEADD() and SAMEPERIODLASTYEAR()

DATEADD()

This function is also used as a <filter> argument to CALCULATE(), and shifts your date filter context forward or backward in time.

 DATEADD(<Date Column>, <number of intervals>, <interval type>)

- <Date Column> - the usual. Put your date column from your calendar table here.

- <Number of Intervals> - Set this to 1 to move one interval later in time, -1 to move back one, etc.

- <Interval Type> - Set this to Year, Quarter, Month, or Day – no quotes

Example measure that shows us last year's [Total Sales]:

```
[Total Sales DATEADD 1 Year Back] =

CALCULATE([Total Sales], DATEADD(Calendar[Date], -1,
          Year))
```

Here are its results for 2003 side-by-side with a pivot showing the original [Total Sales] measure for 2002:

CalendarYear 2003		CalendarYear 2002	
Month	**Total Sales DATEADD 1 Year Back**	**Month**	**Total Sales**
January	$596,747	January	$596,747
February	$550,817	February	$550,817
March	$644,135	March	$644,135
April	$663,692	April	$663,692
May	$673,556	May	$673,556
June	$676,764	June	$676,764
July	$500,365	July	$500,365
August	$546,001	August	$546,001
September	$350,467	September	$350,467
October	$415,390	October	$415,390
November	$335,095	November	$335,095
December	$577,314	December	$577,314
Grand Total	**$6,530,344**	**Grand Total**	**$6,530,344**

Figure 206 DATEADD() version filtered to 2003 matches the original measure filtered to 2002

And now the same comparison, but with Quarter on Rows instead:

CalendarYear 2003		CalendarYear 2002	
Quarter	**Total Sales DATEADD 1 Year Back**	**Quarter**	**Total Sales**
1	$1,791,698	1	$1,791,698
2	$2,014,012	2	$2,014,012
3	$1,396,834	3	$1,396,834
4	$1,327,799	4	$1,327,799
Grand Total	**$6,530,344**	**Grand Total**	**$6,530,344**

Figure 207 Same comparison, just with Quarter on Rows rather than Month. Again, perfect match.

Growth Versus Last Year (Year-Over-Year, YOY, etc.)

One obvious application of DATEADD() and similar functions is the calculation of growth versus the prior year.

```
[Pct Sales Growth YOY] =

([Total Sales] - [Total Sales DATEADD 1 Year Back]) /
       [Total Sales DATEADD 1 Year Back]
```

CalendarYear 2003			CalendarYear 2002	
Month ▾	**Pct Sales Growth YOY**	**Total Sales**	**Month** ▾	**Total Sales**
January	-26.5 %	$438,865	January	$596,747
February	-11.2 %	$489,090	February	$550,817
March	-24.6 %	$485,575	March	$644,135
April	-23.7 %	$506,399	April	$663,692
May	-16.4 %	$562,773	May	$673,556
June	-18.0 %	$554,799	June	$676,764
July	77.2 %	$886,669	July	$500,365
August	55.2 %	$847,414	August	$546,001
September	188.3 %	$1,010,258	September	$350,467
October	160.1 %	$1,080,450	October	$415,390
November	257.2 %	$1,196,981	November	$335,095
December	200.0 %	$1,731,788	December	$577,314
Grand Total	**49.9 %**	**$9,791,060**	**Grand Total**	**$6,530,344**

Figure 208 [Pct Growth YOY] displayed for 2003 and compared to 2002 in the second pivot

Quirks and Caveats

There are a few things you will discover about DATEADD() that might make you scratch your head a bit, so I'll give some advanced notice.

You must have contiguous date ranges on your pivot

If I filter a Quarter out of my pivot I will get an error:

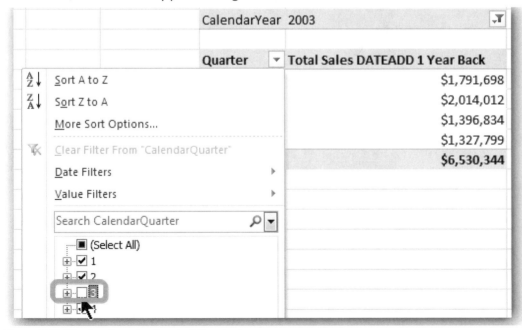

Figure 209 Filtering Quarter 3 out of the pivot...

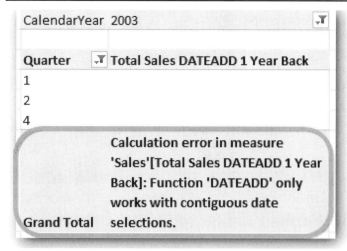

Figure 210 ...yields an error with DATEADD()

The same thing would happen if I were using Month on rows and filtered out one or more months.

> *(i)* Note that the error occurs in the Grand Total cell. There is *nothing* wrong with each of the single-Quarter measure cell calculations, but when the Grand Total fails, the entire pivot fails. The filter context of the Grand Total cell is Quarter={1,2,3} and Year={2003}, and when DATEADD() goes back a year, that "skips" Quarter 4 of 2002, which DATEADD() cannot do.

> *(i)* Merely hiding the Grand Total (using the pivot Design tab on the ribbon) will *not* fix this problem. The only way to fix this is to prevent the Grand Total from even being calculated in the first place, which I will explain in the chapter on IF().

DATEADD() has special handling for "complete" months/quarters/years

This one and the next one are really subtle. If you struggle to understand, don't worry about it – just remember that there's something special going on here, so that if/when you discover this on your own, you can come back here and re-read this section.

2004 is a leap year, in which February contains 29 days. Let's add a simple measure to the Calendar table that shows this:

```
[Number of Days] =

  COUNTROWS(Calendar)
```

Figure 211 29 days in Feb 2004

And now I will add the DATEADD() measure we created before, [Total Sales DATEADD 1 Year Back]:

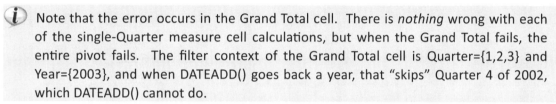

Year	2004	
Month	**Number of Days**	**Total Sales DATEADD 1 Year Back**
January	31	$438,865
February	29	$489,090
March	31	$485,575
April	30	$506,399
May	31	$562,773
June	30	$554,799
July	31	$886,669
August	31	$847,414
Grand Total	**244**	**$4,771,584**

Figure 212 Question: does $489,090 represent 28 days of 2003 sales, or 29?

Let's compare that to a 2003 pivot for the "raw" [Total Sales] measure:

lendarYear 2004				CalendarYear 2003		
onth ▼	Number of Days	Total Sales DATEADD 1 Year Back		Month ▼	Total Sales	Number of Days
nuary	31	$438,865		January	$438,865	31
bruary	29	$489,090		February	$489,090	28
arch	31	$485,575		March	$485,575	31
ril	30	$506,399		April	$506,399	30
ay	31	$562,773		May	$562,773	31

Figure 213 DATEADD() is returning 28 days' worth of Feb 2003 sales even though it starts out with a 29-day filter context in 2004!

DATEADD() Lacks intelligence for Weeks

CalendarYear 2004		CalendarYear 2003	
WeekNum ▼	Total Sales DATEADD 1 Year Back	WeekNum ▼	Total Sales
1	$45,668	1	$64,297
2	$100,546	2	$95,893
3	$107,535	3	$106,530
4	$101,609	4	$94,935
5	$83,508	5	$95,348
6	$135,289	6	$134,367
7	$118,548	7	$119,924
8	$132,961	8	$135,850

Figure 214 With WeekNum on Rows, the DATEADD() measure does NOT match!

To see why the numbers don't match, we need to add Date to Rows as well:

CalendarYear 2004		CalendarYear 2003	
WeekNum ▼	Total Sales DATEADD 1 Year Back	WeekNum ▼	Total Sales
⊟1	$45,668	⊟1	$64,297
Thursday	$12,445	Wednesday	$12,445
Friday	$19,703	Thursday	$19,703
Saturday	$13,520	Friday	$13,520
⊟2	$100,546	Saturday	$18,629
Sunday	$18,629	⊟2	$95,893
Monday	$13,497	Sunday	$13,497
Tuesday	$4,363	Monday	$4,363
Wednesd	$14,623	Tuesday	$14,623
Thursday	$15,733	Wednesday	$15,733
Friday	$18,142	Thursday	$18,142
Saturday	$15,558	Friday	$15,558
⊟3	$107,535	Saturday	$13,977

Figure 215 Both pivots report Sunday through Monday, but the DATEADD() measure is returning 2003's Sunday sales in the context of 2004 Monday

Stated another way, the weeks are misaligned by one day:

CalendarYear 2004		CalendarYear 2003	
WeekNum ▾ **Total Sales DATEADD 1 Year Back**		**WeekNum** ▾ **Total Sales**	
⊟ **1**	**$45,668**	⊟ **1**	**$64,297**
Thursday	$12,445	Wednesday	$12,445
Friday	$19,703	Thursday	$19,703
Saturday	$13,520	Friday	$13,520
⊟ **2**	**$100,546**	Saturday	$18,629
Sunday	$18,629	⊟ **2**	**$95,893**
Monday	$13,497	Sunday	$13,497
Tuesday	$4,363	Monday	$4,363
Wednesd	$14,623	Tuesday	$14,623
Thursday	$15,733	Wednesday	$15,733
Friday	$18,142	Thursday	$18,142
Saturday	$15,558	Friday	$15,558
⊟ **3**	**$107,535**	Saturday	$13,977
Sunday	$13,977	⊟ **3**	**$106,530**

Figure 216 **Why doesn't this work, if it works for Month and Quarter?** *Well for starters, 52 weeks in a year times 7 days per week = 364. So we are never going to get weeks quite right unless we change years to be 364 days long instead of 365 (which some custom calendars actually do).*

So the concept of "week" is defined only in my Calendar table, in the WeekNumOfYear column. Look at the pivots above – Week 1 of 2004 has only 3 days in it! And Week 1 of 2003 has only 4!

That's purely the "fault" of my Calendar table:

D... 🔒 ▾	DayNameOfWeek ▾	WeekNumberOfYear 🔽	CalendarYear 🔽
1/1/2004	Thursday	1	2004
1/2/2004	Friday	1	2004
1/3/2004	Saturday	1	2004

Figure 217 My Calendar table DOES only have 3 days in it for Week 1 of 2004

Whereas the time intelligence functions can intrinsically "know" what we mean by Month/Quarter/Year, they rely on the calendar table for all other concepts, so there isn't any "magic fixup" when I navigate using DATEADD() in a filter context involving weeks.

SAMEPERIODLASTYEAR()

ⓘ SAMEPERIODLASTYEAR(<Date Column>)

This is a shortcut function that is just a wrapper to DATEADD(). It is 100% equivalent to DATEADD() with "-1, Year" as the last two arguments:

```
SAMEPERIODLASTYEAR(Calendar[Date])
```

Is exactly the same as:

```
DATEADD(Calendar[Date], -1, Year)
```

PARALLELPERIOD(), NEXTMONTH(), PREVIOUS YEAR(), etc.

PARALLELPERIOD()

This one is *almost* a wrapper to DATEADD(), but it differs in one crucial way that is best shown by example.

 PARALLELPERIOD(<Date Column>, <number of intervals>, <interval type>)

Let's create an example measure:

```
[Total Sales PARALLELPERIOD Back 1 Year] =

CALCULATE([Total Sales], PARALLELPERIOD(Calendar[Date], -1, Year))
```

CalendarYear	2003		CalendarYear	2002
Row Labels	Total Sales PARALLELPERIOD Back 1 Year		Month	Total Sales
January	$6,530,344		January	$596,747
February	$6,530,344		February	$550,817
March	$6,530,344		March	$644,135
April	$6,530,344		April	$663,692
May	$6,530,344		May	$673,556
June	$6,530,344		June	$676,764
July	$6,530,344		July	$500,365
August	$6,530,344		August	$546,001
September	$6,530,344		September	$350,467
October	$6,530,344		October	$415,390
November	$6,530,344		November	$335,095
December	$6,530,344		December	$577,314
Grand Total	$6,530,344		Grand Total	$6,530,344

Figure 218 PARALLELPERIOD() always fetches the full year when you go back 1 year, no matter what "size" your filter context is (Month in this case).

So PARALLELPERIOD() *navigates* **just like DATEADD(), but when it gets to its "destination," it expands the filter context to the size of the specified <interval type> - Year, Quarter, or Month.**

 Reminder: you don't have to remember all of the details of all of these functions. (I sure don't!) You just need to know that they exist, then be able to find the one that serves your current purpose, and quickly re-familiarize yourself as needed.

NEXTMONTH(), PREVIOUSYEAR(), etc.

These functions are all just wrappers to PARALLELPERIOD() – they navigate and expand in exactly the same way.

```
[Total Sales NEXTMONTH]=

CALCULATE([Total Sales], NEXTMONTH(Calendar[Date]))
```

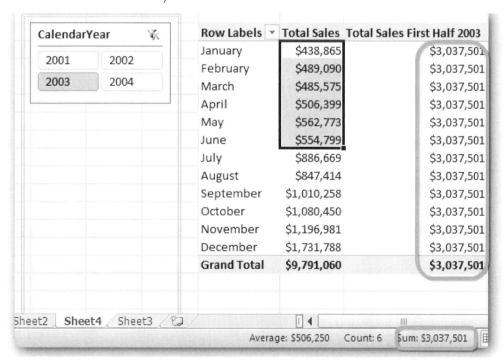

Figure 219 NEXTMONTH() always grabs the FULL next month, even if we start in the context of a single day.

DATESBETWEEN()

Ah, I have a special place in my heart for DATESBETWEEN(). Sometimes, you don't want anything special – you just want total control over the date range in a measure. And DATESBETWEEN() delivers just that.

> *DATESBETWEEN(<date column>, <start date expr>, <end date expr>)*

Let's start with a very simple example:

```
[Total Sales First Half 2003] =

CALCULATE([Total Sales],
        DATESBETWEEN(Calendar[Date],
        "1/1/2003","6/30/2003")
        )
```

CalendarYear		Row Labels	Total Sales	Total Sales First Half 2003
2001 2002		January	$438,865	$3,037,501
2003 2004		February	$489,090	$3,037,501
		March	$485,575	$3,037,501
		April	$506,399	$3,037,501
		May	$562,773	$3,037,501
		June	$554,799	$3,037,501
		July	$886,669	$3,037,501
		August	$847,414	$3,037,501
		September	$1,010,258	$3,037,501
		October	$1,080,450	$3,037,501
		November	$1,196,981	$3,037,501
		December	$1,731,788	$3,037,501
		Grand Total	**$9,791,060**	**$3,037,501**

Sheet2 Sheet4 Sheet3

Average: $506,250   Count: 6   Sum: $3,037,501

Figure 220 Note how DATEBETWEEN() completely overrides existing filter context on the Calendar table, otherwise it would be blank for July-December (and for January-June would match [Total Sales] for each month)

"Life to Date" Calculations

Earlier, we used DATESYTD() to calculate "year to date" sales, but what if you want a running total that does not reset at the start of each year, but instead just keeps piling up year after year?

Fortunately, DATEBETWEEN() lets us use expressions for the endpoint arguments:

```
[Total Sales Life to Date] =

CALCULATE([Total Sales],
          DATESBETWEEN(Calendar[Date], "1/1/1900",
                       LASTDATE(Calendar[Date])
          )
)
```

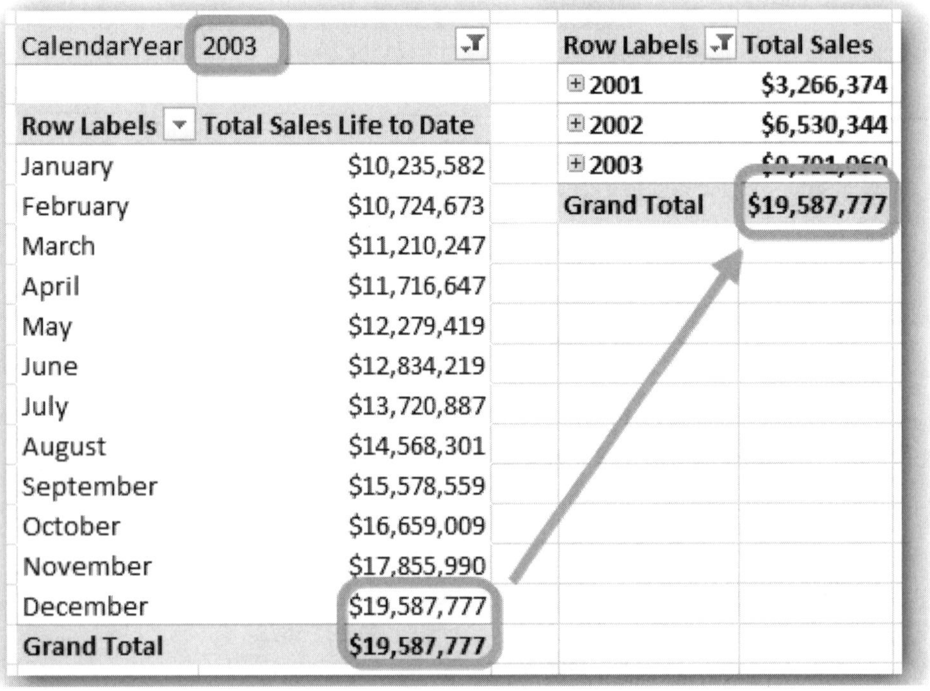

Figure 221 "Life to Date" using DATESBETWEEN() matches grand total across 2001-2003, as expected

Figure 222 Expanding to Month level, "Life to Date" measure still returns expected results

Removing That Hardwired 1/1/1900

Yeah, that's ugly. Let's replace it with FIRSTDATE(ALL(Calendar[Date])):

```
[Total Sales Life to Date] =
 CALCULATE([Total Sales],
           DATESBETWEEN(Calendar[Date],
                        FIRSTDATE(ALL(Calendar[Date])),
                        LASTDATE(Calendar[Date])
                       )
          )
```

Why ALL(Calendar[Date])? Because otherwise we'd just get the first date in the filter context, (which would be January 1, 2003 in the $10,235,582 cell highlighted in the pivot above). We need to apply ALL() in order to clear the current filter context and literally find the first date in the entire Calendar table.

 Note that we do *not* want ALL() on the LASTDATE() in the <end date> argument of DATEBETWEEN() in this case, otherwise it would always return sales for all time, and not sales up until the current filter context date.

DATESBETWEEN() is Fantastic with Disconnected Tables too!

You remember the Min/Max Threshold version of disconnected tables? You can do the same thing with dates, using a disconnected DateRange table, your normal Calendar table, and DATESBETWEEN().

I won't belabor that here, since it's a repetition of a familiar pattern, but for a detailed example, see http://

ppvt.pro/ABCampaign

15- IF(), SWITCH(), BLANK(), and Other Conditional Fun

Using IF() in Measures

It is time to introduce conditional/branching logic into our measure formulas. This starts out as simple as you would expect.

Consider our [Pct Sales Growth YOY] measure from last chapter:

```
[Pct Sales Growth YOY] =

([Total Sales] - [Total Sales DATEADD 1 Year Back]) /
        [Total Sales DATEADD 1 Year Back]
```

Row Labels ▾	Pct Sales Growth YOY
2001	#NUM!
2002	99.9 %
2003	49.9 %
2004	104.8 %
Grand Total	**101.5 %**

Figure 223 We get a #NUM error for 2001

We get an error because [Total Sales DATEADD 1 Year Back] is 0 for 2001 – there were no sales in 2000, so this is really a "div by 0" error.

 Technically speaking, [Total Sales DATEADD 1 Year Back] is *not* returning 0 for 2001, it is returning blank – when there are no rows in the source tables corresponding to the filter context, measures return blank. But when we divide by blank, that's the same as dividing by zero in terms of causing an error.

This is an easy fix – we just edit the formula, and wrap our original formula in an IF():

```
[Pct Sales Growth YOY] =

IF([Total Sales DATEADD 1 Year Back]=0, 0,
    ([Total Sales] - [Total Sales DATEADD 1 Year Back]) /
    [Total Sales DATEADD 1 Year Back]
    )
```

And the results:

Row Labels ▾	Pct Sales Growth YOY
2001	0.0 %
2002	99.9 %
2003	49.9 %
2004	104.8 %
Grand Total	**101.5 %**

Figure 224 Now returns 0% instead of an error

The BLANK() Function

We can do better than 0% though can't we? 0% implies that we had 0 growth, when in reality, this calculation makes no sense at all for 2001.

So rather than return 0, we can return the BLANK() function.

135

Let's edit the formula accordingly:

```
[Pct Sales Growth YOY] =
IF([Total Sales DATEADD 1 Year Back]=0, BLANK(),
    ([Total Sales] - [Total Sales DATEADD 1 Year Back]) /
     [Total Sales DATEADD 1 Year Back]
  )
```

And the results:

Row Labels ▾	Pct Sales Growth YOY
2002	99.9 %
2003	49.9 %
2004	104.8 %
Grand Total	**101.5 %**

Figure 225 Aha! Now 2001 is gone completely, nice!

Why does 2001 disappear from the pivot completely? Because all displayed measures return BLANK() for 2001.

 This is a VERY helpful trick. Retuning BLANK() in certain situations will become one of your most relied-upon techniques.

If we add a measure that is not BLANK() for 2001, 2001 is displayed once again:

Row Labels ▾	Pct Sales Growth YOY	Total Sales
2001		$3,266,374
2002	99.9 %	$6,530,344
2003	49.9 %	$9,791,060
2004	104.8 %	$9,770,900
Grand Total	**101.5 %**	**$29,358,677**

Figure 226 2001 is displayed as long as any single measure returns a non-blank result

You can force 2001 to display, however, even if all measures are blank. Under Pivot Options, on the Pivot Options tab, are the following two checkboxes:

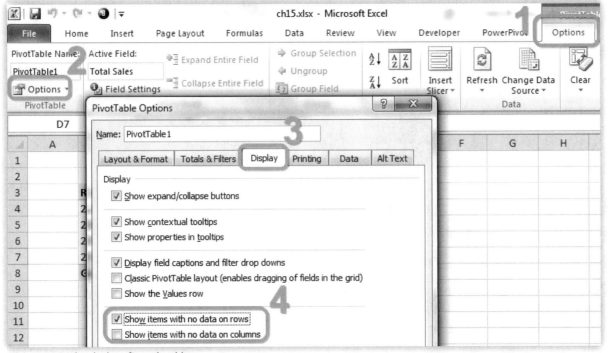

Figure 227 Check that first checkbox…

Row Labels ▼	Pct Sales Growth YOY
2001	
2002	99.9 %
2003	49.9 %
2004	104.8 %
Grand Total	**101.5 %**

Figure 228 ...and 2001 will be displayed even when all measures are blank.

The ISBLANK() Function

Excel has this function too, of course, but it's worth bringing up here. When I test for "=0" as I did in the formulas above, and the measure returns BLANK(), the IF() evaluate to True.

I could have tested for ISBLANK() instead of "=0", but that would still leave me exposed to an error in the case where [Total Sales DATEADD 1 Year Back] returned a legitimate 0 (meaning, there were rows, but the sum of the SalesAmt column was 0 – rare but possible).

So most of the time, I just test for "=0." But when you want to distinguish between 0 and BLANK(), ISBLANK() is what you need.

HASONEVALUE()

Another new function in PowerPivot V2. Primarily you can think of this as the "am I in a subtotal or grand total cell?" function, although it definitely comes in handy elsewhere too.

To demonstrate, first let me create the following measure:

```
[Subcategory pct of Category Sales] =

[Total Sales] /
CALCULATE([Total Sales],
          ALL(Products[SubCategory])
          )
```

And here it is with along with [Total Sales], and Category/Subcategory on Rows:

Row Labels ▼	Total Sales	Subcat pct of Cat Sales
⊟ **Accessories**	**$700,760**	**100.00 %**
Bike Racks	$39,360	5.62 %
Bike Stands	$39,591	5.65 %
Bottles and Cages	$56,798	8.11 %
Cleaners	$7,219	1.03 %
Fenders	$46,620	6.65 %
Helmets	$225,336	32.16 %
Hydration Packs	$40,308	5.75 %
Tires and Tubes	$245,529	35.04 %
⊟ **Bikes**	**$28,318,145**	**100.00 %**
Mountain Bikes	$9,952,760	35.15 %
Road Bikes	$14,520,584	51.28 %
Touring Bikes	$3,844,801	13.58 %
⊟ **Clothing**	**$339,773**	**100.00 %**
Caps	$19,688	5.79 %
Gloves	$35,021	10.31 %
Jerseys	$172,951	50.90 %
Shorts	$71,320	20.99 %
Socks	$5,106	1.50 %
Vests	$35,687	10.50 %
Grand Total	**$29,358,677**	**100.00 %**

Figure 229 Each Subcategory is calculated as a percentage of its parent Category, in terms of [Total Sales]

Those 100.0% subtotals and grand total are useless though. I'd love to suppress them.

To do this, I am going to detect when my filter context contains more than one Subcategory, because having more than one Subcategory is the definition of a subtotal/grand total cell for that field, as explained in the chapter on ALL().

So I edit my original measure to detect that condition, using the HASONEVALUE() function:

```
[Subcategory pct of Category Sales] =

IF(HASONEVALUE(Products[SubCategory]),
    [Total Sales] /
      CALCULATE([Total Sales], ALL(Products[SubCategory]))
    , BLANK()
    )
```

 HASONEVALUE() is equivalent to IF(COUNTROWS(VALUES())=1 – we used to have to use this latter approach, but now in PowerPivot v2, HASONEVALUE() is much better.

Results:

Row Labels	Total Sales	Subcat pct of Cat Sales
⊟ Accessories	$700,760	
Bike Racks	$39,360	5.62 %
Bike Stands	$39,591	5.65 %
Bottles and Cages	$56,798	8.11 %
Cleaners	$7,219	1.03 %
Fenders	$46,620	6.65 %
Helmets	$225,336	32.16 %
Hydration Packs	$40,308	5.75 %
Tires and Tubes	$245,529	35.04 %
⊟ Bikes	$28,318,145	
Mountain Bikes	$9,952,760	35.15 %
Road Bikes	$14,520,584	51.28 %
Touring Bikes	$3,844,801	13.58 %
⊟ Clothing	$339,773	
Caps	$19,688	5.79 %
Gloves	$35,021	10.31 %
Jerseys	$172,951	50.90 %
Shorts	$71,320	20.99 %
Socks	$5,106	1.50 %
Vests	$35,687	10.50 %
Grand Total	$29,358,677	

Figure 230 Subtotals and grand totals suppressed for just this measure, still "on" for [Total Sales]

 I could turn off Subtotals and/or Grand Totals via the Pivot Design tab on the ribbon, but that would turn off totals for [Total Sales] as well. I want to do this *just* for [Subcat pct of Cat Sales].

IF() Based on Row/Column/Filter/Slicer Fields

Our first use of IF() in this chapter tested against the value of a measure. But what if we want to test where we "are" in the pivot in terms of filter context?

For example, what if we want to calculate something a little differently for a specific country?

I've added a new lookup table to my model, one named SalesTerritory. It contains a Country column, which I am displaying on Rows, along with my [Sales to Parents] measure:

Country	Sales to Parents
Australia	$2,486,889
Canada	$762,530
France	$1,400,775
Germany	$1,460,348
United Kingdom	$1,666,415
United States	$3,655,420

Figure 231 I don't trust that number for Canada...

All right, let's invent a problem. Pretend for a moment that I cannot trust the [NumberOfChildren] column in my Customers table for Canadian customers – something about the way I collect data in Canada makes that number not trustworthy. And that column is the basis for my [Sales to Parents] measure.

So for Canada, and Canada only, I want to substitute a different measure, [Sales to Married Couples], for that measure. (And of course, everyone in my organization is "on board" with this change – I'm not deliberately misleading anyone!)

So, how do I detect when Country=Canada? I'll give you the measure formula first and then explain it.

```
[Sales to Parents Adj for Canada]=

IF(HASONEVALUE(SalesTerritory[Country]),
    IF(VALUES(SalesTerritory[Country])="Canada",
        [Sales to Married Couples],
        [Sales to Parents]
        )
    ,
    BLANK()
    )
```

The VALUES() Function

First, let's explain what this VALUES() function is all about. Quite simply, it returns the filter context as specified by the pivot. So sometimes it returns a single value for a column, and other times it returns multiple values (if you are in a total cell).

Examples:

Country	Sales to Parents
Australia	$2,486,889
Canada	$762,530
France	$1,400,775
Germany	$1,460,348
United Kingdom	$1,666,415
United States	$3,655,420
Grand Total	**$11,432,377**

Figure 232 For the highlighted measure cell, VALUES(SalesTerritory[Country]) returns "Canada"

Country	Sales to Parents
Australia	$2,486,889
Canada	$762,530
France	$1,400,775
Germany	$1,460,348
United Kingdom	$1,666,415
United States	$3,655,420
Grand Total	**$11,432,377**

Figure 233 In this case though, it returns multiple values: {"Australia"," Canada", "France"... , "United States"}

OK, now let's work from the inside out and explain the formula.

1. **IF(VALUES(SalesTerritory[Country])="Canada"** – we cannot directly test IF(SalesTerritory[Country]) – that violates the "no naked columns" rule of measures. And since Country is a text string, we need to use something other than MIN, MAX, etc., so we use VALUES().

2. **IF(HASONEVALUE(SalesTerritory[Country])** – If we perform an IF(VALUES()) ="Canada" test in a case where there is more than one value, we will get an error. So we need to "protect" our IF(VALUES()) test with the IF(HASONEVALUE()) test, and only let the IF(VALUES()) test "run" in cases where there is only one value.

OK, let's see the measure in action:

Country	Sales to Parents	Sales to Parents Adj for Canada
Australia	$2,486,889	$2,486,889
Canada	$762,530	$1,078,215
France	$1,400,775	$1,400,775
Germany	$1,460,348	$1,460,348
United Kingdom	$1,666,415	$1,666,415
United States	$3,655,420	$3,655,420

Figure 234 Our special measure differs only for Canada, as desired.

Using VALUES() for Columns That Are Not on the Pivot

You are *not* restricted to using VALUES() with columns that are on the pivot. In fact it is often quite useful to use VALUES() with a column that is *not* used.

For instance, let's look at this pivot that has two fields from the Products table on Rows (Category and Color), and the simple [Product Count] measure:

Category - Color	Product Count
⊟Accessories	35
Black	3
Blue	3
Grey	1
NA	24
Red	3
Silver	1
⊟Bikes	125
Black	43
Blue	13
Red	27
Silver	19
Yellow	23
⊟Clothing	48
Black	19
Blue	2

Figure 235 Simple Products pivot

Now let's focus on a single cell:

Figure 236 For the highlighted measure cell, what does VALUES(Products[Color]) return?

In this case, VALUES(Products[Color]) returns {"Black", "Blue", "Red", "Silver", "Yellow"}.

 Note how "Grey" and "NA" are *not* returned for this "Bikes" measure cell, but those two colors *are* returned for Accessories. This is because Category and Color (the fields on Rows) are both columns from the Products table, which means that a Category filter has an impact on what is valid for Color. Category="Bikes" filters the Products table, and there are no Bikes of Color "Grey" or "NA".

The same sort of thing would be true if Color came from Products and Category came from a related table, one that had a Lookup Table role with respect to Products (since Lookup tables filter their partner Data tables).

Now, if I remove Color from the pivot, what does VALUES(Products[Color]) return?

Category - Color ▼	Product Count
Accessories	35
Bikes	125
Clothing	48
Components	189
Grand Total	**397**

Figure 237 Same pivot cell after Color has been removed – what does VALUES(Products[Color]) return?

It returns exactly the same list as before: {"Black", "Blue", "Red", "Silver", "Yellow"}.

Whether Color was on the pivot or not, the cell we had highlighted did *not* have any direct filters applied for Color. The only Color filters were those implied by the Category filter context, which is still there.

 So if we had Calendar[Year] on the pivot in place of Products[Category], VALUES(Products[Color]) would return all colors, since Calendar and Products have no relationship between them.

VALUES() Only Returns Unique Values

I had the [Product Count] measure on the pivot for a reason:

Category - Color ▼	Product Count
⊟Accessories	35
Black	3
Blue	3
Grey	1
NA	24
Red	3
Silver	1
⊟Bikes	125
Black	43

Figure 238 There are 35 Products in the Accessories Category, which is 35 rows of the Products table, but only 6 different values for Color.

So even though the filter context has 35 rows of the Products table "active" for the highlighted cell, COUNTROWS(VALUES(Products[Color])) would return 6.

To drive that home, let's do exactly that:

[Color Values] =

COUNTROWS(VALUES(Products[Color]))

Category - Color ▾	Product Count	Color Values
⊟ Accessories	35	6
Black	3	1
Blue	3	1
Grey	1	1
NA	24	1
Red	3	1
Silver	1	1

Figure 239 Proof that VALUES() only returns the unique values

SWITCH()

What if we want to do something different for multiple different countries though, and not just Canada? Nested IF()'s are one way of course, but the new function SWITCH() is *much* cleaner.

Here's a completely arbitrary example, since it's hard to come up with something realistic using sample data:

```
[Different Number per Country] =

IF(HASONEVALUE(SalesTerritory[Country]),
    SWITCH(VALUES(SalesTerritory[Country]),
        "Australia", 6,
        "Canada", 12,
        "France", 18,
        "Germany", 24,
        100
    ),
  BLANK()
)
```

Notes:

1. **Starting with the second argument, SWITCH()'s arguments operate in pairs** – if it matches "Australia" it returns 6, if it matches "Canada" it returns 12

2. **If you end SWITCH() with an "odd" argument, that is treated as the "ELSE"** – the 100 is by itself, not paired with another argument. So if the current value doesn't match any of the prior tests, 100 will be returned.

3. **SWITCH() still needs the "protection" of IF(HASONEVALUE()) if you are using a VALUES() as the first argument to SWITCH** – if I were using an arithmetic function like AVERAGE(), it would not be necessary (just as it's not necessary with IF). Really, you should think of SWITCH() as a multi-branch version of IF().

And the results:

Country ▾	Different Number per Country
Australia	6
Canada	12
France	18
Germany	24
NA	100
United Kingdom	100
United States	100

Figure 240 Results of the SWITCH() measure

16- SUMX() and Other X ("Iterator") Functions

Need to Force Totals to Add Up "Correctly?"

Remember our [Sales per Day] measure? Let's take another look at it:

Row Labels	Sales per Day
⊟ 2001	$18,046
Mountain-100	$6,104
Road-150	$14,533
Road-650	$963
⊟ 2002	$17,891
Mountain-100	$5,993
Mountain-200	$5,077
Road-150	$16,381
Road-250	$8,829
Road-550-W	$1,475
Road-650	$1,329
⊟ 2003	$26,825
All-Purpose Bike Stand	$210
Bike Wash	$20
Classic Vest	$111
Cycling Cap	$44
Fender Set - Mountain	$109

Smaller than sum of its children

These obviously sum to a lot more than $17,891

Figure 241 The subtotals do not match the sum of their parts

As your measures get more sophisticated, this will happen a lot: you will get subtotals and grand totals that don't equal the sum (or even the average) of their children. (In this case, it's because [Sales per Day] has a different denominator for each ModelName of bike).

Of course, many times that is 100% desirable. If you have an average temperature for each of the 12 months of the year, for instance, averaging those 12 numbers will *not* give you the average temperature for the year, since each month consists of a different number of days.

But again, in sophisticated measures (and business contexts) sometimes the correct logic for the smallest granularity is not correct for the next level up.

In other words, sometimes you need to *force* a total to equal the sum (or the average, etc.) of its children.

SUMX(), and other "X" functions like it, will help you do just that.

Anatomy of SUMX()

 SUMX(\<table or table expression\>, \<arithmetic expression\>)

That's it. Two arguments.

SUMX() operates as follows:

1. It steps through every single row in \<table or table expression\>, one at a time. You can pass a raw table name for this argument, or use a function that returns a table, such as VALUES() or FILTER(). The contents of \<table or table expression\> are subject to the filter context of the current measure cell. (This "stepping through" behavior is often described as "iterating.")

2. For each row, it evaluates \<arithmetic expression\> using the filter context of the current row.

3. It remembers the result of \<arithmetic expression\> from each row, and when done, it adds them all up.

143

SUMX() in Action

Returning to the subtotals example, let's look at the pivot again:

Year - ModelName	Sales per Day
⊟2001	$18,046
Mountain-100	$6,104
Road-150	$14,533
Road-650	$963
⊟2002	$17,891
Mountain-100	$5,993
Mountain-200	$5,077
Road-150	$16,381
Road-250	$8,829
Road-550-W	$1,475
Road-650	$1,329
⊟2003	$26,825

Figure 242 [Sales per Day] with Calendar[Year] and Products[ModelName] on Rows

Now we write a new measure:

```
[Sales per Day Totals Add Up] =

IF(HASONEVALUE(Products[ModelName]),
    [Sales per Day],
    SUMX(VALUES(Products[ModelName]), [Sales per Day])
)
```

So if we're in the context of a single ModelName, it just uses the [Sales per Day] measure like the pivot already does. But when there is more than one ModelName, that means we're in a total cell, and the SUMX() clause kicks in.

Note that I used VALUES(Products[ModelName]) for the <table or table expression> argument. That lets me be very specific – I want this SUMX() to step through all of the unique values of ModelName from the current filter context. If I specified the entire Products table instead (and no VALUES function), SUMX() would step through every row of the Products table from the current filter context, which might be a different number of rows.

Results:

Figure 243 New measure: the totals are the sum of the individual models

Year - ModelName	Sales per Day	Sales per Day Totals Add Up
⊟2001	$18,046	$21,600
Mountain-100	$6,104	$6,104
Road-150	$14,533	$14,533
Road-650	$963	$963
⊟2002	$17,891	$39,085
Mountain-100	$5,993	$5,993
Mountain-200	$5,077	$5,077
Road-150	$16,381	$16,381
Road-250	$8,829	$8,829
Road-550-W	$1,475	$1,475
Road-650	$1,329	$1,329
⊟2003	$26,825	$41,754
All-Purpose Bike Stand	$210	$210
Bike Wash	$20	$20
Classic Vest	$111	$111
Cycling Cap	$44	$44
Fender Set - Mountain	$109	$109

Average: $6,514   Count: 6   Sum: $39,085

Detailed Stepthrough

Just to drive it home, let's walk through the evaluation of the SUMX() portion of the measure above, for the highlighted cell in the pivot:

Year - ModelName	Sales per Day	Sales per Day Totals Add Up
⊟ 2001	$18,046	$21,600
Mountain-100	$6,104	$6,104
Road-150	$14,533	$14,533
Road-650	$963	$963

Figure 244 We are going to step through how the SUMX() clause of the measure arrived at $21,600

Following the 3 points outlined in the "anatomy of SUMX()" section:

1. **SUMX() steps through every row in VALUES(Products[ModelName]).** The filter context provided by the pivot in this case is a completely unfiltered Products table because this cell is Year=2001, Products=All (it has no "coordinates" in the pivot from the Products table). So VALUES(Products[ModelName]) returns every single unique value of [ModelName] from the Products table.

How many values *is* that, actually? Let's check.

```
[ModelName Values] =

    COUNTROWS(VALUES(Products[ModelName]))
```

Year - ModelName	Sales per Day	Sales per Day Totals Add Up	Model Name Values
⊟ 2001	$18,046	$21,600	119
All-Purpose Bike Stand			1
Bike Wash			1
Cable Lock			1
Chain			1

Figure 245 That is 119 values, even though we only see 3 on the pivot below 2001 in the prior screenshot!

> (i) Why 119 versus 3? All 119 are evaluated even in the original pivot, but because only 3 return non-blank results for [Sales per Day], that's all the pivot showed us.

2. **For each of those 119 values, SUMX() evaluates the [Sales per Day] measure.** The Year=2001 filter context is maintained throughout this process, for every row. But the Products[ModelName] filter context changes every time SUMX() moves to the next of the 119 rows.

So it evaluates [Sales per Day] with filter context Year=2001, ModelName="All-Purpose Bike Stand", and that returns blank, because that model was not sold in 2001 (there are no rows in the Sales table with Year=2001, ModelName="All-Purpose Bike Stand".) Then it moves on to Year=2001, ModelName="Bike Wash", then Year=2001, ModelName="Cable Lock", etc.

Only three of those 119 rows in VALUES(Products[ModelName]) return non-blank results for [Sales per Day], and those are the three we saw displayed on the original pivot: "Mountain-100", "Road-150", and "Road-650".

3. **All 119 results of [Sales per Day] are then summed up.** 116 blank values sum to 0 of course, and then the other three sum to $21,600.

MINX(), MAXX(), AVERAGEX()

These three operate in *precisely* the same manner as SUMX.

The only difference is in that last step – rather than summing up all of the results returned by each step, they then apply a different aggregation: MIN(), MAX(), or AVERAGE().

STDEVX.P(), STDEVX.S(), VARX.P(), VARX.S()

Again, these are exactly the same as all of the other "X" functions discussed so far, but I separated them out because of the ".P versus .S" flavors.

The difference between the P and S versions is precisely the same difference as that between the STDEVP() and STDEVS() functions in normal Excel. You use the P version when your data set represents the entire population of results, and the S function when all you have is a sample of the data.

It's a statistics thing, not a DAX thing.

COUNTX() and COUNTAX()

Technically speaking, these are no different from the others mentioned so far. But there is a subtle difference when you think about it carefully.

Let's return to our SUMX() example from before. Remember the formula? It was:

```
SUMX(VALUES(Products[ModelName]), [Sales per Day])
```

And it iterated through 119 unique values of ModelName, of which only 3 had non-blank values for [Sales per Day].

If we replaced SUMX() with COUNTX(), what would we get for an answer?

We'd get 3, because COUNTX() does not "count" blanks.

So we can think of COUNTX() as being "COUNT *NONBLANK* X()" really.

Why is This Different From COUNTROWS(), Then?

COUNTROWS() cannot take a measure as an argument, so it cannot be used to evaluate how many times that measure returns a non-blank value, which COUNTX() can do.

COUNTAX() versus COUNTX()

COUNTAX() *also* will also return 3 in this case, so it's really no different in the vast majority of cases. There is one specific kind of case where COUNTAX() returns something different – I will use that as an example at the end of this chapter.

 COUNTAX() treats the absence of rows, and blank results from a measure, *exactly* the same way as COUNTX(). The only place where COUNTAX() differs from COUNTX() is when you are counting text values in a column, and there are rows with text values of "" – rows that exist, but which contain an empty string. There will be an example of that at the end of this chapter.

Using the X Functions on Fields That Aren't Displayed

In the one set of illustrations so far, you've seen SUMX() used to make totals add up "correctly."

But you can also use an X function to loop over a field that is *not* on the pivot, then report back on what it found.

Let's take the pivot we used for SUMX():

Year - ModelName	Sales per Day	Sales per Day Totals Add Up
⊟ 2001	$18,046	$21,600
Mountain-100	$6,104	$6,104
Road-150	$14,533	$14,533
Road-650	$963	$963
⊟ 2002	$17,891	$39,085
Mountain-100	$5,993	$5,993
Mountain-200	$5,077	$5,077

Figure 246 Where we left off with our completed SUMX() measure

And let's add a new measure:

```
[Max Single-Country Sales] =
    MAXX(VALUES(SalesTerritory[Country]), [Total Sales])
```

Results:

Year - ModelName	Sales per Day	Sales per Day Totals Add Up	Max Single-Country Sales
⊟ 2001	$18,046	$21,600	$1,309,047
Mountain-100	$6,104	$6,104	$304,749
Road-150	$14,533	$14,533	$984,024
Road-650	$963	$963	$27,265
⊟ 2002	$17,891	$39,085	$2,154,285
Mountain-100	$5,993	$5,993	$365,749
Mountain-200	$5,077	$5,077	$286,231
Road-150	$16,381	$16,381	$1,123,577
Road-250	$8,829	$8,829	$524,360
Road-550-W	$1,475	$1,475	$49,021
Road-650	$1,329	$1,329	$105,00

Figure 247 Interesting new measure, but is it correct?

Let's check by adding Country to the pivot:

Year - ModelName	Sales per Day	Sales per Day Totals Add Up	Max Single-Country Sales
⊟ 2001	$18,046	$21,600	$1,309,047
⊟ Mountain-100	$6,104	$6,104	$304,749
Australia	$4,233	$4,233	$304,749
Canada	$3,379	$3,379	$20,275
France	$3,383	$3,383	$30,450
Germany	$3,387	$3,387	$44,025
United Kingdom	$3,877	$3,877	$54,275
United States	$4,006	$4,006	$132,200
⊟ Road-150	$14,533	$14,533	$984,024
Australia	$6,649	$6,649	$984,024
Canada	$4,055	$4,055	$121,661
France	$3,868	$3,868	$143,131
Germany	$3,959	$3,959	$186,070
United Kingdom	$4,026	$4,026	$225,431
United States	$6,920	$6,920	$941,085
⊟ Road-650	$963	$963	$27,265
Australia	$780	$780	$20,274
Canada	$699	$699	$4,894
France	$699	$699	$6,991
Germany	$699	$699	$7,690
United Kingdom	$743	$743	$11,885
United States	$737	$737	$27,265

Figure 248 It is indeed reporting the max single-country sales

But *Which* Country?

Since this is most "magical" when the Country field is *not* on the pivot, one of the most common questions I get is "ok but how can I display which Country was the max when Country is not on the pivot? Knowing which one is just as important as knowing the amount."

As of PowerPivot v2 there isn't a function that just *does* that for you.

I did write a post on this though, that won't fit here for space reasons. It uses the function FIRSTNON-BLANK() – check it out here if you are interested:

http://ppvt.pro/WhatDidXFind

RANKX()

OK, this one is actually quite a bit different from the others even though its syntax is similar.

Let's do that whole "work backward from desired result" thing again:

Customer FullName	Total Sales	Customer Sales Rank
Jordan Turner	$15,999	1
Willie Xu	$13,490	2
Nichole Nara	$13,295	3
Kaitlyn Henderson	$13,294	4
Margaret He	$13,269	5
Randall Dominguez	$13,266	6
Adriana Gonzalez	$13,243	7
Rosa Hu	$13,216	8
Brandi Gill	$13,196	9
Brad She	$13,173	10
Francisco Sara	$13,165	11
Maurice Shan	$12,910	12
Janet Munoz	$12,489	13

Figure 249 We want a measure that ranks customers by [Total Sales]

Here's the formula for that rank measure:

```
[Customer Sales Rank] =
RANKX(ALL(Customers[FullName]), [Total Sales])
```

The Use of ALL()

The only difference we see so far is that I used ALL() instead of VALUES() in the first argument.

Why is that?

Because if I use VALUES(), I get 1's for everyone:

Customer FullName	Total Sales	Customer Sales Rank
Bradley Kumar	$3,345	1
Bradley Lal	$2,664	1
Aaron Alexander	$70	1
Bradley Luo	$3,400	1
Aaron Baker	$1,751	1
Bradley Nara	$5,898	1
Aaron Butler	$15	1
Bradley Pal	$124	1
Aaron Carter	$40	1
Bradley Rai	$79	1
Aaron Coleman	$62	1

Figure 250 If I replace ALL() with VALUES(), everybody's our #1 customer!

OK, why is *that*?

Well it makes *some* sense actually – for each row of the pivot, there is only one value of Customer[FullName] – so the RANKX measure ranks each customer as if he/she were the only customer in the world :-)

So by applying ALL(), I rank each customer against everyone else. I guess that's intuitive, but the more I think about it, the more even *that* doesn't feel right.

The pragmatic thing to do here is not worry about it. Just use ALL() and be happy we have the function :-)

Ties

Let's look at the bottom of that same pivot, with ALL() restored so not everyone is #1:

Xavier White	$4	18326
Trisha Zhao	$4	18326
Ronald Mehta	$4	18326
Trevor Coleman	$4	18326
Omar Zhao	$4	18326
Shane Mehta	$4	18326
Abigail Morris	$2	18390
Abigail Bennett	$2	18390
Alex Collins	$2	18390
Brad Kumar	$2	18390
Cody Sanders	$2	18390
Dylan Taylor	$2	18390
Hunter Miller	$2	18390
Marcus Morgan	$2	18390
Natalie Bryant	$2	18390
Melanie Peterson	$2	18390
Natalie Rivera	$2	18390
Grand Total	**$29,358,677**	**1**

There are 64 people tied with $4 of sales, so rank "skips" to 18,390

Figure 251 By default, ties are handled like this, but you can override that with the fifth (and optional argument), by setting it to Dense

The Optional Parameters

RANKX() actually has five parameters instead of the two possessed by the other X functions, but the last three are optional:

 RANKX(<table or table expression>, <arithmetic expression>, <*optional* alternate arithmetic expression>, <*optional* sort order flag>, <*optional* tie-handling flag>

<optional alternate arithmetic expression> - The third argument to RANKX() may be the most mysterious thing in all of PowerPivot. If I weren't writing this book, I would happily continue to ignore that I don't understand it. I recommend always leaving it blank. Seriously. (But I will return to it in Chapter 17, because completely taking a "pass" on it doesn't feel right).

<*optional* sort order flag> -This allows you to control rank order (ascending/descending) by setting to 1 or 0. It defaults to 0 if you leave it blank, which ranks largest values highest.

<*optional* tie-handling flag> - This can be set to Skip or Dense. It defaults to Skip, which is the behavior seen in the previous picture. If I change it to Dense, this is what the ties look at near the bottom of the pivot:

```
RANKX(ALL(Customers[FullName]), [Total Sales],,,Dense)
```

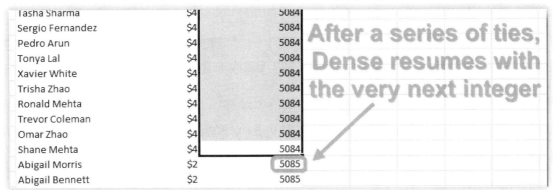

Tasha Sharma	$4	5084
Sergio Fernandez	$4	5084
Pedro Arun	$4	5084
Tonya Lal	$4	5084
Xavier White	$4	5084
Trisha Zhao	$4	5084
Ronald Mehta	$4	5084
Trevor Coleman	$4	5084
Omar Zhao	$4	5084
Shane Mehta	$4	5084
Abigail Morris	$2	5085
Abigail Bennett	$2	5085

After a series of ties, Dense resumes with the very next integer

Figure 252 Dense tie handling – resumes with the very next integer after a series of tied ranks

Duplicate FullNames?

Very dangerous, this one. If you have two customers with the same FullName, they will be combined into a single customer and ranked unfairly high by their combined sales.

So make sure you rank by a unique field. I recommend concatenating CustomerKey or something unique with FullName so that you can still recognize the customer by name, and still maintain uniqueness.

> I will be completely honest with you and say that as of PowerPivot v2, I don't completely trust the RANKX() function yet. There are times when it does mysterious things – such as returning ties that I do not expect. I am not saying you shouldn't use it, but that you should watch the results you get and make sure they meet your expectations before sharing. This may reflect the limits of my understanding of this function of course, in which case I think we need a version of RANKX() that is a bit more straightforward to use. I will update the blog if/when I hear something from my former colleagues at Microsoft.

Non-measure second arguments to the X functions.

So far, I've only used measures for that second argument to these X functions.

But actually this is one place where you can break the "no naked columns" rule. You actually can just put a column name in for that second argument. And SUMX() will happily sum it.

In fact, you can even put a calculated column style formula in there, like Customers[YearlyIncome] / Customers[NumberOfChildren], and that will also work.

The COUNTAX() Mystery Solved!

The ability to use a non-measure expression as that final argument helps us solve the COUNTAX() conundrum. When you use a *measure* as the second argument, I do not believe there is *any* situation in which COUNTX() and COUNTAX() will return different results.

But COUNTAX() will let you use a text column as the second argument, whereas COUNTX(), if you use a column as the second argument, requires that it be numeric or date type.

So here's a silly little table I added to the PowerPivot window as a test:

Figure 253 CountTest table – a testbed for COUNTAX()

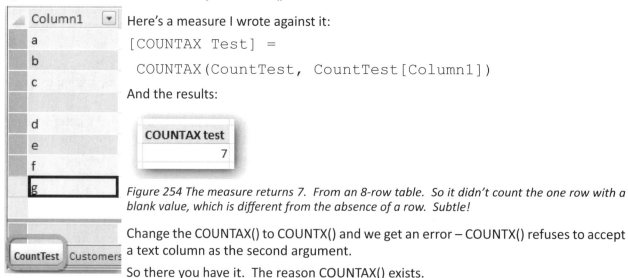

Here's a measure I wrote against it:

```
[COUNTAX Test] =
    COUNTAX(CountTest, CountTest[Column1])
```

And the results:

Figure 254 The measure returns 7. From an 8-row table. So it didn't count the one row with a blank value, which is different from the absence of a row. Subtle!

Change the COUNTAX() to COUNTX() and we get an error – COUNTX() refuses to accept a text column as the second argument.

So there you have it. The reason COUNTAX() exists.

(It's actually more useful in calculated columns than measures, so this wasn't really a "fair" test of its value).

17- Multiple Data Tables

Example1: Budget versus Actuals

Here's a common problem: you have a Sales table, where each row represents an individual transaction. In my case that's about 60 thousand rows. But then you also have a Budget table, where each row is typically captured at a coarser granularity, and is much smaller in terms of row count.

For instance, here's a sample Budget table that I've imported into PowerPivot:

CalendarYear	MonthNumberOfYear	SalesTerritoryRegion	Subcategory	Budgeted Sales
2001	7	Australia	Mountain Bikes	$71,510
2001	7	Australia	Road Bikes	$190,248
2001	7	Canada	Mountain Bikes	$4,183
2001	7	Canada	Road Bikes	$15,429
2001	7	France	Mountain Bikes	$7,916
2001	7	France	Road Bikes	$31,825
2001	7	Germany	Mountain Bikes	$4,384
2001	7	Germany	Road Bikes	$36,068
2001	7	Northwest	Mountain Bikes	$12,058
2001	7	Northwest	Road Bikes	$49,089
2001	7	Southwest	Mountain Bikes	$3,059
2001	7	Southwest	Road Bikes	$59,190
2001	7	United Kingdom	Mountain Bikes	$5,893
2001	7	United Kingdom	Road Bikes	$28,572
2001	8	Australia	Mountain Bikes	$54,200
2001	8	Australia	Road Bikes	$163,254
2001	8	Canada	Mountain Bikes	$8,031
2001	8	Canada	Road Bikes	$22,168
2001	8	France	Mountain Bikes	$8,196
2001	8	France	Road Bikes	$10,289
2001	8	Germany	Road Bikes	$46,872

CountTest | Customers | Sales | Products | Calendar | Exch Rates | MinListPrice | PriceTier | Budget | SalesTerritory | CompetitorSales

Record: 1 of 1,877

Figure 255 Budget table: 1,877 rows at Year/Month/Territory/SuCategory granularity

And now the common question: how are my products selling compared to budget?

Difficult in Normal Excel

Solving that problem in normal Excel is tedious. The normal VLOOKUP() routine that we used in Excel for combining a Data table (like Sales) with a Lookup table (like Products) does not work in this case.

The problem is essentially that Sales and Budget are *both* Data tables. Which one would you VLOOKUP() "into" the other? Plus, each table has multiple rows that correspond to multiple rows in the other, so even if you decided which way VLOOKUP() should "flow," you wouldn't be able to successfully construct a single VLOOKUP() formula.

So a common solution involves creating *two* pivots – one to measure Sales, the other to measure Budget, and then writing formulas that index into each pivot to form one unified "Sales vs. Budget" report. Takes awhile to get it right, and then when someone inevitably wants to see a slightly different report format or rollup level, it's almost as much work to modify as it was to create the first time!

Much Faster *and* More Flexible in PowerPivot

Hey, I wouldn't be bringing it up if I didn't have a solution for you :-)

The short version is that with PowerPivot, Sales and Budget can co-exist in the same pivot. And you still don't need to combine them into one table.

Creating Relationships – We Need Some New Lookup Tables

The next piece of good news is that we can achieve everything we need with relationships. No fancy disconnected tables or "dotted line" relationships through measures.

But we do have a problem: the Budget table refuses to relate to any of our Lookup tables.

For instance, let's try relating Budget to Products using the only Product-related column in Budget: the SubCategory column.

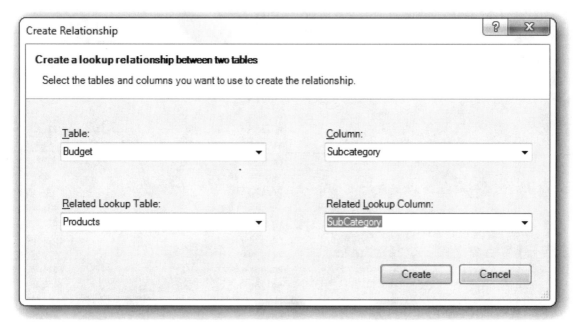

Figure 256 Attempting to relate Budget to Products...

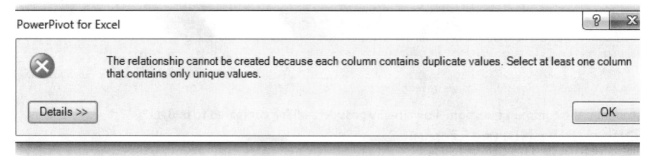

Figure 257 ...results in the dreaded "many to many" error.

Well that makes sense: each SubCategory value (like "Mountain Bikes") *does* appear many times in each table.

We have a mismatched granularity problem between Budget and the rest of our model that's existed so far. Which is why it's such a tough problem in normal Excel actually. So how do we solve it? We need a SubCategories Lookup table!

Figure 258 A single-column SubCategories table:

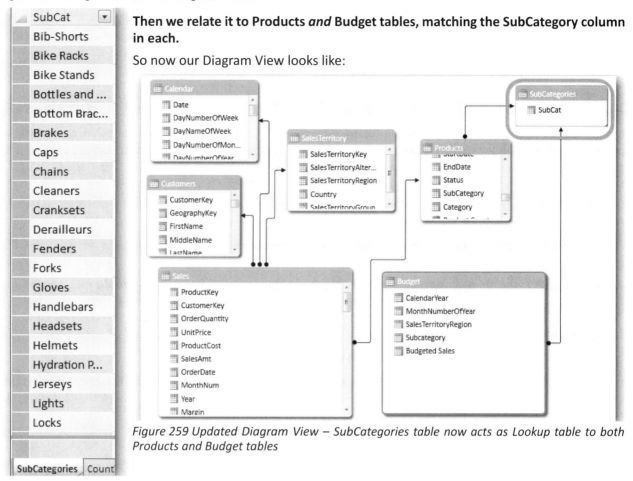

Then we relate it to Products *and* Budget tables, matching the SubCategory column in each.

So now our Diagram View looks like:

Figure 259 Updated Diagram View – SubCategories table now acts as Lookup table to both Products and Budget tables

Remember, filter context "flows" in the *opposite* direction of the relationship arrows. Let's visualize that:

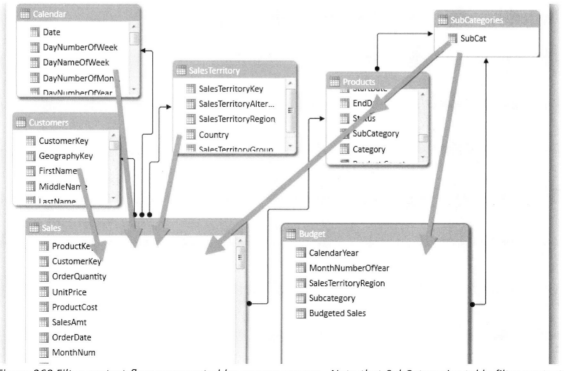

Figure 260 Filter context flow represented by orange arrows. Note that SubCategories table filter context DOES flow through to Sales, even though it's a "multi-step" flow.

Filter context flows from SubCategories to Products, and then from Products to Sales. In other words, the SubCategories still influences Sales (in terms of filter context) as if SubCategories were directly related to Sales. Stated more generally, filter context is transitive: if table A is a Lookup table for table B, and table B is a Lookup table for table C, a filter on table A *will* impact table C.

Where Do We *Get* This New Lookup Table? Consider a Database.

It's mighty tempting to create this SubCategories table via copy/paste. But this is another one of those places where a database really shines. A table or query in a database that always returns the unique list of SubCategory values in your company is an absolute lifesaver, since it saves you from manual update work in the future when you gain new SubCategories (or retire old ones).

In absolute terms, it isn't a ton of manual effort to update the SubCategories table that you created via copy/paste. So compared to the normal Excel way, it's not a big deal.

But little manual stuff like that starts to stand out a *lot* more once the other 95% of your spreadsheet life now lacks manual drudgery.

When you get to the point where an entire family of sophisticated Excel reports would just be running themselves every day if it weren't for this one manual step, suddenly that one manual step becomes a big win to eliminate, whereas that same task would have been hardly noticeable in the old world of constant tedious effort.

SalesTerritory is at Same Granularity Already

For SalesTerritory, we do *not* need to create a new Lookup table. SalesTerritory is the one place where Budget *does* match our existing granularity. So we just create the relationship for that one, no new table required.

Repeating the "New Table" Process for Calendar

Budget's granularity in terms of time only goes down to Year/Month pairs. So again, we need a new lookup table at that same granularity.

Here is the newly-create YearMonths table:

[YearMonth] ▼		*f*	=[Year]&FORMAT([Month], "00")	
Year ▼	**Month** ▼	**YearMonth** ▼	**Add Col**
2001	10	200110	
2001	11	200111	
2001	12	200112	
2001	7	200107	
2001	8	200108	
2001	9	200109	
2002	1	200201	
2002	10	200210	
2002	11	200211	
2002	12	200212	

SubCategories | CountTest | **YearMonths** | Customers | Sales | Products | Calen

Record: ◄ ◄ 5 of 37 ► ►

Figure 261 The new YearMonths table. Note the rowcount of 37, and the calculated column I will use to create relationships.

That YearMonth calculated column is a pattern I find myself repeating a lot. The FOR-MAT() function is used to add the extra zero in front of single-digit month numbers. That isn't strictly necessary here – I use it just to make Year/Month combos sort prop-erly – but it's become such force of habit for me that I figured I would share it.

I add that same sort of YearMonth calculated column to my Budget table, *and* my Calendar table, then create both relationships, yielding the following Diagram View:

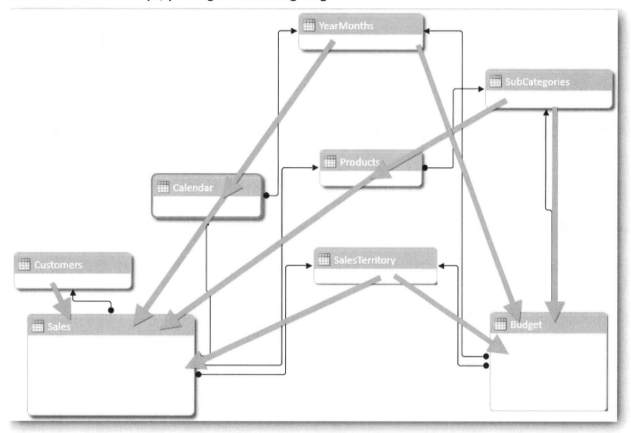

Figure 262 Diagram View updated to show new tables, relationships, and filter context flow (orange arrows). Note that with this many tables, I have turned off the details on each table so that more can fit on a single screen.

Integrated Pivot

I can now construct a single pivot using measures from both Sales and Budget, as long as I *only* use fields from shared Lookup tables on Rows/Column/Filters/Slicers.

What's a shared Lookup table? It's a table that filters both of my Data tables.

In this case, there are three shared Lookup tables: YearMonths, SalesTerritory, and SubCategories, all marked with asterisks in this diagram:

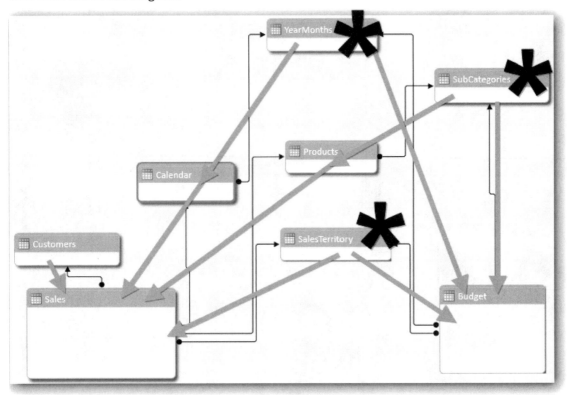

Figure 263 When constructing a pivot that displays measures from both Budget and Sales, only the three tables marked with asterisks should be used on Rows/Columns/Filters/Slicers, because only those three filter both Sales and Budget.

I have created a single, simple measure on the Budget table:

```
[Total Budgeted Sales] =
=SUM(Budget[Budgeted Sales])
```

Let's put that on a new pivot, along with [Total Sales] from the Sales table:

Total Budgeted Sales	Total Sales
$29,991,136	$29,358,677

Figure 264 These measures come from different Data tables: Budget and Sales

But the real test comes when I start adding fields to Rows, for instance. Here I have Year on rows:

Row Labels ▼	Total Budgeted Sales	Total Sales
2001	$3,236,761	$3,266,374
2002	$6,635,482	$6,530,344
2003	$10,001,112	$9,791,060
2004	$10,117,781	$9,770,900
Grand Total	**$29,991,136**	**$29,358,677**

Figure 265 Year on Rows, and both measures still work! But note that in this case, Year comes from the YearMonths table and NOT from the Calendar table!

Once you have the same sort of field (like Year) in more than one table in your model, you need to make sure you are using the right one for the measures in your pivot. The Calendar[Year] column will not work properly with your Budget measures, for instance.

Integrated Measures

This next part is either going to make you yawn and say "yeah, that's obvious" or make you scream "that is the most awesome thing I have EVER seen!" Or somewhere in between perhaps. For me, I still get a smile on my face every single time I do this.

I can write new measures that reference (and compare) measures from these separate tables, Budget and Sales.

For instance:

```
[Sales vs. Budget] =
 ([Total Sales] - [Total Budgeted Sales]) / [Total Budgeted
 Sales]
```

Results:

Row Labels ▼	Total Budgeted Sales	Total Sales	Sales vs Budget
2001	$3,236,761	$3,266,374	0.9 %
2002	$6,635,482	$6,530,344	-1.6 %
2003	$10,001,112	$9,791,060	-2.1 %
2004	$10,117,781	$9,770,900	-3.4 %
Grand Total	**$29,991,136**	**$29,358,677**	-2.1 %

Figure 266 [Sales vs. Budget] in action. (I added the conditional formatting, that was not automatic).

Now I can remove the original two measures, then pile some more fields onto Rows and Columns:

Sales vs Budget	Column Labels ▼				
SubCat - Region ▼	**2001**	**2002**	**2003**	**2004**	**Grand Total**
⊟**Mountain Bikes**	3.8 %	-3.3 %	-3.5 %	-3.0 %	-2.9 %
Australia	8.4 %	-8.6 %	-6.3 %	-4.2 %	-4.9 %
Canada	-10.0 %	3.3 %	-8.5 %	-10.3 %	-8.0 %
France	0.5 %	-4.6 %	-4.7 %	-9.5 %	-6.6 %
Germany	-15.7 %	8.5 %	-3.2 %	11.6 %	4.1 %
United Kingdom	7.6 %	6.3 %	-11.0 %	-7.1 %	-6.5 %
United States	3.4 %	-1.7 %	3.2 %	-2.1 %	0.2 %
⊟**Road Bikes**	0.3 %	-1.0 %	0.1 %	-1.8 %	-0.6 %
Australia	-6.5 %	-1.5 %	-0.1 %	-1.4 %	-2.1 %
Canada	-3.1 %	0.7 %	-6.2 %	-12.1 %	-2.8 %
France	-3.9 %	-7.6 %	0.2 %	1.8 %	-2.5 %
Germany	-10.8 %	-3.7 %	2.4 %	-4.2 %	-2.9 %
United Kingdom	1.1 %	4.0 %	-4.9 %	-3.7 %	-1.5 %
United States	12.7 %	-0.0 %	3.9 %	-0.1 %	3.4 %
⊞**Bike Racks**		3.9 %	-2.5 %		0.1 %
⊞**Bike Stands**		-4.7 %	1.2 %		-1.7 %
⊞**Bottles and Cages**		-5.1 %	-1.0 %		-2.7 %
⊞**Caps**		-7.8 %	-3.8 %		-5.5 %

Figure 267 Sales vs. Budget, made criminally simple. Under- and Over- Performers just jump out at you. And this pivot can be rearranged/restructured at will – the formulas will just keep working, as long as you only use Lookup tables that filter both Data tables.

Example 2: Making Use of that Mysterious RANKX() Third Argument

All right, this has become a matter of honor. The third argument will be put to good use. But I had to invent new data in order to put together a credible example.

First, here is the new data. Pretend I have acquired sales figures for my chief competitor, and how well their bikes have been selling over the past few years.

That is here in the CompetitorSales table:

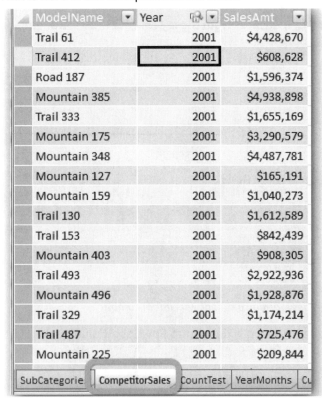

ModelName	Year	SalesAmt
Trail 61	2001	$4,428,670
Trail 412	2001	$608,628
Road 187	2001	$1,596,374
Mountain 385	2001	$4,938,898
Trail 333	2001	$1,655,169
Mountain 175	2001	$3,290,579
Mountain 348	2001	$4,487,781
Mountain 127	2001	$165,191
Mountain 159	2001	$1,040,273
Trail 130	2001	$1,612,589
Trail 153	2001	$842,439
Mountain 403	2001	$908,305
Trail 493	2001	$2,922,936
Mountain 496	2001	$1,928,876
Trail 329	2001	$1,174,214
Trail 487	2001	$725,476
Mountain 225	2001	$209,844

SubCategorie | CompetitorSales | CountTest | YearMonths | Cu

Figure 268 CompeitorSales is just three columns: ModelName, Year, and SalesAmt

The Problem: Ranking MY Products Against Theirs!

So… what if I want to see how MY products rank against my competitors in terms of sales?

For example, if one of my models sold $3M worth of product, and their top three Models sold $4M, $3.5M, and $2.5M, that means my model would rank 3rd against their models.

(Credit goes to Scott Senkeresty for breaking the logjam and suggesting a scenario in which the third param could be used.)

Year Granularity Mismatch Means a New Lookup Table

Just like in Sales vs. Budget, since we have a granularity mismatch, we need a new Lookup table. This time is the simplest one yet: Years.

Year
2001
2002
2003
2004

Figure 269 The new Lookup table, Years

Now I relate that to CompetitorSales, and also to Calendar (so I can filter Sales), yielding the following table diagram:

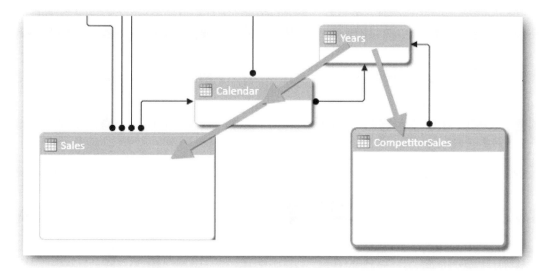

Figure 270 Table diagram (other tables moved aside to highlight just this "corner" of the model)

Simple Measure

Now I add a very simple measure on the CompetitorSales table:

```
[Compete Sales] =

    SUM(CompetitorSales[SalesAmt])
```

And here it is on a simple pivot:

Model	Compete Sales
Trail 412	$11,064,747
Trail 153	$10,935,275
Mountain 385	$10,773,383
Trail 487	$10,328,574
Trail 222	$9,966,929
Trail 333	$9,955,816
Trail 61	$9,925,752
Mountain 175	$9,632,946
Trail 493	$8,872,714
Mountain 403	$8,648,188
Mountain 496	$8,262,950
Road 101	$8,220,904

Figure 271 [Compete Sales] with CompetitorSales[ModelName] on Rows

Now the Absolutely Amazing "Cross-Rank" Measure

Back on the Sales table (or the Products table if I prefer):

```
[Model Sales Rank vs Competition] =

    RANKX(VALUES(CompetitorSales[ModelName]),
        [Compete Sales],
        [Total Sales]
        )
```

What does that formula *mean*? It starts out like it's going to just rank competitive products against each other and then takes a twist:

- **VALUES(CompetitorSales[ModelName])** – this means that the "entities" being ranked are in fact the unique ModelNames from the CompetitorSales table.

- **[Compete Sales]** – this means that the measure by which those competitive models will be ranked will be their own [Compete Sales] measure. So far, this is just normal, totally understandable usage of RANKX().

- **[Total Sales]** – but whoa! This means we're going to take the value of [Total Sales] in our current filter context (which on the left-side pivot, is a ModelName from *my* company), and insert it into the pecking order established by the first two arguments! Essentially, treat the value of this measure, in the current filter context, as if it were a participant in the normal evaluation of RANKX() as controlled by the first two arguments.

And results:

My Products' Sales		Model Sales Rank vs Competition		Their Sales	
Model	Total Sales			Model	Compete Sales
Mountain-200	$7,929,475		14	Trail 412	$11,064,747
Road-150	$5,549,897		19	Trail 153	$10,935,275
Road-250	$4,451,260		19	Mountain 385	$10,773,383
Touring-1000	$2,992,008		20	Trail 487	$10,328,574
Road-350-W	$1,580,220		20	Trail 222	$9,966,929
Road-550-W	$1,514,622		20	Trail 333	$9,955,816
Mountain-100	$1,341,121		20	Trail 61	$9,925,752
Road-750	$779,206		20	Mountain 175	$9,632,946
Road-650	$645,380		20	Trail 493	$8,872,714
Touring-2000	$451,924		20	Mountain 403	$8,648,188
Mountain-400-W	$417,833		20	Mountain 496	$8,262,950
Touring-3000	$400,869		20	Road 101	$8,220,904
Mountain-500	$264,330		20	Road 187	$7,955,912
Sport-100	$225,336		20	Mountain 127	$7,296,954
Long-Sleeve Logo Jersey	$86,783		20	Mountain 348	$6,882,475

Figure 272 New Cross-Rank measure compared to pivot displaying competitive sales. My top product would indeed be behind their 13 best products, earning a rank of 14.

And Since Both Are Filtered by the Years Table...

I can add Years[Year] as a slicer to both pivots!

Let's see if it still works when I slice to a different year:

My Products' Sales		Model Sales Rank vs Competition	Their Sales	
Model	Total Sales		Model	Compete Sales
Mountain-200	$3,723,271	4	Trail 487	$4,506,831
Road-250	$2,144,214	9	Trail 333	$3,989,343
Touring-1000	$1,058,527	13	Road 187	$3,971,737
Road-550-W	$676,096	16	Trail 153	$3,710,833
Road-350-W	$540,915	17	Trail 412	$3,172,682
Road-750	$326,154	19	Mountain 403	$3,050,286
Road-650	$264,651	19	Trail 423	$2,982,821
Touring-2000	$195,591	20	Trail 329	$2,736,560
Touring-3000	$163,317	20	Mountain 496	$1,722,153
Mountain-400-W	$159,284	20	Trail 222	$1,343,252
Mountain-500	$107,083	20	Mountain 127	$1,287,586
Sport-100	$92,584	20	Mountain 348	$1,085,922

Figure 273 Shared Year slicer: measure still works

Wow.

18- Time Intelligence with Custom Calendars: Advanced Use of FILTER()

Perhaps My Favorite Thing in DAX

Working with custom calendars in DAX has become something that I'd almost do for free, it's so much fun. Specifically, it just feels *powerful*, like you can do just about anything.

That said, it took me a little while to discover the magic formula. It took some experimentation. But you won't have to do any of that – I will give you the secret, and explain how it works.

It also provides a platform to explain a few more things about FILTER() that I left unaddressed in that chapter.

The Periods Table

A "4/4/5" Example

OK, let's say my company operates on a "4/4/5" calendar, which is very common in retail. "4/4/5" refers to the number of weeks in each period, where a period is roughly a month. These calendars rotate through four quarters in a year, each consisting 13 total weeks.

Here's an example – a Periods table imported into PowerPivot:

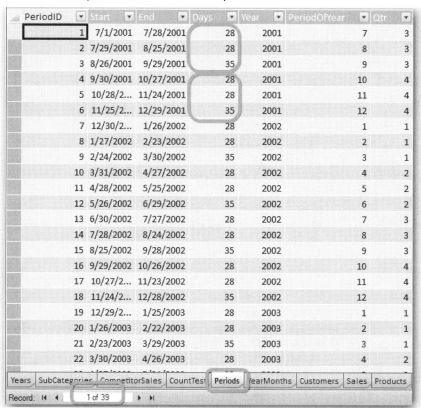

Figure 274 Periods table – 39 rows spanning from 7/1/2001 to 9/25/2004 – note the repeating 28/28/35 pattern, which is 4/4/5 weeks

How This Changes Things: We Need to "Write" Our Own Time Intelligence Functions

The critical point is not merely the existence of this table. The "wrinkle" here is that all "sales for period X" reports, as well as all comparisons of growth – versus last year, versus prior periods – must be performed according to the periods defined in this table. Likewise, all "year to date" and similar calculations must respect this table.

The "smarter" time intelligence functions like DATESYTD(), DATEADD(), and SAMEPERIODLASTYEAR() – the ones with built-in knowledge of the standard calendar – will *not* work properly in this regard.

So we will need to essentially write our own versions of those functions from scratch, using other more primitive functions like FILTER(), ALL(), and DATESBETWEEN().

Simple "Sales in Period" Measure

Let's start with the basics. We want a pivot that shows something like this:

Year - Qtr - Period	Sales in Period
⊟ 2001	$3,219,717
⊟ Q3	$1,417,740
P7	$426,286
P8	$448,953
P9	$542,501
⊟ Q4	$1,801,977
P10	$481,475
P11	$516,537
P12	$803,964
⊟ 2002	$6,526,854
⊟ Q1	$1,824,424
P1	$552,898
P2	$534,463
P3	$737,062
⊟ Q2	$2,009,710
P4	$582,060
P5	$687,716
P6	$739,934

Figure 275 Simplest pivot: just display sales data according to the custom Periods table (the 4/4/5 calendar)

This is pretty straightforward actually, it's just another example of a disconnected table.

Let's start with two measures on the Periods table that report the Start/End dates for each period:

        [PeriodStartDate] =

        FIRSTDATE(Periods[Start])

And:

        [PeriodEndDate] =

        LASTDATE(Periods[End])

With results:

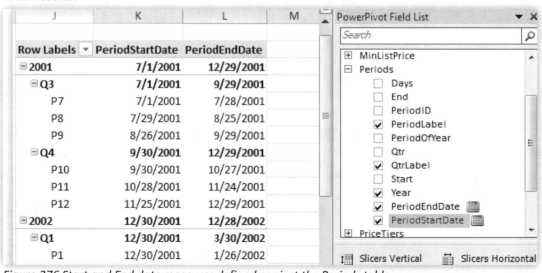

Figure 276 Start and End date measures defined against the Periods table

Note that I added a couple of text columns via formula (QtrLabel and PeriodLabel), to make the pivot display a little nicer than just a jumble of numbers on Rows:

Formatting | Measures | View

=“Q” & [Qtr]

PeriodOfYear	Qtr	QtrLabel	PeriodLabel
7	3	Q3	P7
8	3	Q3	P8
9	3	Q3	P9
10	4	Q4	P10
11	4	Q4	P11

Figure 277 QtrLabel and PeriodLabel – better label fields for the pivot, defined using simple concatenation formulas

Then let’s define a [Sales in Period] measure on the Sales table, one that respects [PeriodStartDate] and [PeriodEndDate]:

```
[Sales in Period] =
 CALCULATE([Total Sales],
           DATESBETWEEN(Calendar[Date],
                        [PeriodStartDate],
                        [PeriodEndDate]
                        )
          )
```

Displayed with conditional formatting, and filtered to just 2003 and 2004 to highlight differences:

Row Labels	PeriodStartDate	PeriodEndDate	Sales in Period
2003	**12/29/2002**	**12/27/2003**	**$9,614,218**
Q1	**12/29/2002**	**3/29/2003**	**$1,421,937**
P1	12/29/2002	1/25/2003	$411,802
P2	1/26/2003	2/22/2003	$485,488
P3	2/23/2003	3/29/2003	$524,647
Q2	**3/30/2003**	**6/28/2003**	**$1,632,944**
P4	3/30/2003	4/26/2003	$483,894
P5	4/27/2003	5/24/2003	$488,796
P6	5/25/2003	6/28/2003	$660,254
Q3	**6/29/2003**	**9/27/2003**	**$2,701,763**
P7	6/29/2003	7/26/2003	$777,371
P8	7/27/2003	8/23/2003	$747,270
P9	8/24/2003	9/27/2003	$1,177,122
Q4	**9/28/2003**	**12/27/2003**	**$3,857,574**
P10	9/28/2003	10/25/2003	$943,911
P11	10/26/2003	11/22/2003	$1,048,462
P12	11/23/2003	12/27/2003	$1,865,201
2004	**12/28/2003**	**9/25/2004**	**$9,997,888**
Q1	**12/28/2003**	**3/27/2004**	**$4,328,055**
P1	12/28/2003	1/24/2004	$1,261,841

Figure 278 [Sales in Period] – note the highlighted larger values for Year (2003) and Qtr (Q2) relative to Period. Note also the “bump” in the third period of each quarter, due to the 4/4/5 structure.

Visualizing the Relationships

So far this is absolutely the same as what we covered in the chapter on disconnected tables. But just to anchor our understanding, let's take a look at the table diagram:

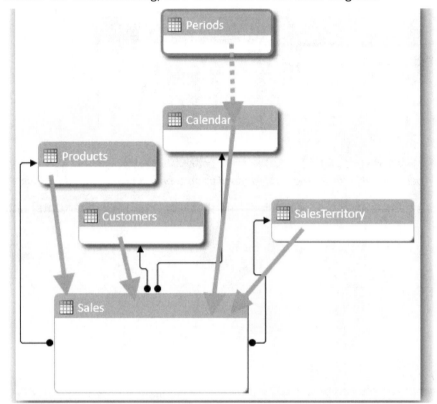

Figure 279 Table diagram updated. Periods table has "dotted line" relationship to Calendar, which has real relationship to Sales. Therefore with certain measures like [Sales in Period], Periods table acts like a Lookup table to Sales. (Several tables from prior chapters removed for clarity).

Another Familiar Concept: Sales per Day

Since our periods are of varying sizes, in order to fairly compare "apples to apples" we should have a measure that compares sales per day (or per week).

First let's write a measure that calculates how many days are currently selected:

```
[Days in Period] =

SUM(Periods[Days])
```

Row Labels .T	Sales in Period	Days in Period
⊟ 2003	$9,614,218	364
⊟ Q1	$1,421,937	91
P1	$411,802	28
P2	$485,488	28
P3	$524,647	35
⊟ Q2	$1,632,944	91
P4	$483,894	28

Figure 280 [Days in Period] measure (Start and End date measures removed from pivot)

OK, now we can write a measure that calculates sales per day in each period:

```
[Sales per Day in Period] =

[Sales in Period]/[Days in Period]
```

Row Labels	Sales in Period	Days in Period	Sales per Day in Period
⊟2003	$9,614,218	364	$26,413
⊟Q1	$1,421,937	91	$15,626
P1	$411,802	28	$14,707
P2	$485,488	28	$17,339
P3	$524,647	35	$14,990
⊟Q2	$1,632,944	91	$17,944
P4	$483,894	28	$17,282
P5	$488,796	28	$17,457
P6	$660,254	35	$18,864
⊟Q3	$2,701,763	91	$29,690
P7	$777,371	28	$27,763
P8	$747,270	28	$26,688
P9	$1,177,122	35	$33,632
⊟Q4	$3,857,574	91	$42,391
P10	$943,911	28	$33,711
P11	$1,048,462	28	$37,445
P12	$1,865,201	35	$53,291
⊟2004	$9,997,888	273	$36,622
⊟Q1	$4,328,055	91	$47,561
P1	$1,261,841	28	$45,066

Figure 281 [Sales per Day in Period] – note how the length of each period does not determine the size of its value. We can now compare "apples to apples" – for "4 vs. 4 vs. 5" but also Period vs. Quarter and Year.

First New Concept: Sales per Day in Prior Period
Getting Organized First

First let's add a PeriodYear column to the Periods table, so that we have a unique label for each period re-gardless of what year it is in:

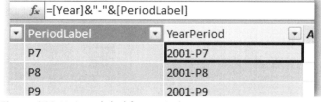

PeriodLabel	YearPeriod	A
P7	2001-P7	
P8	2001-P8	
P9	2001-P9	

Figure 282 Unique label for periods, across years

And use that on rows instead:

PeriodYear	Sales per Day in Period
2001-P7	$15,224
2001-P8	$16,034
2001-P9	$15,500
2001-P10	$17,196
2001-P11	$18,448
2001-P12	$22,970
2002-P1	$19,746
2002-P2	$19,088
2002-P3	$21,059
2002-P4	$20,788
2002-P5	$24,561
2002-P6	$21,141
2002-P7	$16,402
2002-P8	$17,049
2002-P9	$12,911

Figure 283 PeriodYear on Rows, [Sales per Day in Period] on Values

Desired Results

In the context of that pivot, here is what we want to end up with:

PeriodYear ▼	Sales per Day in Period	Prior Period Sales per Day
2001-P7	$15,224	#NUM!
2001-P8	$16,034	$15,224
2001-P9	$15,500	$16,034
2001-P10	$17,196	$15,500
2001-P11	$18,448	$17,196
2001-P12	$22,970	$18,448
2002-P1	$19,746	$22,970
2002-P2	$19,088	$19,746
2002-P3	$21,059	$19,088
2002-P4	$20,788	$21,059
2002-P5	$24,561	$20,788
2002-P6	$21,141	$24,561

Figure 284 This is what we want: a measure that returns the [Sales per Day in Period] value for the immediately prior period. (#NUM makes sense for now since that was our first-ever period).

Revealing the Formula First, Then Explaining

Let's take the "work backwards" theme one step further and just reveal the formula for that measure first:

```
[Prior Period Sales per Day] =

IF(HASONEVALUE(Periods[PeriodID]),
    CALCULATE([Sales per Day in Period],
              ALL(Periods),
              FILTER(ALL(Periods),
                     Periods[PeriodID]=
                      VALUES(Periods[PeriodID])-1
                     )
             ),
    BLANK()
   )
```

The Greatest Formula in the World

Ignore the HASONEVALUE() test for a moment and just focus on the "meat" of the formula:

```
CALCULATE([Sales per Day in Period],
          ALL(Periods),
          FILTER(ALL(Periods),
                 Periods[PeriodID]=
                  VALUES(Periods[PeriodID])-1
                 )
         )
```

On my blog, I only half-jokingly refer to this as the Greatest Formula in the World, or GFITW. It is *by far* the #1 pattern you need to know when dealing with custom calendars.

As you get comfortable with the GFITW, some of you may prefer to treat it as just that: a pattern that you can adapt to your needs. It's not *strictly* necessary that you understand in depth *why* it works, at least not immediately. (I certainly have copied a few normal Excel formulas and macros off the web in my day that I didn't fully understand at the time, no shame in it right?)

So for a moment let's just boil it down to the pattern itself:

i The GFITW Pattern – adapt and reuse this for all your custom calendar needs!

```
CALCULATE(<base measure>,
          ALL(<custom periods table>),
          FILTER(ALL(<custom periods table>),
                 <row test with navigation arithmetic>
                 )
          )
```

Got it? Now to explain how it works, starting from a high level and then getting progressively more detailed.

"Clear Filters Then Re-filter" – Another Name for GFITW

At a high level, here's the way to understand GFITW: you clear *all* existing time-related filter context, then filter it back down to a *new* filter context. That new filter context is one that you control, typically using math that navigates backward in your custom calendar table. For this reason, you can also think of GFITW as "Clear filters, then re-filter."

Another way to say it: first you clear all time-related filter context, yielding a completely "blank slate." Once that is done, you can reconstruct a brand new filter context, from scratch, without worrying about interference from the original filter context.

With that understanding, it's not hard to "parse" the GFITW into its component parts:

- **ALL(<custom periods table>)** – this first ALL(), the one *outside* of the FILTER(), is the first part of the "Clear" phase. (Not shocking given that ALL() is all about clearing filter context right?)

- **FILTER(ALL(<custom periods table>)...** - the second ALL(), the one insider the FILTER(), *also* contributes to the "Clear" phase. (Why we need to "clear" twice is explained in the next section)

- **FILTER(... <row test with navigation arithmetic>)** – this is the "re-filter" phase, the part where you build up a new filter context from scratch, using whatever logic is required.

To get to the next level of detail, we need to revisit the FILTER() function, and form a slightly deeper understanding of it than we did before.

FILTER() – The Ins and Outs

When I first introduced FILTER(), I explained it as "use this function when you need to use an expression on the right side of a CALCULATE() <filter> argument." In a nutshell, that remains true – that's a fair way to describe *when* to use it.

But that doesn't capture every difference between the FILTER() function and the "raw" <filter> arguments to CALCULATE(). There are several key points to understand about the FILTER() function before we can truly understand the GFITW. Let's go one by one.

First Key Characteristic of FILTER() – It Always Subtracts from Filter Context, Never Overrides

Let's go way back to the original discussion of CALCULATE(). Remember this first example?

```
[2002 Sales] =

CALCULATE([Total Sales], Sales[Year]=2002)
```

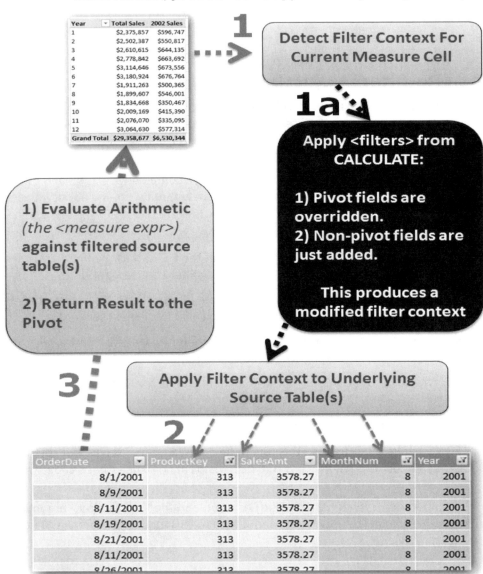

Figure 285 Normal CALCULATE() <filter> behavior is an override: we get 2002's Sales even for 2001

Let's try that same thing with FILTER() instead:

```
[2002 Sales] =

CALCULATE([Total Sales], FILTER(Sales, Sales[Year]=2002))
```

Row Labels	Total Sales	2002 Sales	2002 Sales via FILTER
2001	$3,266,374	$6,530,344	
2002	$6,530,344	$6,530,344	$6,530,344
2003	$9,791,060	$6,530,344	
2004	$9,770,900	$6,530,344	
Grand Total	$29,358,677	$6,530,344	$6,530,344

Figure 286 FILTER() gives us blanks for years other than 2002, because FILTER() always subtracts from filter context rather than overriding it

Note that using FILTER() in this example violates two rules of using FILTER(): one is to never use FILTER() when a simple <filter> will do. The other is to only use FILTER() against Lookup tables. This example is only provided to drive home the particular difference, that FILTER() subtracts from filter context.

Now let's go one step further, and add an additional raw <filter> to CALCULATE() that sets Year=2003:

```
[2002 FILTER with 2003 raw filter] =

CALCULATE([Total Sales],
          FILTER(Sales, Sales[Year]=2002),
          Sales[Year]=2003
          )
```

And the results:

Row Labels ▼	Total Sales	2002 Sales	2002 Sales via FILTER	2002 FILTER with 2003 raw filter
2001	$3,266,374	$6,530,344		
2002	$6,530,344	$6,530,344	$6,530,344	
2003	$9,791,060	$6,530,344		
2004	$9,770,900	$6,530,344		
Grand Total	**$29,358,677**	**$6,530,344**	**$6,530,344**	

Figure 287 FILTER() ALWAYS subtracts from the rest of the filter context, and it does not matter where the rest of the filter context comes from – it can come from the original pivot OR other arguments to CALCULATE(), and FILTER() just keeps subtracting from it. It's like a black hole.

In the following illustration, the left side represents the filter context applied to a source table as determined by the original filter context from the pivot, plus all the other <filter> arguments to CALCULATE(). (Where "other" means "all <filter> arguments other than the FILTER we're currently looking at – technically the other arguments could be FILTER's as well).

And then the right side represents the result of the FILTER() we're focusing on. (Ignore the numbers, they are just random data – focus on the rows).

Results of Original Filter Context and all other arguments to CALCULATE()

Results of FILTER()

Figure 288 Same source table (such as Sales or Periods) – original filter context on the left, results of FILTER() on the right. Each "says" that a different set of rows should be active. When CALCULATE moves into the arithmetic phase, which rows will remain active?

Because FILTER() subtracts from filter context rather than overriding it, only rows that are left active by *both* the original context and the FILTER() will "survive" and remain active:

1	6	4	10	7	8
5	6	10	7	7	8
8	**3**	**8**	**10**	**2**	**8**
8	2	9	8	2	10
1	8	1	2	6	3
3	1	10	7	2	4
7	**2**	**4**	**3**	**1**	**5**
5	7	8	1	9	10
10	7	10	9	7	7
5	6	8	3	8	6
9	**8**	**5**	**3**	**1**	**10**
8	8	8	2	9	1
1	**8**	**8**	**4**	**1**	**8**
4	8	7	2	2	9
6	3	9	6	9	10
5	7	9	3	6	1

Results of Original Filter Context and all other arguments to CALCULATE()

Results of FILTER()

Figure 289 Only the four circled rows were active in the original filter context AND in the result set from FILTER(), so only those four will remain active "when the dust settles"

So this is the final filter context:

1	6	4	10	7	8
5	6	10	7	7	8
8	**3**	**8**	**10**	**2**	**8**
8	2	9	8	2	10
1	8	1	2	6	3
3	1	10	7	2	4
7	**2**	**4**	**3**	**1**	**5**
5	7	8	1	9	10
10	7	10	9	7	7
5	6	8	3	8	6
9	**8**	**5**	**3**	**1**	**10**
8	8	8	2	9	1
1	**8**	**8**	**4**	**1**	**8**
4	8	7	2	2	9
6	3	9	6	9	10
5	7	9	3	6	1

Final filter context

Figure 290 Clean view of the final filter context in the example above

This Explains Why We Needed the ALL() Outside the FILTER() in GFITW

OK, so FILTER() always subtracts from filter context. Another way to say that is "FILTER() can NEVER *add back* to filter context something that was removed by something else."

So this explains why the GFITW starts out with a "Clear filters" phase – if we start out with a filter context of "Period 1 of 2003" and we go backward to "Period 12 of 2002" in our FILTER(), we will end up with nothing in our resulting filter context.

```
CALCULATE(...,ALL(<custom periods table>),…)
```

So that first ALL() in GFITW starts us with a clean slate, so that whatever our FILTER() says can become "the last word" on filter context.

Second Key Characteristic of FILTER(): Its <table> Argument Respects the Existing Filter Context of the Pivot

FILTER() does not start out with an unfiltered table! Instead, it starts with what the *pivot* says in terms of filter context, at least by default, and ignores all other arguments to CALCULATE().

Let's return to the function definition:

> **FILTER(<table>, <single "rich" filter>)**

If you provide just a table name for that first argument, FILTER() will start out with whatever filter context was specified by the pivot – nothing more or less!

Let's step through an example to see what I mean. Pretend for a moment that we had used the following formula instead:

```
CALCULATE([Sales per Day in Period],
          ALL(Periods),
          FILTER(Periods,
                Periods[PeriodID]=
                 VALUES(Periods[PeriodID])-1
                )
          )
```

The only difference from the original formula is that I removed the ALL() around Periods in that first argument to FILTER().

Now with that formula in mind, consider the following pivot, and the filter context of the highlighted measure cell:

PeriodYear	Sales per Day in Period	Prior Period Sales per Day
2001-P7	$15,224	#NUM!
2001-P8	$16,034	$15,224
2001-P9	$15,500	$16,034
2001-P10	$17,196	$15,500
2001-P11	$18,448	$17,196
2001-P12	$22,970	$18,448
2002-P1	$19,746	$22,970

Figure 291 Let's focus on the highlighted measure cell and step through an example

In that cell, the pivot is saying PeriodYear="2002-P1." So here's what the Periods table looks like according to the pivot:

PeriodID	Year	PeriodOfYear	YearPeriod
~~1~~	~~2001~~	~~7~~	~~2001-P7~~
~~2~~	~~2001~~	~~8~~	~~2001-P8~~
~~3~~	~~2001~~	~~9~~	~~2001-P9~~
~~4~~	~~2001~~	~~10~~	~~2001-P10~~
~~5~~	~~2001~~	~~11~~	~~2001-P11~~
~~6~~	~~2001~~	~~12~~	~~2001-P12~~
7	**2002**	**1**	**2002-P1**
~~8~~	~~2002~~	~~2~~	~~2002-P2~~
~~9~~	~~2002~~	~~3~~	~~2002-P3~~
~~10~~	~~2002~~	~~4~~	~~2002-P4~~
~~11~~	~~2002~~	~~5~~	~~2002-P5~~
~~12~~	~~2002~~	~~6~~	~~2002-P6~~

Figure 292 This is the PIVOT's "opinion" of the Periods table filter context

If we have an ALL(Periods) for the first argument to CALCULATE(), that means this is the "combined" filter context from the pivot plus the non-FILTER() arguments to CALCULATE():

PeriodID	Year	PeriodOfYear	YearPeriod
1	2001	7	2001-P7
2	2001	8	2001-P8
3	2001	9	2001-P9
4	2001	10	2001-P10
5	2001	11	2001-P11
6	2001	12	2001-P12
7	2002	1	2002-P1
8	2002	2	2002-P2
9	2002	3	2002-P3
10	2002	4	2002-P4
11	2002	5	2002-P5
12	2002	6	2002-P6

Figure 293 Pivot filter context plus the ALL(Periods) argument yields ALL rows active

BUT if we used FILTER(Periods, ...) as our FILTER(), FILTER() will start out with the original pivot filter context – it ignores all other <filter> arguments to CALCULATE()!

PeriodID	Year	PeriodOfYear	YearPeriod
1	2001	7	2001-P7
2	2001	8	2001-P8
3	2001	9	2001-P9
4	2001	10	2001-P10
5	2001	11	2001-P11
6	2001	12	2001-P12
7	2002	1	2002-P1
8	2002	2	2002-P2
9	2002	3	2002-P3
10	2002	4	2002-P4
11	2002	5	2002-P5
12	2002	6	2002-P6

Figure 294 FILTER() ignores all other <filter> arguments to CALCULATE() and starts from the pivot's original "opinion" of filter context!

Now, of those active rows (just one row), which ones meet the requirement of [PeriodID]=6, which is what the arithmetic test boils down to? None of them do! So this is the result of the FILTER():

PeriodID	Year	PeriodOfYear	YearPeriod
1	2001	7	2001-P7
2	2001	8	2001-P8
3	2001	9	2001-P9
4	2001	10	2001-P10
5	2001	11	2001-P11
6	2001	12	2001-P12
7	2002	1	2002-P1
8	2002	2	2002-P2
9	2002	3	2002-P3
10	2002	4	2002-P4
11	2002	5	2002-P5
12	2002	6	2002-P6

Figure 295 Results of the FILTER() – No rows left active

OK, so that means we have the original pivot context plus the ALL() <filter> param resulting in all rows active, and the FILTER() resulting in no rows active:

PeriodID	Year	PeriodOfYear	YearPeriod
1	2001	7	2001-P7
2	2001	8	2001-P8
3	2001	9	2001-P9
4	2001	10	2001-P10
5	2001	11	2001-P11
6	2001	12	2001-P12
7	2002	1	2002-P1
8	2002	2	2002-P2
9	2002	3	2002-P3
10	2002	4	2002-P4
11	2002	5	2002-P5
12	2002	6	2002-P6

Pivot plus the ALL() <filter> param

PeriodID	Year	PeriodOfYear	YearPeriod
1	2001	7	2001-P7
2	2001	8	2001-P8
3	2001	9	2001-P9
4	2001	10	2001-P10
5	2001	11	2001-P11
6	2001	12	2001-P12
7	2002	1	2002-P1
8	2002	2	2002-P2
9	2002	3	2002-P3
10	2002	4	2002-P4
11	2002	5	2002-P5
12	2002	6	2002-P6

Results of the FILTER() Function

Figure 296 When these two "opinions" of filter context get merged…

PeriodID	Year	PeriodOfYear	YearPeriod
1	2001	7	2001-P7
2	2001	8	2001-P8
3	2001	9	2001-P9
4	2001	10	2001-P10
5	2001	11	2001-P11
6	2001	12	2001-P12
7	2002	1	2002-P1
8	2002	2	2002-P2
9	2002	3	2002-P3
10	2002	4	2002-P4
11	2002	5	2002-P5
12	2002	6	2002-P6

Final filter context

Figure 297 The resulting filter context is NO rows active, which is not what we intend in GFITW

That Explains Why We Need the ALL() Inside the FILTER()

Returning to the GFITW pattern, we apply an ALL() to the Periods table outside the FILTER() function and insider the FILTER() function:

```
CALCULATE(<base measure>,
        ALL(<custom periods table>),
        FILTER(ALL(<custom periods table>),
            <row test with navigation arithmetic>
            )
        )
```

We already saw that the "outside" ALL(), the one provided as a raw <filter> argument, is there because of that first key characteristic of FILTER(), which is that it always subtracts from filter context.

But now we can also understand why there's an ALL() inside FILTER() as well – we want FILTER() itself to start from a clean slate!

OK, let's walk through it again, this time with both ALL()'s in place:

1. **The original pivot filter context:**

PeriodID	Year	PeriodOfYear	YearPeriod
1	2001	7	2001-P7
2	2001	8	2001-P8
3	2001	9	2001-P9
4	2001	10	2001-P10
5	2001	11	2001-P11
6	2001	12	2001-P12
7	2002	1	2002-P1
8	2002	2	2002-P2
9	2002	3	2002-P3
10	2002	4	2002-P4
11	2002	5	2002-P5
12	2002	6	2002-P6

Figure 298 Original filter context from the pivot

2. **The starting point for FILTER(), after the "inside" ALL is applied:**

PeriodID	Year	PeriodOfYear	YearPeriod
1	2001	7	2001-P7
2	2001	8	2001-P8
3	2001	9	2001-P9
4	2001	10	2001-P10
5	2001	11	2001-P11
6	2001	12	2001-P12
7	2002	1	2002-P1
8	2002	2	2002-P2
9	2002	3	2002-P3
10	2002	4	2002-P4
11	2002	5	2002-P5
12	2002	6	2002-P6

Figure 299 FILTER(ALL(Periods)…) starting point – after that inside ALL() is applied to original pivot filter context

3. **The results of FILTER(), after the arithmetic boils down to PeriodID=6:**

PeriodID	Year	PeriodOfYear	YearPeriod
~~1~~	~~2001~~	~~7~~	~~2001-P7~~
~~2~~	~~2001~~	~~8~~	~~2001-P8~~
~~3~~	~~2001~~	~~9~~	~~2001-P9~~
~~4~~	~~2001~~	~~10~~	~~2001-P10~~
~~5~~	~~2001~~	~~11~~	~~2001-P11~~
6	**2001**	**12**	**2001-P12**
~~7~~	~~2002~~	~~1~~	~~2002-P1~~
~~8~~	~~2002~~	~~2~~	~~2002-P2~~
~~9~~	~~2002~~	~~3~~	~~2002-P3~~
~~10~~	~~2002~~	~~4~~	~~2002-P4~~
~~11~~	~~2002~~	~~5~~	~~2002-P5~~
~~12~~	~~2002~~	~~6~~	~~2002-P6~~

Figure 300 Results of the FILTER() function – one row active

4. **Now let's see what the rest of the CALCULATE() <filter> arguments result in:**

PeriodID	Year	PeriodOfYear	YearPeriod
1	2001	7	2001-P7
2	2001	8	2001-P8
3	2001	9	2001-P9
4	2001	10	2001-P10
5	2001	11	2001-P11
6	2001	12	2001-P12
7	2002	1	2002-P1
8	2002	2	2002-P2
9	2002	3	2002-P3
10	2002	4	2002-P4
11	2002	5	2002-P5
12	2002	6	2002-P6

Figure 301 After the "outside" ALL() is applied, all rows are active

5. Lastly, we see what rows are left active after FILTER()'s "opinion" is merged with the rest of the <filter> arguments:

PeriodID	Year	PeriodOfYear	YearPeriod
~~1~~	~~2001~~	~~7~~	~~2001-P7~~
~~2~~	~~2001~~	~~8~~	~~2001-P8~~
~~3~~	~~2001~~	~~9~~	~~2001-P9~~
~~4~~	~~2001~~	~~10~~	~~2001-P10~~
~~5~~	~~2001~~	~~11~~	~~2001-P11~~
6	**2001**	**12**	**2001-P12**
~~7~~	~~2002~~	~~1~~	~~2002-P1~~
~~8~~	~~2002~~	~~2~~	~~2002-P2~~
~~9~~	~~2002~~	~~3~~	~~2002-P3~~
~~10~~	~~2002~~	~~4~~	~~2002-P4~~
~~11~~	~~2002~~	~~5~~	~~2002-P5~~
~~12~~	~~2002~~	~~6~~	~~2002-P6~~

Figure 302 The only row that "survived" pivot filter context plus the other <filter> arguments (the outside ALL), AND the FILTER(), was just this one. Which is what we want.

 Note that the order of arguments to CALCULATE() does not matter at all. If we had the FILTER() as the first <filter>, and the "outside" ALL() as the second, the results would be the same.

Summing Up: FILTER()'s Characteristics Are Why We Need Two ALL()'s in GFITW

- **FILTER() results in a set of "active" rows, and a row will *only* remain active "when the dust settles"** if it was active according to FILTER() *and* active according to the pivot filter context (after the other <filter> arguments are applied to it)

- **The "outside" ALL() is needed because FILTER() can therefore only *subtract* from filter context.**

- **FILTER()'s <table> argument starts out only paying attention to pivot filter context**, and ignores all other <filter> arguments to CALCULATE(), so the "outside" ALL() has no impact on the FILTER() itself

- **That last point is why the "inside" ALL() is also required,** so that FILTER() can start from a truly clean slate.

The Navigation Arithmetic

With all of that understood, the navigation arithmetic really is the simple part.

Let's look at the entire FILTER() that I used in my [Prior Period Sales per Day] GFITW measure:

```
FILTER(ALL(Periods),
       Periods[PeriodID]=
       VALUES(Periods[PeriodID])-1
    )
```

The part of the GFITW pattern that I call "navigation arithmetic is the second argument:

```
Periods[PeriodID]=VALUES(Periods[PeriodID])-1
```

How does that work?

At first, it seems kinda strange: how can there be a row where PeriodID equals itself minus one? The answer lies in another important detail of the FILTER() function.

The Second Argument to FILTER() Respects Original Pivot Filter Context

That's right – even though that "inner" ALL() forces FILTER() to look at all the rows in Periods, when it's inspecting a row via the filter test in the second argument, the original filter context from the pivot still applies. It doesn't care about other <filter> arguments to CALCULATE(), and it doesn't care about the first argument to FILTER() either. So VALUES() works, but so would MIN() and MAX().

And since, in the full measure formula, the GFITW was "guarded" by a HASONEVALUE() test, VALUES(Periods[PeriodID]) in this formula *always* returns a single value for PeriodID. (If not, subtracting 1 from it would yield an error).

Pretty nifty.

> Subtracting 1 from the PeriodID in this case yields the previous period, because my Periods have consecutive PeriodID values.

In Your Periods Table, You Always Need a Numeric PeriodID Column or Equivalent

Since our navigation always comes down to some sort of math, you absolutely need a PeriodID column – one that:

- Contains a unique number for each row
- Increases as time goes on
- Has consecutive numbers for periods that are consecutive in time

Pretty simple – if you don't have a column on which you can perform sensible arithmetic, you aren't going to be able to navigate.

More GFITW Measures – YOY, YTD, and "Multi-granularity"

Let's do a few more custom calendar measures.

YOY (Year over Year) Custom Calendar Measure

This one looks very much the same as our first GFITW example, and only differs in terms of the navigation arithmetic.

```
[YOY Period Sales] =

IF(HASONEVALUE(Periods[PeriodID]),
    CALCULATE([Sales in Period],
              ALL(Periods),
              FILTER(ALL(Periods),
                    Periods[PeriodID]=
                     VALUES(Periods[PeriodID])-12
                     )
              ),
    BLANK()
    )
```

Really the only thing changed here is that we are subtracting 12 rather than 1.

Let's look at the results:

PeriodID ▼	Sales in Period	YOY Period Sales
2001-P7	$426,286	$29,358,677
2001-P8	$448,953	$29,358,677
2001-P9	$542,501	$29,358,677
2001-P10	$481,475	$29,358,677
2001-P11	$516,537	$29,358,677
2001-P12	$803,964	$29,358,677
2002-P1	$552,898	$29,358,677
2002-P2	$534,463	$29,358,677
2002-P3	$737,062	$29,358,677
2002-P4	$582,060	$29,358,677
2002-P5	$687,716	$29,358,677
2002-P6	$739,934	$29,358,677
2002-P7	$459,261	$426,286
2002-P8	$477,370	$448,953
2002-P9	$451,886	$542,501
2002-P10	$383,725	$481,475
2002-P11	$297,905	$516,537
2002-P12	$622,573	$803,964
2003-P1	$411,802	$552,898
2003-P2	$485,488	$534,463

Figure 303 [YOY Period Sales] – the $426,286 is great, but I definitely did NOT expect the grand total to be returned for the first 11 periods – I expected those to be blank.

Fixing That Weird Grand Total Problem for the "Should Be Blank" Cells

Why is this happening? No seriously, why the heck is this happening, please tell me :-)

I'm kidding – I know why. But I don't like it. Folks, I personally believe this is a design mistake in the DAX engine. Not a "red alert" kind of mistake, because it's easily corrected with a formula change, but it's one that I wish we didn't have to work around. (Note that other DAX pros are divided on this controversial topic).

Here's the crux of the problem: DATESBETWEEN(Calendar[Date], BLANK(), BLANK()) returns ALL dates in the Calendar table, rather than no dates!

In the filter context for the measure cells returning the $29M number, we end up with no rows active in our Periods table. Why?   Check out what VALUES(Periods[PeriodID])-12 returns as a measure:

PeriodID ▼	Sales in Period	YOY Period Sales	VALUES - 12
2001-P7	$426,286	$29,358,677	-11
2001-P8	$448,953	$29,358,677	-10
2001-P9	$542,501	$29,358,677	-9
2001-P10	$481,475	$29,358,677	-8
2001-P11	$516,537	$29,358,677	-7
2001-P12	$803,964	$29,358,677	-6
2002-P1	$552,898	$29,358,677	-5
2002-P2	$534,463	$29,358,677	-4
2002-P3	$737,062	$29,358,677	-3
2002-P4	$582,060	$29,358,677	-2
2002-P5	$687,716	$29,358,677	-1
2002-P6	$739,934	$29,358,677	0
2002-P7	$459,261	$426,286	1
2002-P8	$477,370	$448,953	2

Figure 304 There are NO rows in the Periods table with PeriodID=0. Or -1, -2, etc. So the $29M cells have NO rows active in the Periods table.

And when there are no "active" Periods rows in our filter context, our [PeriodStartDate] and [PeriodEnd-Date] measures return blanks, because they are just FIRSTDATE()/LASTDATE() measures against the Periods table.

And that is why we're seeing the grand total (the $29M number) for [YOY Sales in Period] – because the FILTER() in our GFITW returns no rows in the Periods table for those cells, that leads to blanks for the start/end date measures, and then DATESBETWEEN() interprets that as "select everything."

The fix is to return to our original [Sales in Period] measure and substitute the FILTER() function for DATES-BETWEEN().

Original measure:

```
[Sales in Period] =

CALCULATE([Total Sales],
                DATESBETWEEN(Calendar[Date],
                             [PeriodStartDate],
                             [PeriodEndDate]
                             )
                )
```

New version that uses FILTER():

```
[Sales in Period] =

CALCULATE([Total Sales],
                FILTER(Calendar,
                       Calendar[Date]>=[PeriodStartDate] &&
                       Calendar[Date]<=[PeriodSEndDate]
                       )
                )
```

And all is right with the world:

PeriodID	Sales in Period	YOY Period Sales
2001-P7	$426,286	
2001-P8	$448,953	
2001-P9	$542,501	
2001-P10	$481,475	
2001-P11	$516,537	
2001-P12	$803,964	
2002-P1	$552,898	
2002-P2	$534,463	
2002-P3	$737,062	
2002-P4	$582,060	
2002-P5	$687,716	
2002-P6	$739,934	
2002-P7	$459,261	$426,286
2002-P8	$477,370	$448,953
2002-P9	$451,886	$542,501
2002-P10	$383,725	$481,475
2002-P11	$297,905	$516,537
2002-P12	$622,573	$803,964

Figure 305 Ah, MUCH better.

Year to Date (YTD) Measure with Custom Calendar

Let's get right to it. First, I add a new column to my Periods table:

```
ƒx =CALCULATE(MIN(Periods[PeriodID]), FILTER(Periods,
   Periods[Year]=EARLIER(Periods[Year])))
```

PeriodLabel	YearPeriod	FirstPeriodInYear
₽7	2001-P7	1
₽8	2001-P8	1
₽9	2001-P9	1
₽10	2001-P10	1
₽11	2001-P11	1
₽12	2001-P12	1
₽1	2002-P1	7
₽2	2002-P2	7
₽3	2002-P3	7

Figure 306 I will explain this calculated column formula in the chapter on advanced calculated columns. For now, just focus on how it is used in the measure.

 Again, if you have a database as your data source, and the skill (or assistance) to manipulate it, this is the sort of column that I highly recommend be implemented in the database rather than in a DAX column.

And now, the measure:

```
[YTD Period Sales] =

  CALCULATE([Sales in Period],
          ALL(Periods),
          FILTER(ALL(Periods),
              Periods[PeriodID]<=MAX(Periods[PeriodID]) &&
              Periods[PeriodID]>=MAX(Periods[FirstPeriodInYear])
               )
         )
```

And the results:

PeriodID	Sales in Period	YOY Period Sales	YTD Period Sales
⊟ 2001	$3,219,717		$3,219,717
2001-P7	$426,286		$426,286
2001-P8	$448,953		$875,239
2001-P9	$542,501		$1,417,740
2001-P10	$481,475		$1,899,215
2001-P11	$516,537		$2,415,752
2001-P12	$803,964		$3,219,717
⊟ 2002	$6,526,854		$6,526,854
2002-P1	$552,898		$552,898
2002-P2	$534,463		$1,087,361
2002-P3	$737,062		$1,824,424
2002-P4	$582,060		$2,406,483
2002-P5	$687,716		$3,094,199
2002-P6	$739,934		$3,834,133
2002-P7	$459,261	$426,286	$4,293,395
2002-P8	$477,370	$448,953	$4,770,765
2002-P9	$451,886	$542,501	$5,222,651
2002-P10	$383,725	$481,475	$5,606,376
2002-P11	$297,905	$516,537	$5,904,281
2002-P12	$622,573	$803,964	$6,526,854
⊟ 2003	$9,614,218		$9,614,218
2003-P1	$411,802	$552,898	$411,802

Figure 307 YTD Period Sales measure with custom calendar – good stuff.

Fixing YOY Period to Work on Totals, Too

We have three measures on the pivot now. Notice that two of them work at the totals level, and one does not:

PeriodID	Sales in Period	YOY Period Sales	YTD Period Sales
⊟ 2001	$3,219,717		$3,219,717
2001-P7	$426,286		$426,286
2001-P8	$448,953		$875,239
2001-P9	$542,501	???	$1,417,740
2001-P10	$481,475		$1,899,215
2001-P11	$516,537		$2,415,752
2001-P12	$803,964		$3,219,717
⊟ 2002	$6,526,854		$6,526,854

Figure 308 Can we make [YOY Period Sales] work at the totals level?

There are two reasons why [YOY Period Sales] does not work at the totals level.

1. **First, of course, is that we have a IF(HASONEVALUE()) test in the measure,** and return BLANK() for totals.
2. **More importantly, though, we have a VALUES(Periods[PeriodID])-12 in the formula,** which will outright fail in the context of a total cell.

So in order to remove the HASONEVALUE() "guard," we need to fix that VALUES()-12 part.

The best way to do that is to subtract 12 from the beginning of the current time frame *and* 12 from the end of it. So we subtract 12 from the MIN() and 12 from the MAX() of the PeriodID, and select only Periods that fall between that range.

In the single-period case, the beginning and the end are the same PeriodID, so nothing actually changes there. Only when multiple periods are selected, as is the case in a total cell, does this change in formula make a difference.

```
[YOY Period Sales] =

CALCULATE([Sales in Period],
         ALL(Periods),
         FILTER(ALL(Periods),
               Periods[PeriodID]>=MIN(Periods[PeriodID])-12 &&
               Periods[PeriodID]<=MAX(Periods[PeriodID])-12
              )
        )
```

That also allows us to remove the HASONEVALUE() guard.

Results:

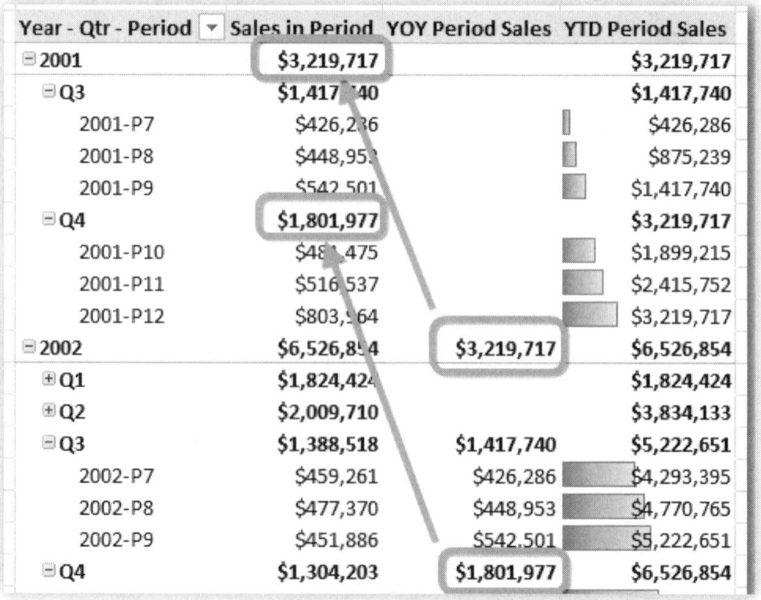

Year - Qtr - Period	Sales in Period	YOY Period Sales	YTD Period Sales
⊟ 2001	$3,219,717		$3,219,717
⊟ Q3	$1,417,740		$1,417,740
2001-P7	$426,286		$426,286
2001-P8	$448,953		$875,239
2001-P9	$542,501		$1,417,740
⊟ Q4	$1,801,977		$3,219,717
2001-P10	$481,475		$1,899,215
2001-P11	$516,537		$2,415,752
2001-P12	$803,964		$3,219,717
⊟ 2002	$6,526,854	$3,219,717	$6,526,854
⊞ Q1	$1,824,424		$1,824,424
⊞ Q2	$2,009,710		$3,834,133
⊟ Q3	$1,388,518	$1,417,740	$5,222,651
2002-P7	$459,261	$426,286	$4,293,395
2002-P8	$477,370	$448,953	$4,770,765
2002-P9	$451,886	$542,501	$5,222,651
⊟ Q4	$1,304,203	$1,801,977	$6,526,854

Figure 309 YOY now works on totals, too – Year and Qtr!

I can now also copy/paste that formula above and change the base measure to create a YOY version of [Sales per Day in Period]:

Year - Qtr - Period ▾	Sales per Day in Period	YOY Period Sales per Day
⊟ 2001	$17,691	
⊟ Q3	$15,580	
2001-P7	$15,224	
2001-P8	$16,034	
2001-P9	$15,500	
⊟ Q4	$19,802	
2001-P10	$17,196	
2001-P11	$18,448	
2001-P12	$22,970	
⊟ 2002	$17,931	$17,691
⊞ Q1	$20,049	
⊞ Q2	$22,085	
⊟ Q3	$15,258	$15,580
2002-P7	$16,402	$15,224
2002-P8	$17,049	$16,034
2002-P9	$12,911	$15,500
⊟ Q4	$14,332	$19,802

Figure 310 Sales per day version of the YOY measure, more useful for "apples to apples" comparisons

Fixing Prior Period to work on totals, too

This is trickier than YOY – if the current total cell is a Quarter, we need to shift back 3 periods. But if the current total cell is a Year, we need to shift back 12.

```
[Prior Period Sales per Day] =

  CALCULATE([Sales per Day in Period],
          ALL(Periods),
          FILTER(ALL(Periods),
                  Periods[PeriodID]>=MIN(Periods[PeriodID])
                                    - COUNTROWS(Periods)
                  &&
                  Periods[PeriodID]<=MAX(Periods[PeriodID])
                                    - COUNTROWS(Periods)
                  )
          )
```

So rather than subtracting a fixed number like in YOY, we subtract COUNTROWS(Periods), which is the number of currently selected periods – the "size" of the current time selection, in other words.

Results:

Year - Qtr - Period ▾	Sales per Day in Period	Prior Period Sales per Day
⊟ 2001	$17,691	
⊟ Q3	$15,580	
2001-P7	$15,224	
2001-P8	$16,034	$15,224
2001-P9	$15,500	$16,034
⊟ Q4	$19,802	$15,580
2001-P10	$17,196	$15,500
2001-P11	$18,448	$17,196
2001-P12	$22,970	$18,448
⊟ 2002	$17,931	$17,691
⊞ Q1	$20,049	$19,802
⊞ Q2	$22,085	$20,049

Figure 311 Prior Period: Now matches at Period, Qtr, and Year levels. No more blank totals.

The Usual "Percent Growth" Formulas

Now you can do the usual "new minus old, divided by old" trick to get the pct growth.

For example,

```
[Sales per Day Growth vs Same Period Last Year] =

IF([YOY Period Sales per Day] = 0, BLANK(),
    ([Sales per Day in Period] –
    [YOY Period Sales per Day])/
    [YOY Period Sales per Day]
  )
```

And results:

Year - Qtr - Period ▾	YOY Period Sales per Day	Sales per Day in Period	Sales per Day Growth vs Same Period Last Year
⊟ 2001		$17,691	
⊟ Q3		$15,580	
2001-P7		$15,224	
2001-P8		$16,034	
2001-P9		$15,500	
⊟ Q4		$19,802	
2001-P10		$17,196	
2001-P11		$18,448	
2001-P12		$22,970	
⊟ 2002	$17,691	$17,931	1.4 %
⊞ Q1		$20,049	
⊞ Q2		$22,085	
⊟ Q3	$15,580	$15,258	-2.1 %
2002-P7	$15,224	$16,402	7.7 %
2002-P8	$16,034	$17,049	6.3 %
2002-P9	$15,500	$12,911	-16.7 %
⊟ Q4	$19,802	$14,332	-27.6 %

Figure 312 Percent growth is as simple a calc as it always was, even though its component measures are quite sophisticated

19- Performance: How to keep things running fast.

How Important is Speed?
"Now" is three seconds in length

Let's start here. Research suggests that human beings perceive the moment of "now" to be three seconds in length. Hugs are even typically three seconds! Think of it as the fundamental unit of human time – something that takes three seconds or less is happening "now," and something that lasts longer than that requires... waiting.

Sound squishy or touchy-feely to you? Well it's relevant to us data crunchers too, in a big way.

Earlier this year, someone at Microsoft emailed and asked me the following question: "For large Power-Pivot workbooks, how long do you think users will expect to wait when they click a slicer?"

My answer: "It must be fast, period. They don't care that there is a lot of data behind it. If it isn't fast, they won't engage. The limits of human patience are not the least bit sympathetic to our data volume or complexity problems."

When we produce interactive reports or dashboards for consumption by the rest of our workgroup, we must keep in mind that the speed of interaction is critical. Anything longer than three seconds, and we risk losing the consumer altogether.

 If you would like to read an interesting article on this "3 seconds" topic, see **http://ppvt.pro/3srule**

What Happens When Something Takes Longer Than Three Seconds?

If a slicer click or related interaction takes too long, three things happen:

1. **The user's train of thought is broken while waiting on the click to complete.** Their mind wanders off topic and they often flip back over to email while they wait. They sometimes forget to come back.

They do not "commit" to the experience, do not get absorbed, and generally decide to remain "shallow" in their thoughts toward it.

2. **If they grow to expect "long" wait times, they will ultimately decide not to click at *all*.** If they know that conducting a slicer click exploration of the data is going to take 15 seconds a click, and they may have to execute 10 clicks over the course of their exploration, they simply decide not to do it at all.

Yeah, if they had invested that 2.5 minutes, they may have discovered something amazing or revolutionary in the data. Tough. Humans aren't built for that. They want their three seconds.

3. **Ultimately, and most importantly, your impact as a professional is severely diminished.** Putting together something amazing that no one uses is the same thing as doing nothing at all. Your work (and you) will be undervalued and viewed as expendable.

So it is important to think of speed as an equal, a "peer," of the content you are delivering. You *cannot* simply tell yourself, "I'm delivering a ton of great information, it's worth the wait for people when they click the slicer." Speed is just as important as having the right numbers.

To underscore that point: it is better to produce something that delivers, say, 10 "points" of information that *everyone* is using than to deliver 50 "points" of information that only 10% of people use. That's not just a point about speed of course – making the report visually clean and understandable is also important. And while I have many opinions about that stuff, I don't have space for it in this book. So we'll stick to performance.

Slicers: The Biggest Culprit

It may surprise you to learn that those innocuous, friendly little slicers on your report are usually far and away the most expensive parts of your report.

 Time to revisit those three terms I introduced in the FILTER() chapter:

Performance: the practice of keeping your reports fast for your users. For instance, if someone clicks a slicer and it takes 30 seconds for the pivot to update, I would refer to that as "poor performance." If it responds instantly, I might call that "excellent performance," or I might say that the pivot "performs well."

Response time: the amount of time it takes a report to respond to a user action and display the updated results. In the example above, I described a "response time" of 30 seconds as poor. Generally we try to keep response times to 3 seconds or less.

Expensive: an operation is said to be "expensive" if it consumes a lot of time and therefore impacts performance/response time. For instance, above I could have described <column> = <static value> tests as "inexpensive" for the DAX engine, and richer comparisons like <column> = <measure> as "potentially expensive."

"Cross-Filtering" Behavior

You've probably seen cross-filtering in action but not given it much thought. Here's an example from the NFL (American football) data that I use occasionally on the blog:

Grouping					
179 lbs and below	180....189 lbs	190....199 lbs	200....209 lbs	210....219 lbs	220....229 lbs
230....239 lbs	240....249 lbs	250....259 lbs	260....269 lbs	270....279 lbs	280....289 lbs
290 299 lbs	300 309 lbs	310....319 lbs	320....329 lbs	340...349 lbs	
330....339 lbs	350 lbs and high...				

CollegeAttendedN...		PlayerName	▼	TD Catches
		Aaron Shea		7
Alabama		Aaron Stecker		2
Alabama State		Aaron Walker		1
Alcorn State		Adam Bergen		1
Appalachian State		Ahman Green		13
Arizona		Alex Bannister		1
Arizona State		Alex Smith		2
Arkansas		Alge Crumpler		23
Arkansas-Monticello		Alvis Whitted		7
Arkansas-Pine Bluff		Amani Toomer		42
Auburn		Amos Zereoue		1
Baylor		Andre' Davis		15
Boise State		Andre Johnson		12
Boston College		Anquan Boldin		16
Bradley		Anthony Becht		18
		Antonio Bryant		16
		Antonio Chatman		5
		Antonio Freeman		28

Figure 313 No selections made on slicers, but no player heavier than 330 pounds has ever caught a Touchdown (TD) Pass (at least not in this data set)

Now I select two "tiles" in the top slicer – the ones at 320 and 340 pounds:

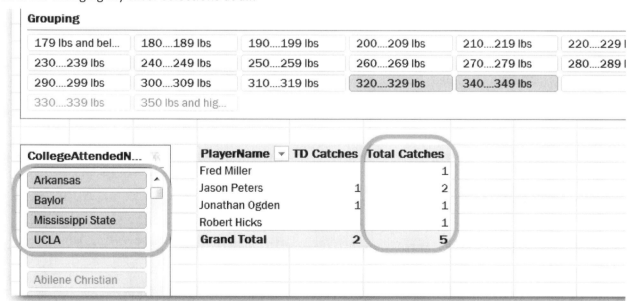

Figure 314 Note that the "CollegeAttended" slicer now has only two selectable values – all other are disabled

Why has the CollegeAttended slicer "filter itself" if I have not made any selection on it?

Well there are only two players in this data set weighing 320 pounds or more who have a TD Catch – Jason Peters and Jonathan Ogden, and they attended Arkansas and UCLA. The slicer is being helpful and showing you that clicking any other CollegeAttended will yield a completely blank pivot.

 If clicking a given "tile" in a slicer would yield a completely blank pivot (every measure returning blank), then that tile will be disabled. That's what I call "cross filtering," and it's a slicer behavior that is enabled for all slicers by default.

Cross-filtering can be, and usually is, a very helpful feature.

Cross-Filtering is Expensive in Terms of Performance

But it's also a LOT of work for the PowerPivot engine. Here, I add another measure to the previous pivot, without changing my slicer selections at all:

Figure 315 Added one measure, [Total Catches], and now two more Colleges are clickable

See that? So the slicers are not just sensitive to each other, they are also sensitive to the measures on the pivot. That means the measures have to be evaluated for each of the Colleges in the slicer (even though I have clicked none) to see if *either* measure would return a value for *each* tile!

(i) In order to enable or disable tiles in a slicer, the cross-filtering behavior actually *re-runs the entire pivot behind the scenes*, as if the tiles in the slicer were on Rows (or Columns)! Those rows of the "behind the scenes" pivot that returned at least one non-blank value are the tiles that will be displayed as clickable.

That "behind the scenes" process is repeated for *every* slicer connected to your pivot, *every* time the report consumer clicks something.

So the short version is this: every slicer you add is just as expensive as adding an entire new pivot. A single pivot with five slicers, in other words, will be about as slow as six pivots. Let that sink in.

Mitigating the Effects of Cross-Filtering

So, what do we do about this? A few possibilities:

1. **Do nothing.** If you're still under 3 seconds, you may not need to worry.

2. **Use fewer slicers.** Always worth considering since they eat so much screen real estate anyway. If a particular slicer is unlikely to be used most of the time, and is there "just in case the consumer needs it," you might consider creating a completely separate report to address that use case.

3. **Turn off cross-filtering for some slicers**. This is simple to do, the question is more about when to do it – for which slicers? Let's cover the "how" first.

How to Turn off Cross-Filtering

1. **Select a slicer.** I do this by clicking somewhere in the label area of the slicer, typically. The key is to get the slicer Options tab to show up in the ribbon:

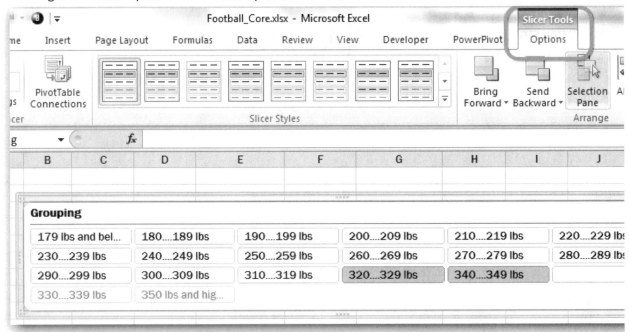

Figure 316 Select a slicer in the sheet itself (not the field list), and this ribbon tab will appear

2. **Click the Slicer Settings button** on that ribbon tab:

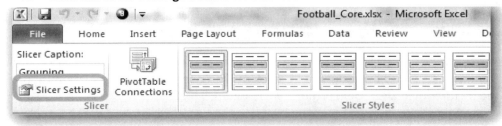

Figure 317 Click this button

3. **On the resulting dialog, uncheck** this checkbox:

Figure 318 Unchecking this checkbox turns off cross-filtering for this slicer

Turning off Cross-Filtering Only Impacts *that* Slicer

To see what I mean by this, check out the slicer after cross-filtering has been turned off:

Grouping					
179 lbs and bel...	180...189 lbs	190...199 lbs	200...209 lbs	210...219 lbs	220...229 lb
230...239 lbs	240...249 lbs	250...259 lbs	260...269 lbs	270...279 lbs	280...289 lb
290...299 lbs	300...309 lbs	310...319 lbs	320...329 lbs	330...339 lbs	340...349 lb
350 lbs and hig...					

Figure 319 The highlighted tile used to be disabled and sorted to the end, but now with cross-filtering off, it's enabled and back to its original position

OK, so disabling cross-filter *did* have an impact there.

But now look at the *other* slicer:

Figure 320 The other slicer is STILL only showing four enabled tiles

So this means this slicer is still affected by the other. For instance, let's clear the selection on the first slicer and see what happens:

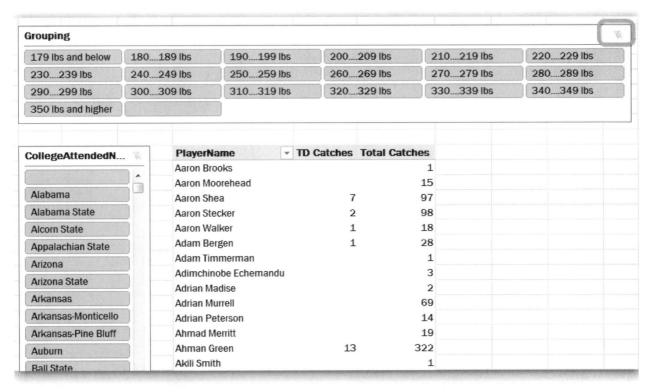

Figure 321 Even though Slicer 1 has cross filtering turned off, selections made in Slicer 1 STILL impact Slicer 2

> A slicer with cross-filtering turned off still impacts all other slicers. Disabling cross-fil-
> ter only impacts whether that slicer is impacted by other slicers. Think of this as turn-
> ing off "incoming" filtering for that slicer, rather than "outgoing" filtering.

Slicers For Which You Should Turn Cross-Filtering Off

At a high level there are three kinds of slicers for which I feel pretty good about disabling cross filtering:

1. **Slicers for which all tiles almost always have data.** If all or most tiles are always going to be active anyway, why have cross-filtering chewing up response time? One common example of this is Calendar/Time related slicers. You generally have data for every month for instance (if not you may want to consider trimming your Calendar table).

2. **Slicers with very few tiles.** The cross-filtering feature is most useful for keeping the consumer from having to scroll the slicer, looking for the tile they want to select. So if there are only four tiles, and there is no scrollbar to worry about, that slicer jumps out at me as a candidate.

3. **Slicers that form the "top" of a hierarchy.** If you have three slicers – one for Country, one for State, and one for City, the consumer tends to make a choice on Country, then State, and then City (assuming they need to filter that deep). It's pretty critical that State and City slicers retain cross-filtering (for the long scrolling reason), but disabling it for Country does not compromise that. Plus, the topmost slicer in a hierarchy tends to have the fewest tiles too.

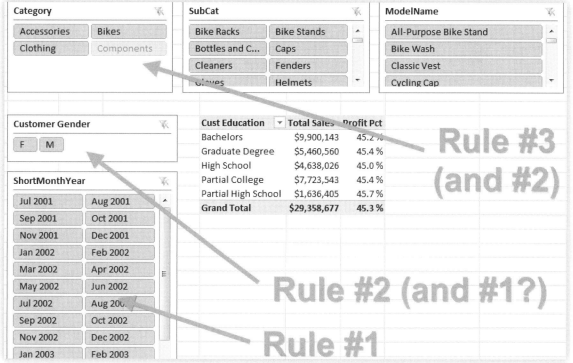

Figure 322 An example of all three kinds of "turn off cross-filter" candidates

OK, that's the easiest/most obvious thing to look at if/when a report is slow. Let's move on to data shaping.

The Shape of Your Source Tables Is Also Important

The shape (and characteristics) of your source tables can also have a tremendous impact on performance. In this section I will list some of my most impactful tips. Some of these changes are easy to make, and others require more up-front planning.

Narrower Tables are Better

- **Don't import columns you aren't going to use.** Leave them out. And yes, it's better to never import them (or edit them out via Table Properties, trigger a re-import) than it is to import then just delete the columns.

- **Move as many columns as you can from Data tables to Lookup tables.** The "narrower is better" rule applies more forcefully to tables that have higher row counts. So if you can move a row from a Data table to a Lookup table, even if it means creating a new Lookup table, it is very often worth doing so.

Here's a quick example:

StoreID	Date	TotalSales	City	State	ZIP
174	4/1/201...	33376	Duvall	WA	98019
187	4/1/201...	89909	Kirkland	WA	98033
205	4/1/201...	44317	Kirkland	WA	98033
276	4/1/201...	74610	Bellevue	WA	98005
302	4/1/201...	53480	Redmo...	WA	98052
309	4/1/201...	29123	Redmo...	WA	98052
323	4/1/201...	91802	Redmo...	WA	98052
325	4/1/201...	52957	Kirkland	WA	98034
377	4/1/201...	70203	Kirkland	WA	98033
400	4/1/201...	34442	Bellevue	WA	98004
407	4/1/201...	10768	Bellevue	WA	98004

Figure 323 A fragment of a Sales table. Note how every time we have 98033 for ZIPCode, City=Kirkland and State=WA

We don't need all three columns (City/State/ZIP) in this Sales table – ZIP is all we need in order to precisely "pin down" City and State. So we can move City and State to another table:

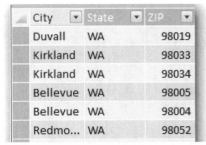

Figure 324 Our new Locations table (could also sensibly have been named ZIPCodes)

And remove City and State columns from Sales:

StoreID	Date	TotalSales	ZIP
174	4/1/201...	33376	98019
187	4/1/201...	89909	98033
205	4/1/201...	44317	98033
276	4/1/201...	74610	98005
302	4/1/201...	53480	98052
309	4/1/201...	29123	98052
323	4/1/201...	91802	98052
325	4/1/201...	52957	98034
377	4/1/201...	70203	98033
400	4/1/201...	34442	98004
407	4/1/201...	10768	98004
467	4/1/201...	59412	98053
542	4/1/201...	69295	98053
651	4/1/201...	79463	98004

Figure 325 City and State columns removed from Sales table

Then we relate Sales to Locations:

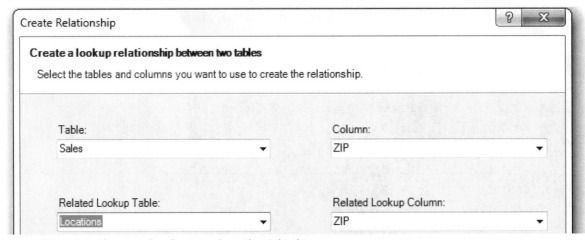

Figure 326 Relate them, and we've now done the right thing

- **Sometimes it may even be worth "pivoting" the source data before import.** There are transformations, such as the SQL command UNPIVOT, that can turn a wide and short table into a tall and narrow table. This sometimes can make a big difference, and other times have no impact, so it requires some experimentation.

Here's an example of a "wide" Sales table:

☑	Date ▾	TotalSales ▾	Normal Sales ▾	Promo Sales ▾	Returns ▾	Rebates ▾	Margin ▾	Discounts ▾
174	4/1/201...	33376	43204	24086	37931	34375	28185	26023
187	4/1/201...	89909	42600	21669	22323	44419	23394	26730
205	4/1/201...	44317	22952	35902	40079	28999	34696	24511
377	4/1/201...	70203	28269	25455	43945	25594	25531	20542
400	4/1/201...	34442	28631	20924	21041	44641	34339	39198
407	4/1/201...	10768	49734	44222	46381	25651	48936	28179
467	4/1/201...	59412	28251	33842	44064	40492	45455	32095
542	4/1/201...	69295	36118	48611	40257	37022	42440	29791

Figure 327 Many numerical columns: a "wide" table (9 columns, 1M rows)

Here's that same table "unpivoted" to be tall and narrow:

StoreID ☑	Date ▾	AmtType ▾	Amt ▾
174	4/1/201...	1	33376
187	4/1/201...	1	89909
205	4/1/201...	1	44317
377	4/1/201...	1	70203
400	4/1/201...	1	34442
407	4/1/201...	1	10768
467	4/1/201...	1	59412
542	4/1/201...	1	69295
651	4/1/201...	1	79463
787	4/1/201...	1	18329
893	4/1/201...	1	27108
174	4/1/201...	2	43204
187	4/1/201...	2	42600
205	4/1/201...	2	22952
377	4/1/201...	2	28269
400	4/1/201...	2	28631
407	4/1/201...	2	49734
467	4/1/201...	2	28251
542	4/1/201	2	36118

Figure 328 Table has been reduced to 4 columns, but now 7M rows

Then, rather than your [Total Sales] measure formula being SUM(Sales[TotalSales]), it will now be CALCULATE(SUM(Sales[Amt]), AmtType=1).

Imported Columns Are Generally Better than Calculated Columns

If you can implement a calculated column in the original data source (typically a database), and then import that column rather than calculate it in PowerPivot, that can surprisingly improve slicer click performance. (Imported columns are compressed more efficiently, leading to smaller file sizes, lower RAM consumption, and usually better slicer click performance).

A few notes on this:

- **Again, the more rows in the table, the more impactful this change can be.** I don't worry about it in small Lookup tables for instance.

- **If the calculated column is commonly used on Rows/Columns/Slicers, that is more impactful than a numeric column.** Converting a column like "Category" from calculated to imported will yield a bigger performance improvement, for instance, than "QuantitySold," which is typically just used as the basis for a SUM() measure. (But if you've moved all of your Row/Column/Slicer/Filter fields to smaller Lookup tables as recommended earlier in the book, this sort of change would be happening in a smaller table anyway and may not be much help.)

- **If the calculated column is the basis for a relationship, that is more impactful.** This is basically an extension of the previous bullet, since a relationship column is used to link a Lookup table to its Data table, and the Lookup table's columns are used on Rows/Columns/Slicers/Filters. So if nearly every column in your Data and Lookup tables is imported, but you created a single calculated column in your Data table so that you could link it to the Lookup table, you're likely paying most of the calculated column penalty despite your efforts elsewhere.

"Star Schema" is Generally Better than "Snowflake Schema"

Longtime database folks already know what I am talking about. Everyone else has no idea, so the following explanation is for you :-)

> (i) Snowflake schema = multiple levels of Lookup tables.
>
> Star schema = one level of Lookup tables.

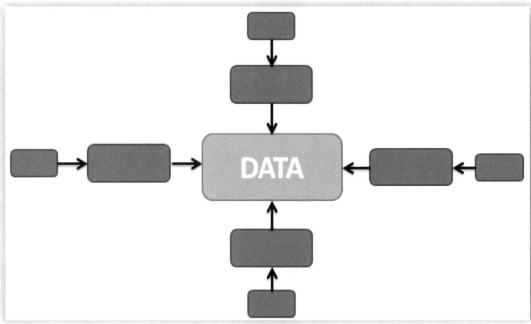

Figure 329 Snowflake schema: multiple levels of Lookup tables

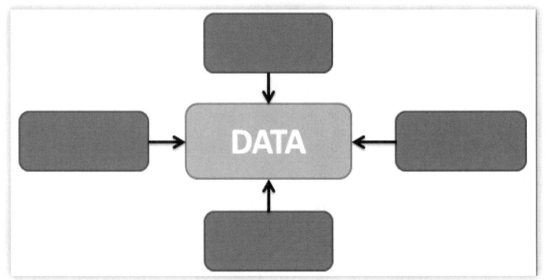

Figure 330 Star schema: if you can "squash" chained lookup tables into single, larger tables, that often can improve performance (yes even though it makes the tables wider – the most important table to keep narrow is the Data table)

Note: in the chapter on Multiple Data Tables (such as Budget versus Sales), it was explained that sometimes you cannot avoid multi-hop Lookup table arrangements. That's fine. Just don't go crazy and create lots of chained Lookup tables because you *can* – do it only when you have to. And if your reports exhibit good response times already, you can ignore this guideline altogether :-)

Measure Performance

I could write many chapters on this, and they still wouldn't be enough. In fact, others such as Marco Russo, Alberto Ferrari, and Chris Webb are the "go to" people when it comes to measure tuning and performance. I learn from them all the time – I don't claim to be the world's greatest at DAX. (My knack is more for explaining it and prioritizing what you need to know first). Their blogs and books are definitely worth checking out if you find yourself "outgrowing" this book :-)

But there are a few quick tips worth sharing.

DISTINCTCOUNT() is Much Faster than COUNTROWS(DISTINCT())

In v1, we had to use COUNTROWS(DISTINCT()), because we lacked a DISTINCTCOUNT() function.

Now though you should always use DISTINCTCOUNT(). It is *dramatically* faster.

FILTER() Should Only Be Used Against Lookup Tables and Other "Small" Columns

This tip has been mentioned before, but the reason behind it has not. Here it is, as briefly as possible.

A "raw" <filter> argument to CALCULATE() has the ability to inspect large "blocks" of rows all at once to see whether those rows should be active according to a specified filter context like Products[Color]="Blue". That is what makes a raw <filter> so blindingly fast to evaluate, even against tens or hundreds of millions of rows of data!

FILTER() lacks that "block inspection" capability, and *always* steps through the rows in its <table> argument *one at a time*. A raw CALCULATE() <filter> that scans 100 million rows might only have to look at 1,000 different blocks in order to decide which of the 100 million rows should be active. But if you use a FILTER() against those same 100 million rows, it will have to make 100 million inspections rather than 1,000, which means it's 100,000 times slower! With FILTER(), smaller tables are your friend.

Remember That the "X" Functions Are Loops

If you have a SUMX() measure in your pivot, for instance, remember that it looks at every row in the <table> argument one at a time, just like FILTER(). Sometimes it's easy to forget how much work SUMX() and similar functions are doing behind the scenes.

It's especially easy to forget how much work is going on if the column or table from the <table> argument is not displayed on the pivot. (It's not actually slower, it's just that you don't *see* what it's looping through.)

In my experience, a single X function is rarely a problem. But when you start "nesting" loops inside of other loops, things can get crazy in a hurry.

For instance, one time I wrote a measure that was essentially a SUMX() of a MAXX() – my formula was something like:

```
SUMX(<table with 1k rows>, [Another Measure])
```

But the formula for [Another Measure] was:

```
MAXX(<table with 1k rows>, <simple SUM measure>)
```

You see where this is going. I had a 1,000 row loop inside another 1,000 row loop, so my measure was doing 1 million loops for every single measure cell in the pivot! That was… not fast.

Similarly, if you have an X function measure as part of the <rich filter> argument inside a FILTER() function, you can again get into nested loops just like this – the FILTER() might step through 1,000 rows, evaluating a 1,000-loop SUMX() at each step, resulting in 1 million loops for each measure cell in the pivot.

20- Advanced Calculated Columns

Perspective: Calculated Columns Are Not DAX's Strength

Let me be clear: I'm not saying that DAX is *bad* at calculated columns. I am just saying that *measures* are the magic in DAX, which is why I've spent the vast majority of the book on measures. I mean, we've always had calculated columns in Excel right?

OK, PowerPivot Calc Columns *Are* a Strength in Some Ways.

Well, even I have to stop for a moment and say: we've never had the ability to write a calc column against a 141 million row table now have we?

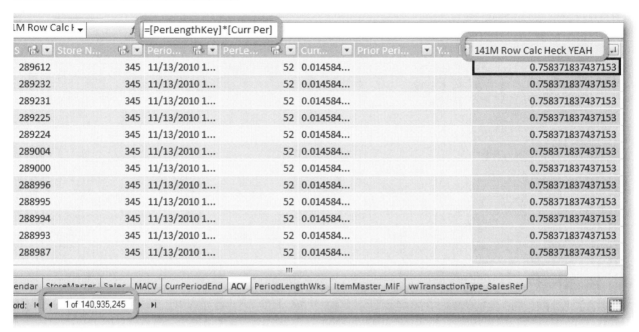

Figure 331 Calculated column written against a table with 141 million rows in it! (And this wasn't some beast of a computer - I did this on my featherweight, 4 GB RAM Ultrabook that cost $899 retail in January 2012! Requires 64-bit of course.)

OK, so I'll refine my point: *other than* the benefits provided by massive data capacity, seamless refresh, named reference, and relationships, PowerPivot calculated columns are nothing new to us :-)

But More Difficult in Some Cases

Actually, to be completely honest, PowerPivot calculated columns are actually a bit *more* difficult than normal Excel columns, at least in some circumstances, because PowerPivot lacks "A1" style reference.

In completely "row-wise" calcs, like [Column1] * [Column2], PowerPivot is no more difficult than normal Excel. But when you want to do something like "sum all the rows in this table where the [ProductID] is the same as this current row," it gets a bit trickier.

 I'm *not* criticizing PowerPivot for lacking A1-style reference. No, that was absolutely the correct decision. I just want to set your expectations – sometimes you will have to work a little harder in a PowerPivot calc column than you would in an Excel calc column, but even then, only when your calc goes beyond a single row.

Anyway, we'll get to that. But first, some simple stuff that just didn't fit anywhere else.

Start Out With "Not so Advanced"

OK, there are a couple of calculated column quick topics I'd like to cover that don't really deserve the label "advanced" – they're more "useful things I didn't cover before because I was dying to get to measures."

Grouping Columns

My favorite example of this is the Sales by Temperature, aka "Temperature Mashup" demo. In that demo, I import a table of temperature (weather) data, relate it to my Sales table, and then report [Sales per Day] broken out by temperature:

Temperature ▼	Sales per Day
14	$3,543
15.8	$4,677
19.4	$3,558
25.4	$98
25.8	$4,630
26.6	$2,785
27.5	$5,956
28	$87
29.3	$5,329
30.2	$3,951
31.9	$38
32.3	$7
33.3	$7,640
33.7	$4,486
33.8	$4,303
35.6	$3,228
36.1	$6,559

Figure 332 Sales per Day with Temperature on Rows, but the temperature is very precise

OK, I obviously do NOT care to see temperature ranges broken out by a tenth of a degree. I want to group them into more useful ranges.

You can do this with a calculated column. In the demo, here's the formula I use in the Temperature table:

```
IF([Avg Temp]<40,"Cold",
    IF([Avg Temp]<55,"Cool",
        IF([Avg Temp]<70,"Warm",
            "Hot"
            )
        )
    )
```

Here's what it looks like in the Temperature table as a calc column:

| fx =IF([Avg Temp]<40,"Cold",IF([Avg Temp]<55,"Cool",IF([Avg Temp]<70,"Warm","Hot"))) |

nth	MonthNumber	Avg Temp	TempKey	TempRange
	1	26.3	Northeast1	Cold
)	2	25.4	Northeast2	Cold
r	3	31.4	Northeast3	Cold
r	4	48.1	Northeast4	Cool
y	5	52.8	Northeast5	Cool
ie	6	66.8	Northeast6	Warm
	7	70.4	Northeast7	Hot
g	8	66	Northeast8	Warm
)	9	61.2	Northeast9	Warm
:	10	47.2	Northeast10	Cool
v	11	38.1	Northeast11	Cold
c	12	28	Northeast12	Cold
	1	30.5	Central1	Cold
)	2	31.9	Central2	Cold
r	3	41.9	Central3	Cool
		52.4	Central4	Cool

Figure 333 Grouping column in the Temperature table

And here's what it looks like used on Rows instead of the Avg Temp column:

Temperature	Sales per Day
Cold	$13,527
Cool	$9,485
Hot	$6,662
Warm	$14,739
Grand Total	**$26,120**

Figure 334 TempRange on Rows – MUCH better

 I've used many kinds of formulas along these lines – ROUND() has been a very popular
function for me in this regard, for instance.

To see the whole "Temperature Mashup" demo end to end that first debuted in 2009 (!), visit http://ppvt.
pro/TempMash

Unique Columns for Sorting

Did you notice that the sort order is "off" in that Temperature report? Here it is again:

Temperature	Sales per Day
Cold	$13,527
Cool	$9,485
Hot	$6,662
Warm	$14,739
Grand Total	**$26,120**

Figure 335 I would prefer the sort order to be Cold, Cool, Warm, Hot

OK, so let's use the Sort by Column feature, and use AvgTemp to sort the TempRange column:

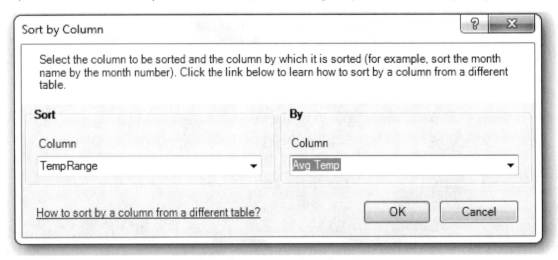

Figure 336 Attempting to use AvgTemp as the Sort By Column for TempRange

This yields an error:

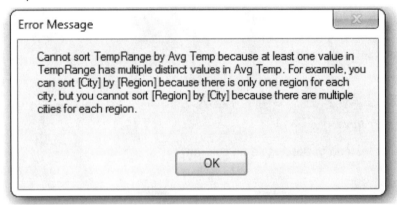

Figure 337 It does not like Green Eggs and Ham – not in a box, not with a fox. OK and it also doesn't like AvgTemp as a Sort By Column.

I guess it *could* have used AvgTemp, since no single AvgTemp corresponds to two different TempRange values (48.1 for instance *always* maps to "Cool"), but PowerPivot doesn't want to trust me. It wants each value of TempRange to have a *single* value in the Sort By Column, and as a former (and sometimes current) software engineer myself, I can understand why it doesn't want to trust me :-)

So in this case, a SWITCH() does the trick –giving me a column with values 1-4:

```
SWITCH([TempRange], "Cold", 1, "Cool", 2, "Warm", 3, "Hot", 4)
```

fx =SWITCH([TempRange], "Cold", 1, "Cool", 2, "Warm", 3, "Hot", 4)		
TempRange	TempRangeSeque...	Add Col
Cold	1	
Cold	1	
Cold	1	
Cool	2	
Cool	2	
Warm	3	
Hot	4	

Figure 338 A valid candidate for a sorting column – this one works

Another Sort by Column Example

For a slightly more sophisticated problem, consider the "QtrYearLabel" column in my Periods table:

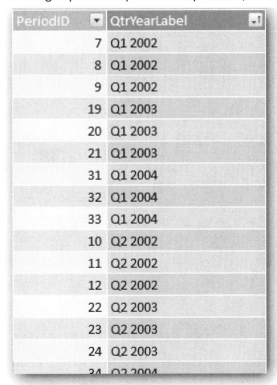

PeriodID	QtrYearLabel
7	Q1 2002
8	Q1 2002
9	Q1 2002
19	Q1 2003
20	Q1 2003
21	Q1 2003
31	Q1 2004
32	Q1 2004
33	Q1 2004
10	Q2 2002
11	Q2 2002
12	Q2 2002
22	Q2 2003
23	Q2 2003
24	Q2 2003
34	Q2 2004

Figure 339 QtrYearLabel – note how each value matches multiple PeriodID values

I deliberately positioned it next to the PeriodID column so you could see that I have the same "matches multiple" problem here as what I had in the Temperature example.

But a SWITCH() isn't going to save me this time. I need to do some math. Here's a pattern that I use over and over again.

```
([Year] * 4) + [Qtr]
```

 OK, in pattern form that is:

(<Year Column> * <number of periods per year>) + <period column>

Where "period" can be quarter (of which there are 4 per year), month (12), week (52), semester (2), whatever.

That gives me:

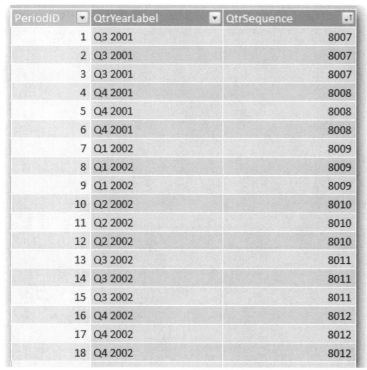

PeriodID	QtrYearLabel	QtrSequence
1	Q3 2001	8007
2	Q3 2001	8007
3	Q3 2001	8007
4	Q4 2001	8008
5	Q4 2001	8008
6	Q4 2001	8008
7	Q1 2002	8009
8	Q1 2002	8009
9	Q1 2002	8009
10	Q2 2002	8010
11	Q2 2002	8010
12	Q2 2002	8010
13	Q3 2002	8011
14	Q3 2002	8011
15	Q3 2002	8011
16	Q4 2002	8012
17	Q4 2002	8012
18	Q4 2002	8012

Figure 340 Unique sort id/sequence column for my QtrYearLabel column

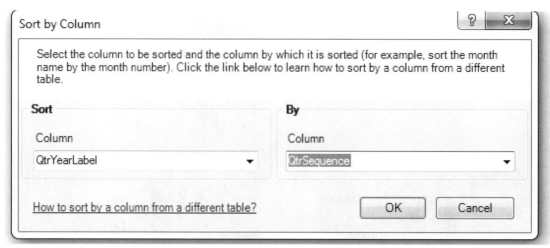

Figure 341 And this one works

Now For the Advanced Examples

Summing Up In a Lookup Table

Let's say you wanted to create a Total Sales column in your Products table, reflecting the sales for each Product.

First, Rob would scold you. That's what measures are for! Why would you summarize a value in your Lookup table? But then I would calm down and admit that there are definitely cases where you might *occasionally* need to do this :-)

It turns out that SUMX() can be used here, combined with the RELATEDTABLE() function:

```
SUMX(RELATEDTABLE(Sales), Sales[SalesAmt])
```

| f_x =SUMX(RELATEDTABLE(Sales), Sales[SalesAmt]) | | | |

e ▾	SubCategory ▾	Category ▾	SalesPerProduct ▾
)0 Bl...	Mountain Bikes	Bikes	$165,374.51
)0 Bl...	Mountain Bikes	Bikes	$151,874.55
)0 Bl...	Mountain Bikes	Bikes	$202,499.40
)0 Bl...	Mountain Bikes	Bikes	$192,374.43

Figure 342 SUMX() – not just for measures anymore!

 RELATEDTABLE() – you can think of this as a function that looks "backwards" across a relationship, from Lookup table to Data table, and returns all rows from the Data table corresponding to the current row in the Lookup table.

Note the use of a regular column reference for the second argument of SUMX(), which was something I introduced back in the chapter on the X functions. If you're really curious as to why this all works, read the next section. If you're just happy to have a pattern that works, just give it a skim.

Row Context – A Concept That's Partly Critical but Mostly Ignorable :-)

The reason SUMX() allows a raw column reference in that second argument is that SUMX(), just like FILTER(), operates on a "one row at a time" basis when working its way through the rows in its first argument (the <table> argument). We've been talking a lot about filter context throughout the book, but technically there's also another concept known as "row context."

At a simple level, we can understand that a calc column implicitly calculates one row at a time. If I write a calc column formula like [PeriodId] + 1, the value of [PeriodId] from the current row is used to calculate each row of the new column. I mean, that's just how calculated columns work. And that is the simplest example of row context.

I'm pretty sure that when you start writing more complex measures than those covered in this book, understanding row context as clearly as you understand filter context becomes important. But I've made it a long way without being able to expound in depth on the intricacies of row context in measures. Instead I say things like "FILTER() works one row at a time." And row context just seems to make intuitive sense, most of the time, in calc columns.

So this little detour about row context is really an apology: when/if you discover that you really need to understand row context at that "next level," I'm just not the guy to explain it to you. Or at least not yet. You can safely ignore it for now – I have for three years and am no worse for the wear, but guys like Marco Russo, Alberto Ferrari, and Chris Webb can do things in DAX that I can only copy. Go get one of their books if you outgrow what I have to teach you, and godspeed – think of me as a booster-phase rocket :-)

Simple Use of the EARLIER() Function

Ah, the EARLIER() function. It was two years before I understood how/when to use it, and even today, I admit that this function and I have only an uneasy peace. I've caught myself a few times using it when I didn't actually have to, so mastery is still elusive.

That said, I am pretty confident in certain patterns for its use, and that's really all you are going to need, at least for a long time.

Let's extend the prior example from the Products table, and this time calculate a column that represents the total sales from all products with a matching Category.

In other words, you want something like this:

ProductName	Category	SalesPerProduct	TotalCategorySales
Patch Kit/8 Patches	Accessories	$7,307.39	$700,759.96
Road Tire Tube	Accessories	$9,480.24	$700,759.96
Water Bottle - 30 oz.	Accessories	$21,177.56	$700,759.96
Mountain Tire Tube	Accessories	$15,444.05	$700,759.96
Touring Tire Tube	Accessories	$7,425.12	$700,759.96
Bike Wash - Dissolver	Accessories	$7,218.60	$700,759.96
Road Bottle Cage	Accessories	$15,390.88	$700,759.96
Mountain Bottle Cage	Accessories	$20,229.75	$700,759.96
Taillights - Battery-Po..	Accessories		$700,759.96
Minipump	Accessories		$700,759.96
LL Road Tire	Accessories	$22,435.56	$700,759.96
Fender Set - Mountain	Accessories	$46,619.58	$700,759.96
Mountain Pump	Accessories		$700,759.96
LL Mountain Tire	Accessories	$21,541.38	$700,759.96
ML Road Tire	Accessories	$23,140.74	$700,759.96

Figure 343 Every row with Category=Accessories sums to the same amount, which is the sum of all Accessories rows

ProductName	Category	SalesPerProduct	TotalCategorySales
Mountain-500 Black, 40	Bikes	$25,919.52	$28,318,144.65
Mountain-500 Black, 42	Bikes	$26,459.51	$28,318,144.65
Mountain-500 Black, 44	Bikes	$31,319.42	$28,318,144.65
Mountain-500 Black, 48	Bikes	$30,239.44	$28,318,144.65
Mountain-500 Black, 52	Bikes	$22,139.59	$28,318,144.65
Road-750 Black, 58	Bikes	$180,356.66	$28,318,144.65
Road-750 Black, 44	Bikes	$194,396.40	$28,318,144.65
Road-750 Black, 48	Bikes	$196,016.37	$28,318,144.65
Road-750 Black, 52	Bikes	$208,436.14	$28,318,144.65
Mountain-500 Silver, 40	Bikes	$25,424.55	$28,318,144.65
Mountain-500 Silver, 42	Bikes	$25,424.55	$28,318,144.65
Mountain-500 Silver, 44	Bikes	$22,034.61	$28,318,144.65
Mountain-500 Silver, 48	Bikes	$28,249.50	$28,318,144.65
Mountain-500 Silver, 52	Bikes	$27,119.52	$28,318,144.65
Road-650 Red, 58	Bikes	$13,282.87	$28,318,144.65
Road-650 Red, 60	Bikes	$11,884.67	$28,318,144.65

Figure 344 Filtered to Bikes

OK, here's the formula:

```
CALCULATE(SUM(Products[SalesPerProduct]),
        FILTER(ALL(Products),
            Products[Category]=
            EARLIER(Products[Category])
            )
        )
```

Whoa! CALCULATE() in a calc column! Yeah, things are getting crazy now :-) I have some explaining to do. I mean, this pattern looks a lot like the GFITW, but different. **In fact, let's think of it that way – we're doing a "clear then re-filter," just like in the GFITW.** I can hear your questions now though...

- **"Why no ALL(Products) *outside* the FILTER()?"** – the last time we saw this sort of pattern, it was in the GFITW and it was in a measure. And there was an ALL() outside the FILTER() as well. So why not here? **Well, in a calc column, there *is* no filter context. In other words, the filter context in a calc column is always set to ALL(), for everything!** So we don't need that ALL() outside the FILTER() – its role in the GFITW was to clear the existing filter context, which is already done for us in a calc column. (You can add an "outside" ALL here and it won't impact your result).

- **"OK then, why is the *inside* ALL() still there?"** – you always ask the *smartest* questions! Well, inside a FILTER(), the notion of row context *does* exist. And we use the inside ALL() to get rid of our row context so that we're looking at all rows in the table. Without the inside ALL(), our result for [TotalCategorySales] would be the same as [SalesPerProduct], which is not what we want.

- **"Hmm, OK, I think I get that enough to at least use it. But what the heck is EARLIER()?"** – this function basically says "hey you know that row context we're using right now? I want to undo that, almost like hitting ctrl-Z, and go *back* to the *previous* row context we were using before." Which is like a quantum physics explanation when all we really wanted to hear was **"EARLIER() removes that inside ALL() we just applied so we can inspect the current row again."**

 I really do think that all of this stuff could/should be made easier in a future version of PowerPivot. There should just be dedicated functions for these advanced calc column scenarios, named things like CALCSIMILARROWS() for this particular example. We don't really need to understand these particular concepts as deeply as we understand the measure stuff, we just need them to work. And this FILTER() / EARLIER() stuff is really overkill – it forces us to get a bit "closer" to the DAX engine than we need to. Don't feel bad if your head hurts a little right now. Just use the patterns here and don't worry too much – it really is fine to do that. I have the credentials (or guts?) to call myself PowerPivotPro and yet that's how *I* roll when it comes to advanced calc columns. You can too.

An Even More Advanced Example

I had to include this one, both because it shows a few twists on the previous technique, and because it is one of the coolest, most inspiring examples of the potential we all now have as Excel Pros.

I have a neighbor who's a neuroscientist. In his field, he's kind of a big deal, like Will Ferrell in the movie "Anchorman." His name is Dan Wesson, he runs a research lab at Case Western Reserve University (CWRU), and his lab made it onto CNN earlier this year with some exciting developments in Alzheimer's research. (See? People know him).

This is a well-funded lab with all kinds of expensive equipment. It's an impressive place – I've toured it. He even has individual software packages that cost $10,000 for a single seat!

And oh yeah, with my help he's converted most of his data analysis over to PowerPivot. You know, the next generation of spreadsheet. That thing that costs approximately $10,000 *less* than his other software. That's right, Excel Pros – we even do Alzheimer's research!

Here are a few of my favorite pictures of all time:

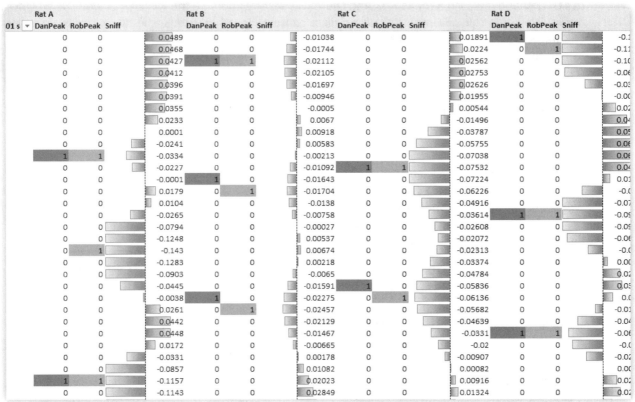

Figure 345 This "DNA" view is data from the Neuroscience lab at CWRU. The red and blue "waves" are rats inhaling and exhaling – red is inhale, blue is exhale, and each row represents 1/100 of a second!

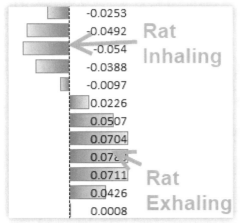

Figure 346 Zoomed in on one of the inhale/exhale waves.

Now here's the one that makes me the happiest:

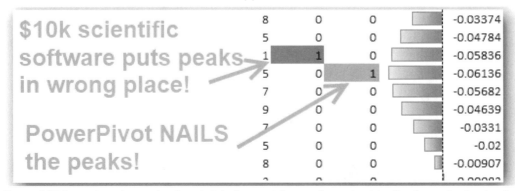

Figure 347 Detecting the peak of each inhale event is very important to Dan's work. Look where the $10,000, purpose-built scientific software places the peaks versus where PowerPivot puts them!

That "peak detection" is just a calc column. Here's what the data looks like:

Time	Rat	Value
0	E	0.0189
0.01	E	0.02238
0.02	E	0.02561
0.03	E	0.02752
0.04	E	0.02627
0.05	E	0.01959
0.06	E	0.00553
0.07	E	-0.01486
0.08	E	-0.03775
0.09	E	-0.05746
0.1	E	-0.07033
0.11	E	-0.07531

Figure 348 Time (in hundredths of a second), RatID, and Value - negative for inhale, positive for exhale. The bigger the absolute value, the more forceful the inhale/exhale.

The most critical component of detecting an inhale peak is finding the most negative value in any given timeframe. Think of it as like a moving average, except that it's a moving minimum!

And here's my calc column formula for moving minimum:

```
=CALCULATE(MIN(Data[value]),

        FILTER(ALL(Data),

                Data[Rat]=EARLIER(Data[Rat])

                ),

        FILTER(ALL(Data),

                Data[TimeID] <= EARLIER(Data[TimeID]) +5
                &&

                Data[TimeID] >= EARLIER(Data[TimeID]) -5

                )

        )
```

Hey, it's still the same old "GFITW modified for calc column use," just like the first example I showed you for the EARLIER() function. But there are a few wrinkles:

- **Two FILTER() functions** – don't let this scare you. You can do as many as you want and the rules are still the same. A row has to "survive" *both* FILTER()'s in order to be eventually "fed" to the MIN() function that's the first argument to the CALCULATE().

- **The first FILTER()** - is just like our previous example. Only rows for the current rat should be counted, otherwise we're looking at someone else's breathing :-)

- **The Second FILTER() is kinda cool** – it basically says "only count the five rows that happened sequentially before me, and the five rows that happened right after me." So we end up looking at a window in time that is 11 rows "long," which is actually 0.11 seconds.

The net result of the formula is that it tells us the smallest value in the current 11-row window.

From there, other calc columns can detect if the current row's Value column matches the new 11-row minimum column, in which case we're probably looking at a peak inhale.

See http://ppvt.pro/PkSniff for the full blog post, and see if you can spot the one mistake I made back then that I corrected in the formula above :-)

If you're interested in reading more about this project, see:

http://ppvt.pro/Peak2Freq - where we move on to use our peak calc columns to produce frequency and amplitude measures.

http://ppvt.pro/FzzyTime - where we correlate the inhale/exhale data with events in another table that cannot be directly related (more calc column wizardry ensues)

There's going to be another update on that project at some point, when Dan publishes the paper, so keep an eye on the Medical/Scientific category as well: http://ppvt.pro/MedSciCat

Memory and CPU Consumption of Complex Calc Columns

I think it's appropriate to mention that certain kinds of calculated columns can eat a truly staggering amount of RAM when they're running.

Take my "moving minimum" example from the peak detection scenario above for instance. That formula is written to only look at the previous five rows and the next five rows, plus the current row. **So I'm only inspecting 11 rows at a time.**

But to find those 11 rows to inspect, PowerPivot starts from scratch and goes looking through the *entire* table, one row at a time, and deciding whether each row belongs in that current window of 11.

In normal Excel, relative reference takes care of this – Excel literally goes and looks five rows up and five rows down. It does *not* have to scan the entire worksheet, row by row, in order to find the right 11 rows. When it comes to "look at the rows close to me," PowerPivot is just fundamentally less intelligent than normal Excel. That's a consequence of lacking A1-style reference, which I've said before is a necessary evil in order to get a truly robust environment.

I'll leave you with one last observation on this topic: if you have one million rows in your table, that means scanning a million rows to calculate just a single row of the calc column. And since there are a million rows to calc, you have a million loops, each of which is a million rows of loop in itself. That's literally a *trillion* comparisons! Not only does that take a lot of time and processor power, but it takes a lot of RAM too.

Ultimately, with Dan's project, we had to abandon using PowerPivot calc columns for peak detection and implement the same "moving minimum" formula in SQL Server. That inhale/exhale table of his grew to be over 100 million rows! **But we still use PowerPivot for all of the measures and reporting, which after all is PowerPivot's strength.**

21- The Final Transformation: One Click That Will Change Your Life Forever

In chapter one, I set the stage: the world needs Excel Pros more than anyone realizes yet, and needs us dramatically more than ever (thanks to the twin forces of 'Big Data' and economic pressure).

In order to meet that need, and claim proper recognition (and compensation!) for doing so, I said we required a dramatic expansion in the power of our toolset. Specifically, I highlighted four key problems with 'traditional' Excel that are holding us back:

1. Too much manual effort goes into creating and maintaining traditional Excel reports.
2. Integration of multiple data sources into unified insight is particularly tedious.
3. Truly "Big" Data does not fit because of the 1 million row limit.
4. Excel has an image problem that undermines the perceived importance of your work.

In the pages between that first chapter and this one, I have shown you how PowerPivot addresses the first three problems:

1. The centralized, sophisticated, and 'portable' logic provided by DAX measures cuts manual effort to 10% or less of traditional levels.
2. Integration of multiple data sources now requires only three clicks for each new data source. This is thanks to the power of Relationships, which even solve the dreaded 'granularity mismatch' problem such as that posed by 'Budget vs. Actuals' situations.
3. Hundreds of millions of rows of data can be addressed and analyzed.

Along the way, I hope you've also seen that PowerPivot lives up to my analogy of 'biplane upgraded to jet plane, but with a familiar cockpit.'

However, I haven't yet addressed the fourth problem: image. In this chapter, I will explain what that image problem *is*, and how PowerPivot can provide a brand new perception of our work.

The Hidden Credibility Thief Steals From You Every Day

Excel Pros are at war every day with an unseen enemy, one that does more harm to us as professionals than every other problem combined. More than office politics. More than even the most dreadful formula mistake.

This sinister force operates right under our noses, hidden in plain sight, all day, every day. I will first unmask this villain, and then explain how we will put him away forever.

Let's start in an innocuous place: once upon a time, there was a spreadsheet...

A Common Practice: Making Spreadsheets Look Less Like... Spreadsheets

Here's a relatively sophisticated PowerPivot workbook that I created.

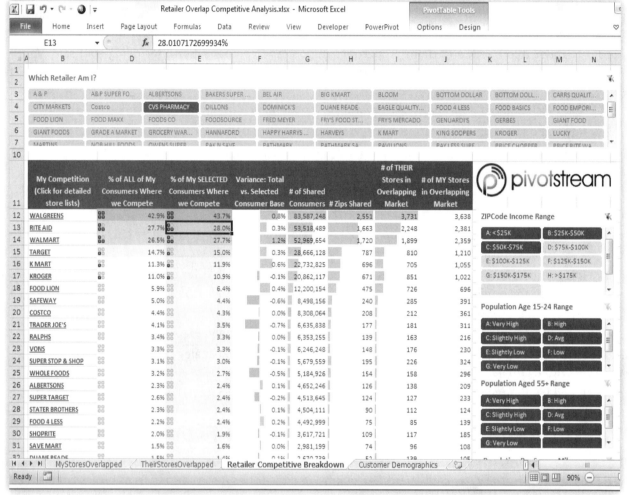

Figure 349 This PowerPivot workbook tells retailers their top competitors in certain demographics.

It's a slick looking workbook (if I do say so myself), and offers slick functionality. But let's make it look a little bit less 'spreadsheet-y.'

Figure 350 Turn off Gridlines and Headers.

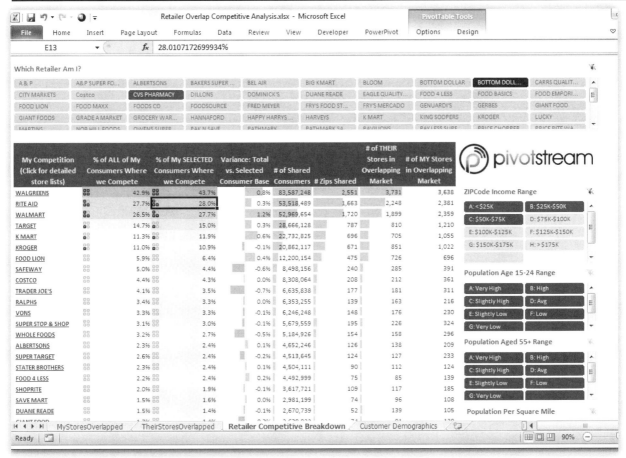

Figure 351 Looking less like a spreadsheet!

I'll even park the selected cell behind that slicer up top, so that I don't see it:

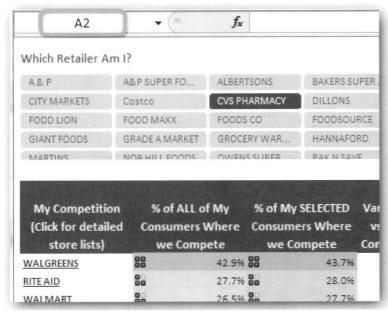

Figure 352 Cell A4 is behind the slicer, so you don't see a selected cell.

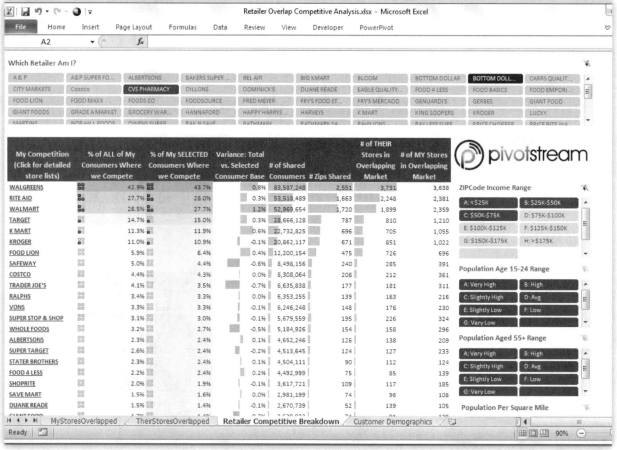

Figure 353 Looking good! But there are a few lingering 'spreadsheet' artifacts...

Have I Succeeded? Does It No Longer Seem Like a Spreadsheet?

Um, no. I've done everything I can and *still* have not succeeded. Let's highlight some of the things I *can't* control:

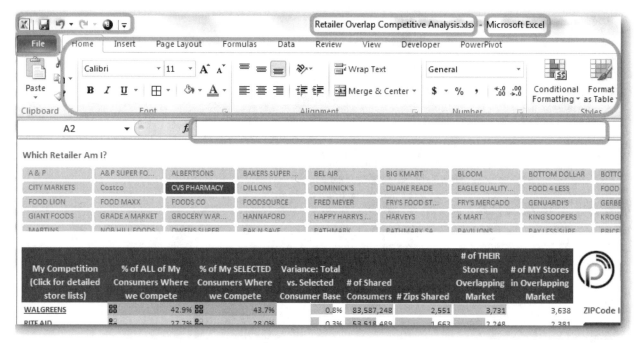

Figure 354 Toolbar, File Menu, the Ribbon, Filename ending in 'XLSX', Microsoft Excel's name itself (a dead giveaway) and a Formula Bar!

This is definitely still Excel. No one is going to miss that.

Why Does It *Matter*?

Why do we care that it still looks like Excel? Why do we bother with even the minor aesthetic steps I went through? For that matter, why is a post on formatting spreadsheets (http://ppvt.pro/FormatXL) – one that doesn't contain the word "PowerPivot" – one of the top 5 all-time most viewed posts on PowerPivotPro. com?

Well, spreadsheets are what we do. They are where our work meets the world. Indeed, those spreadsheets running around are almost *synonymous* with us: very often, when a consumer is looking at one of them, they are inherently equating the spreadsheet with your contributions to the team. In the consumer's head, the spreadsheet is **you;** and since we all know that appearances matter a lot more than they should, we put a lot of effort into formatting. As our spreadsheets are our representatives to the rest of the organization (maybe even to customers and partners), the way our spreadsheets *look* reflects on us.

That's an important point to keep in mind. However, we're going to dig a few steps deeper.

Sharing It with Others

Okay, I've got the spreadsheet set up as nicely as I can. Now it's time to share. So I fire up my email and compose a little message:

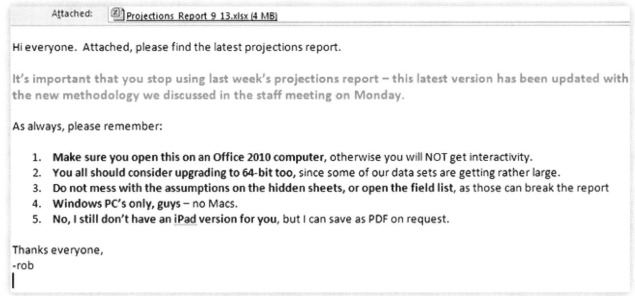

Figure 355 Does this look familiar to you? I bet it does.

Wow, look at all that. All those *instructions*. The do's and don'ts. Above all, the unmet desires of my poor coworkers who just want the data in a convenient format.

On the Receiving End: Excel = Word = PowerPoint

All right. Now let's put ourselves in someone else's shoes: one of our consumers, who receives the spreadsheet. Let's call him Jim.

Jim comes back to his desk to find these three messages at the top of his inbox:

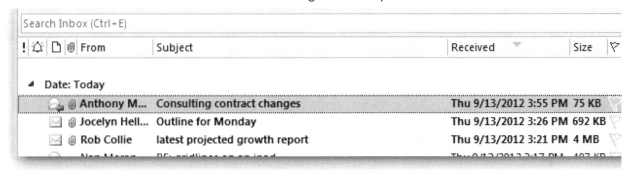

Figure 356 "Hmm, looks like a few things for me to review."

Then Jim opens those messages:

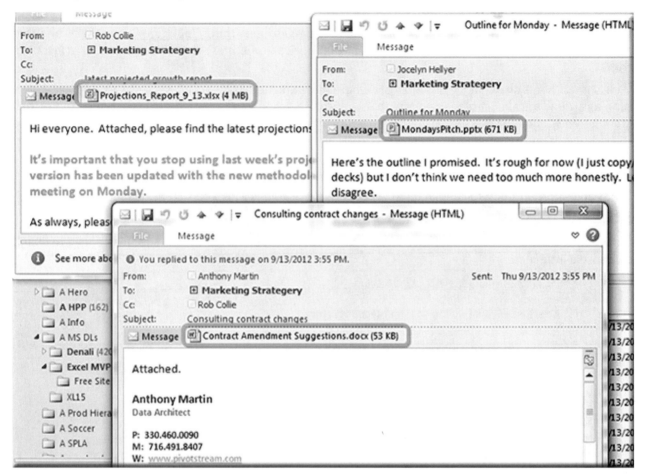

Figure 357 Three messages, three coworkers, three Office documents: "Oh great. Attached documents. At least they're all probably short."

That word 'document' – it covers a lot of ground doesn't it? Here's a Word doc that is just edits to a long-standing document, and a slide deck that's a Frankenstein's monster of copy/paste from other decks. And sitting right next to both of those is just another Office doc, produced in just another Office app.

This tight psychological association between Word, Excel, and PowerPoint is quite unfortunate, for they are actually very different. Word and PowerPoint documents are containers for *static content* – stuff that was *entered* via one method or another (typing, pasting, clicking for formatting, etc.) A well-constructed spreadsheet, by contrast, is an *application* in itself. Excel Pros, whether we realize it or not, are *programmers*. We produce logical systems – our spreadsheets are *machines* that we created.

Excel Pros are the dominant business programmers of the world. We are *engineers*. Our spreadsheets are, in and of themselves, a form of *software* – software that happens to be created in an environment known as Excel, and that happens to also run (for consumers) in that same environment.

Yet this close association with the other Office apps, and with the notion of a 'document', dumbs that all down in the eyes of the consumer. It's not their fault: this is just how the human brain digests the unfamiliar – it filters it through the lens of the familiar. Docs are docs. Office apps are Office apps.

Even at Microsoft, on the Office team, people who worked on Word, PowerPoint and / or Outlook really didn't regard Excel as being any different. (Except the people who worked on Excel – we were definitely regarded as different. That may *also* sound familiar to you).

From Magical to Mundane

It is clear then that our perceived value is even damaged by the fact that it's the same Excel for creating docs as it is for consuming docs. Why? Because Excel has a million buttons and control surfaces – ways by which consumers can become confused. By which they can break things.

While we might hope that this complexity would heighten the respect for our skills, consumers' lack of understanding actually just harms the reputation of Excel; and, by extension, its users. My friend Dick Moffat complained to me recently that "back in the day" someone could call themselves an Excel Developer and it was a "cool" thing to say. Being an Excel Pro was a cutting edge profession that could earn you a top-notch living, even as a freelancer. Yet, he lamented, very few people call themselves that today.

Something has clearly eroded over the years. When the spreadsheet first exploded onto the scene, it felt like absolute magic – it came in with the original PC tide, an absolutely revolutionary force.

People have been making pretty spreadsheets since the 1980s, and since the 1990s they've been emailing them around. Or saving them to file shares. In other words, treating them just like Word docs.

Throughout that entire timeframe, the notion that Excel = PowerPoint = Word has been pervasive; and constantly reinforced.

Furthermore, the focus of the world, since about 1996, has been rapidly moving away from the desktop, and onto … the internet.

The Web: From Enemy to Opportunity
Siphoning Mindshare Away From Us Since 1996

Part of the problem we face is not an Excel problem – it is a desktop problem, period. Consider the following charts that I ran on Indeed.com's job trends search:

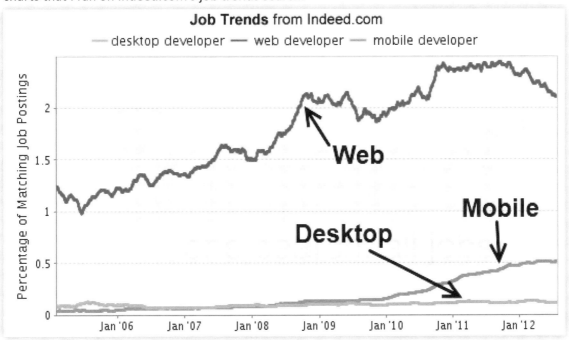

Figure 358 Job listing trends since 2005 for three different kinds of programmer.

I wish Indeed.com's data went back farther, but this still shows the point: desktop development isn't exactly the rage. The only thing cutting into web development as a career is mobile development.

Here's another:

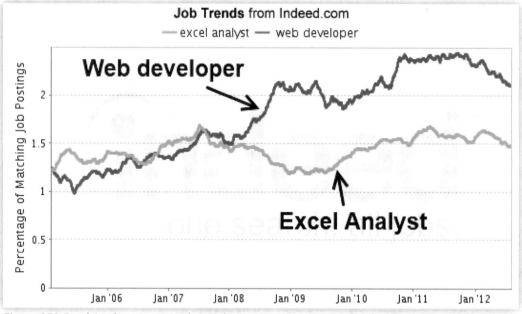

Figure 359 Excel Analyst versus Web Developer.

Interesting that Excel has been holding steady, and Web Developer didn't 'pass' it until late 2006.

Web Developers dominate the job listings because web *applications* are what the world demands. Although none of us are 'desktop developers' in the sense of this chart, this reflects a broader shift in the way the world does its computing, which *does* affect us.

Erosion of the desktop's perceived importance means erosion of Excel's perceived importance (but not usage). When I arrived at Microsoft in 1996, expense reporting was driven by an Excel template. By 2000, the Excel template was gone, replaced by a pure web-based format.

If Excel can be removed from a process, it has been by now. What's left is the stuff I talked about in the introduction – people who are embedded in the business, know the business, and are able to directly provide digested data (using Excel).

To view the graph above, and run your own searches like this, visit http://ppvt.pro/XLvsWebDev.

Our Bridge to the Future

Let's return to the scenario of me emailing around a report, and this time, imagine me sending the following instead:

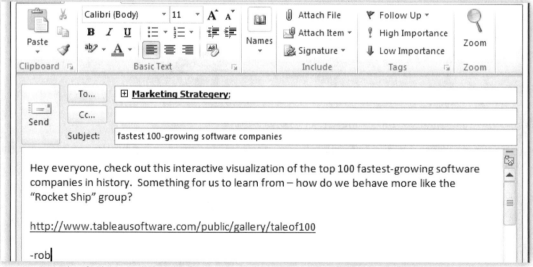

Figure 360 This feels very different than emailing a document, especially on the receiving end.

Jim opens the mail, and right off the bat he's more enthusiastic about clicking a link than opening an attachment. The web just feels 'light.' Documents that open in desktop apps feel heavy by comparison.

He clicks the link, and sees:

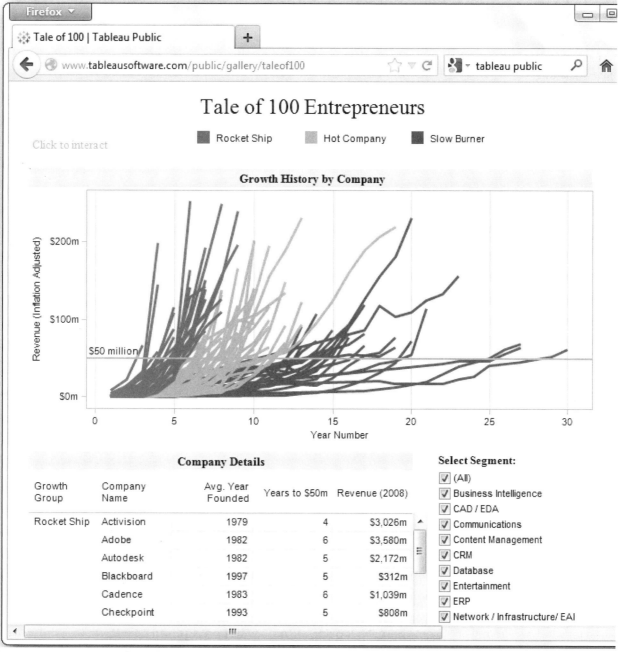

Figure 361 Interactive web application displaying the data.

This is a superior experience in many ways:

- **'Lighter' than opening a document**, so right from the beginning the consumer feels more engaged, and less taxed.

- **Requires no installation** – it's a thing you visit, not something you bring to you (and configure!) before you can use it.

- **Works on virtually every operating system** – no apologies or disclaimers required in my email.

- **Does *not* suffer from a close association with 'content containers'** like Word and PowerPoint.

- **Feels modern**, unlike the 1980s technology of Excel docs.

- **Less intimidating and error-prone**, since it provides a clean consumer experience, without the clutter and danger of the tools that were used to *produce* the report.

- **Quite simply feels much more *legitimate*** – web-based applications are not the sort of thing the average office worker can produce. They require teams to build. And basically every computing experience that we trust these days is a web experience.

The screenshot above is from a company named Tableau, a company that many consider to be a competitor to Excel and PowerPivot. Why do I include them, of all people? Because I want to clearly highlight what we have *lacked*.

That is, until now. :-)

Back to My Retail Competitive Spreadsheet

Let's circle back to my final formatted version:

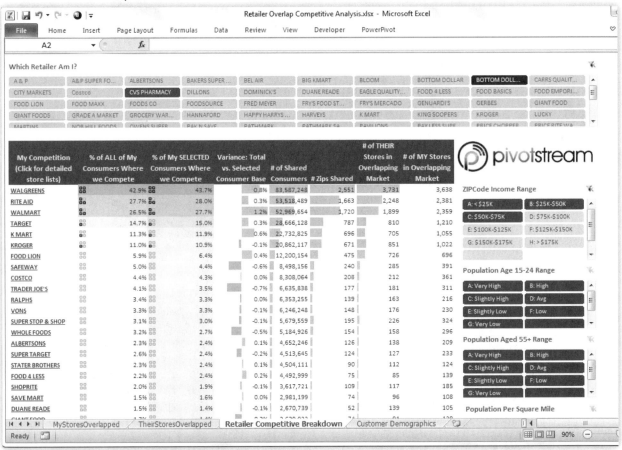

Figure 362 Best we can do on the desktop.

Then let's flip over to my browser, where I'm looking at some workbooks stored on a cloud website.

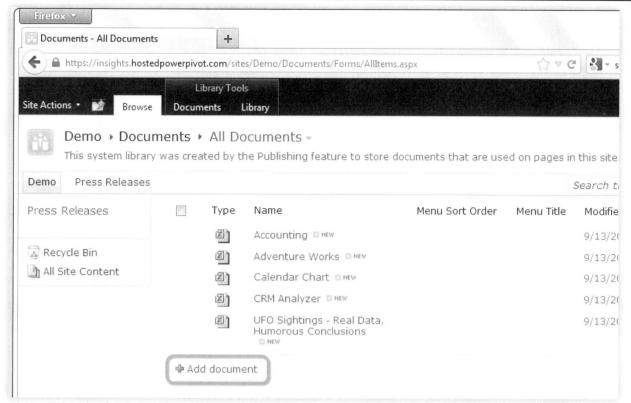

Figure 363 A cloud website where some XLSX files are stored. Note the highlighted "Add Document" link.

I click that Add Document link and am prompted for a file path:

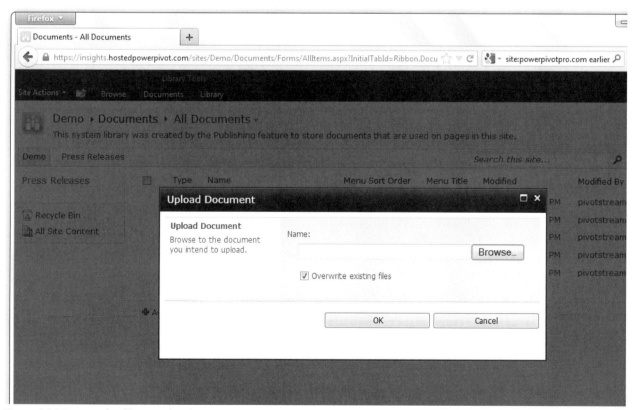

Figure 364 Prompt for file to upload.

I browse to the location where I have saved my retail competitive workbook, then click OK:

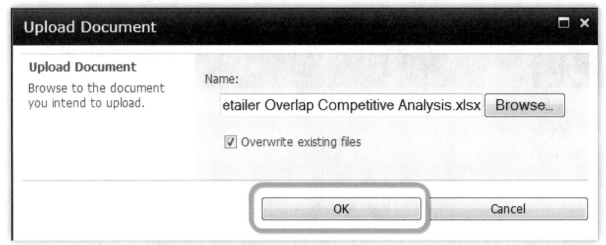

Figure 365 Just the usual upload to a web storage location.

And, as expected, my file is now stored up there as well:

	Type	Name	Menu Sort Order	Menu Title	Modified
☐					
	⊠	Accounting ☐ NEW			9/13/2012 1:33 PM
	⊠	Adventure Works ☐ NEW			9/13/2012 1:33 PM
	⊠	Calendar Chart ☐ NEW			9/13/2012 1:33 PM
	⊠	CRM Analyzer ☐ NEW			9/13/2012 1:33 PM
	⊠	UFO Sightings - Real Data, Humorous Conclusions ☐ NEW			9/13/2012 1:34 PM
	⊠	Retailer Overlap Competitive Analysis ☐ NEW			9/13/2012 6:56 PM

✛ Add document

Figure 366 Workbook uploaded successfully.

Flip to Consumer View

Up until now I've been looking at the 'behind the scenes' mode of this website, a place where people like me can put workbooks that we've made.

However, this is a very special kind of website, and has a much bigger purpose than just storing workbooks. This website is a PowerPivot *server* website!

To show you what I mean, let's look at the homepage of the site; a place that all of my consumers can see, and which is geared toward their needs. The link to the homepage is here:

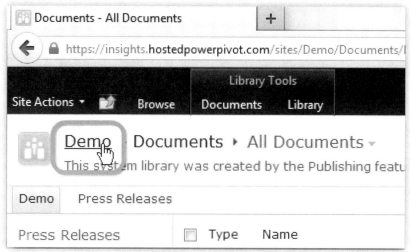

Figure 367 Link back to the consumer-oriented homepage.

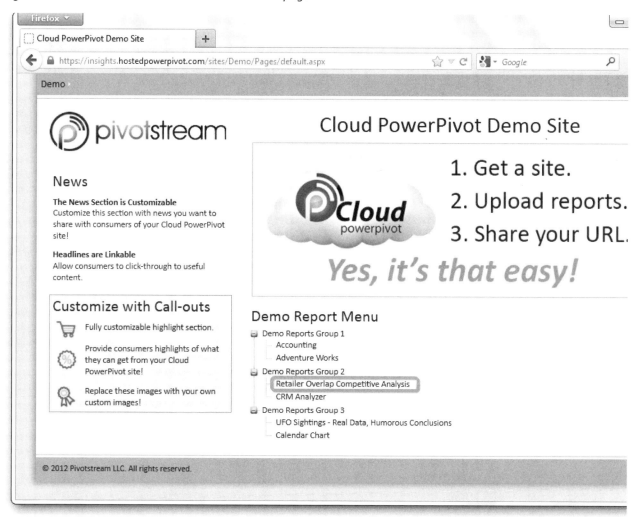

Figure 368 Note the retailer competitive link! Clicking that gives me...

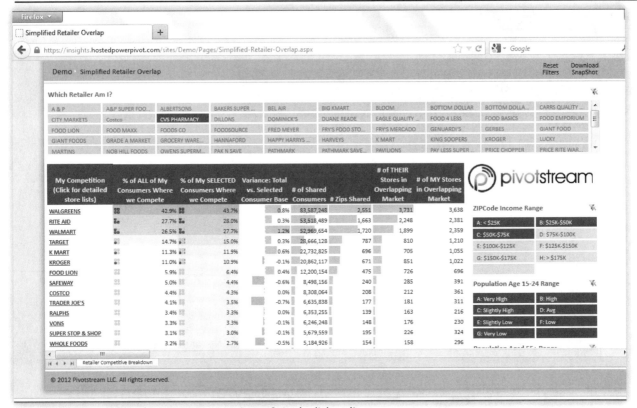

Figure 369 The workbook! But is it just a picture? Let's click a slicer.

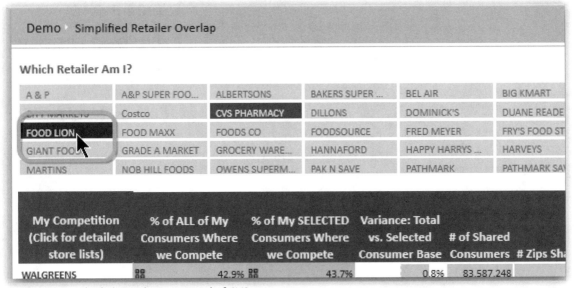

Figure 370 Let's click Food Lion instead of CVS.

Demo ▸ Simplified Retailer Overlap

Which Retailer Am I?

A & P	A&P SUPER FOO…	ALBERTSONS	BAKERS SUPER …	BEL AIR	BIG K
CITY MARKETS	Costco	CVS PHARMACY	DILLONS	DOMINICK'S	DUAN
FOOD LION	FOOD MAXX	FOODS CO	FOODSOURCE	FRED MEYER	FRY'S
GIANT FOODS	GRADE A MARKET	GROCERY WARE…	HANNAFORD	HAPPY HARRYS …	HARV
MARTINS	NOB HILL FOODS	OWENS SUPERM…	PAK N SAVE	PATHMARK	PATHI

My Competition (Click for detailed store lists)	% of ALL of My Consumers Where we Compete	% of My SELECTED Consumers Where we Compete	Variance: Total vs. Selected Consumer Base	# of Shared Consumers #
CVS PHARMACY	42.5%	42.5%	-0.1%	12,200,154
RITE AID	38.9%	38.8%	-0.1%	11,134,380
WALMART	34.3%	34.3%	0.0%	9,851,689
WALGREENS	33.9%	33.8%	-0.1%	9,712,869
K MART	16.6%	16.7%	0.1%	4,800,589
KROGER	12.7%	12.6%	0.0%	3,626,632
TARGET	12.6%	12.6%	0.0%	3,617,772

*Figure 371 Yes, it **is** fully interactive. In my browser. (Even though this computer does **not** have PowerPivot installed!)*

I'll slice it to Whole Foods next:

Demo ▸ Simplified Retailer Overlap   Reset Filters   Download SnapShot

Which Retailer Am I?

GIANT FOODS	GRADE A MARKET	GROCERY WARE…	HANNAFORD	HAPPY HARRYS …	HARVEYS	K MART	KING SOOPERS	KROGER	LUCKY
MARTINS	NOB HILL FOODS	OWENS SUPERM…	PAK N SAVE	PATHMARK	PATHMARK SAVE…	PAVILIONS	PAY LESS SUPER …	PRICE CHOPPER	PRICE RITE WAR…
QUALITY FOOD C…	RALEY'S	RALPHS	RANDALLS	REIDS	RITE AID	SAFEWAY	SAVE MART	SCOTT'S	SHOPRITE
SMITHS FOOD &…	STATER BROTHERS	STOP & SHOP	SUPER FRESH	SUPER GIANT	SUPER K	SUPER STOP & S…	SUPER TARGET	SWEET BAY	
THE MARKET	TOM THUMB	TOPS MARKETS	Trader Joe's	VONS	WALDBAUMS	WALGREENS	Walmart	WEGMANS	**Whole Foods**

My Competition (Click for detailed store lists)	% of ALL of My Consumers Where we Compete	% of My SELECTED Consumers Where we Compete	Variance: Total vs. Selected Consumer Base	# of Shared Consumers	# Zips Shared	# of THEIR Stores in Overlapping Market	# of MY Stores in Overlapping Market
CVS PHARMACY	70.5%	69.8%	-0.7%	5,184,926	154	296	158
WALGREENS	61.1%	64.1%	3.0%	4,762,978	145	325	151
RITE AID	41.4%	41.9%	0.5%	3,112,340	91	152	95
TRADER JOE'S	31.5%	32.3%	0.8%	2,402,774	72	75	74
TARGET	26.0%	25.8%	-0.2%	1,918,598	58	63	60
WALMART	22.3%	23.1%	0.8%	1,714,555	49	133	51
SAFEWAY	21.4%	22.3%	0.9%	1,656,303	47	60	50

pivotstream

ZIPCode Income Range

A: < $25K	B: $25K-$50K
C: $50K-$75K	D: $75K-$100K
E: $100K-$125K	F: $125K-$150K
G: $150K-$175K	H: > $175K

Figure 372 Note how Walgreens jumps to #2, and Trader Joe's jumps all the way into the fourth slot.

I can also 'drill across' to another detailed report by clicking the hyperlinks on the left, such as the 'Trader Joe's' entry circled in the image above.

My Competition (Click for detailed store lists)
CVS PHARMACY
WALGREENS
RITE AID
TRADER JOE'S
TARGET

Figure 373 This hyperlink is just a HYPERLINK() formula in Excel that references into the pivot, but the consumer doesn't know that…

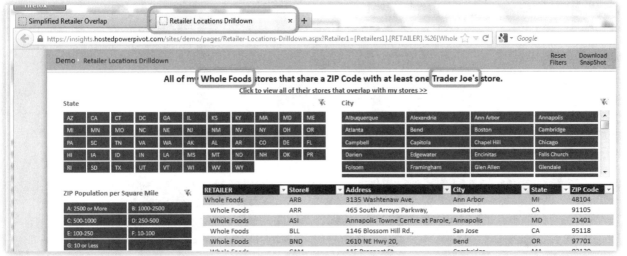

*Figure 374 Opens a new browser tab and shows me a completely different report, **but** parameterized to the Retailer I picked on the slicer (Whole Foods) and the Retailer whose hyperlink I clicked (Trader Joe's).*

Want More Evidence?

Here's another PowerPivot *application* on that same demo site:

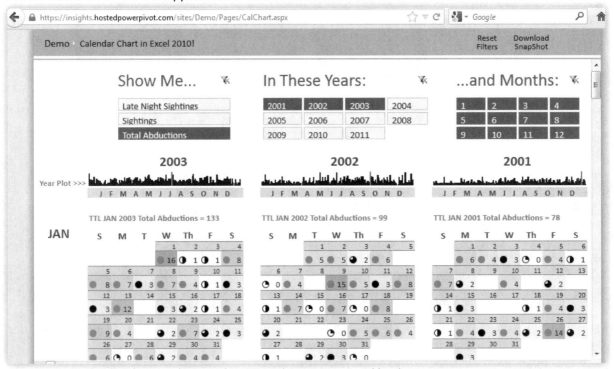

Figure 375 A calendar chart implemented in an Excel PowerPivot workbook.

And here's that same application *displaying on an iPad*!

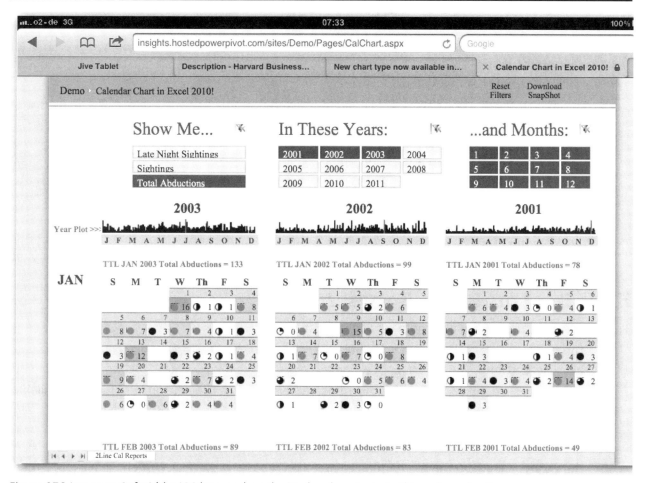

Figure 376 Just open Safari (the iOS browser) on the iPad and navigate to this web application.

 What's in a name?

Notice how I keep using the word 'application' instead of 'workbook' or 'spreadsheet?' That's how your consumers will think of this, too, as long as *you* describe it as such from the beginning. Tell them you've "built a new PowerPivot application and it's available on the web to use." Don't say that you've "uploaded a workbook." Got it?

To try this application in your own browser, visit http://ppvt.pro/CalChartDemo. To see how it was built in Excel/PowerPivot (and download the original workbook so you can modify it to fit your data), see this post: http://ppvt.pro/CalChartHowTo.

 We can now answer the question, 'what is the one click that will change your life as an Excel Pro?' It's the first time you click 'Upload Document' on a PowerPivot server.

The net effect is this: you've built an interactive, data-driven web application. It is available to whoever you decide (you have to give them access; it is not wide open to the world). It would take a team of programmers *weeks* (if not months) to deliver something of equivalent quality.

The fact that Excel/PowerPivot was your programming environment is not something you have to keep secret, but as long as you don't constantly use old-fashioned words like 'doc' and 'spreadsheet' with your consumers, web delivery shifts perception *dramatically* in your favor. Do not waste this.

Beyond Perception: Other Server Benefits

- **An end to the distribution problem** – even just getting workbooks to your consumers is often a lot of work with normal Excel. With the server, you put the workbook one place and then send around a single URL to the *application*.

- **Automatic refresh** – you can schedule your applications on the server to refresh themselves with the latest data, without you (or anyone else) having to intervene. When you go on vacation, you can actually *be* on vacation.

- **Security** – you can provide users with interactive access to the application but still prevent them from downloading the workbook. Thus your formulas and other sensitive business logic, as well as all the data itself, is safely secured on the server, instead of running around on everyone's laptop, threatening every day to be leaked.

- **One version of the truth** – because everyone is always using the server copy, there is no doubt that everyone is using the latest. Nor is there any doubt they are using the same formulas as everyone else. If you're using the same URL, it's the same application.

How Do You Get a Server?

Right now there are a few options; more may open up over time.

1. **You can buy SharePoint Enterprise Server plus SQL Server BI** Edition from Microsoft and install your own server. Unless you have a lot of experience here (and a deep budget), this won't work for you.

2. **You can use Office 365.** At the time of writing, this offering is still in beta and not formally available. Nor has anything related to pricing been disclosed. I do know that there are some limitations – files must be no bigger than 10MB, you cannot auto refresh anything except linked tables, and the overall aesthetics still scream 'spreadsheet.'

3. **Third Party Cloud Offerings.** I'm not going to promote any particular offerings here but there are a few out there. Also, I might just have something up my sleeve as well. Keep an eye on http://ppvt.pro/CloudPPV for news.

The future for Excel Pros is bright, and it's here. Take off in your new jet plane and enjoy the ride.

A1- Further Proof That the Game is Changing

In this book I've made some bold claims about PowerPivot's impact on your career. I've used words like "programmer," "engineer," and "developer" to describe your changing role. (I should also add terms like "Business Intelligence Professional," "Data Scientist," and "Big Data Specialist" to that list).

All of that may sound like an attractive exaggeration to you – nothing more than a pleasant metaphor. But in reality it is quite literally the truth.

Microsoft, you see, has redesigned their industrial-strength data analysis programming toolset to simply be... PowerPivot.

SQL Server Analysis Services (SSAS) – Complex but Lucrative

Early in this book, I mentioned that PowerPivot grew out of an existing Microsoft product, SSAS. For years, SSAS has been the most widely-adopted product in a high-end market known as "OLAP databases." (That's a fancy name, but you and I can think of "OLAP" as "pivot calculation engines.")

While PowerPivot and SSAS share a lot of common ancestry, the traditional SSAS product is **not** friendly to Excel Pros. It uses a formula language known as MDX that is quite foreign and difficult for us. Furthermore, traditional SSAS is fundamentally very formal and rigid. It does not operate on Tables; instead it uses Dimensions, Measure Groups, and Hierarchies – concepts that carry a lot of complexity, rigidity, and side effects. Lastly, it is very abstract – you invest large amounts of effort (and thinking) before you ever see results, in contrast to Excel and PowerPivot's instant and ongoing feedback.

Of course, the handful of SSAS Pros in the world typically earn more money than Excel Pros. For example, in 2006 I hired an SSAS Pro for two months of work and paid him $50,000. That's good money!

SSAS is Now Becoming PowerPivot

Hey, let's open up a **real** development tool: Visual Studio Ultimate. This is where SSAS Pros do their work, as well as web developers, mobile app developers, etc. – this is **the** programming tool from Microsoft:

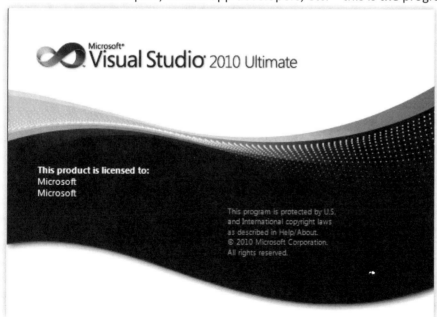

Figure 377 Visual Studio Ultimate: Even the name sounds impressive

But rather than build something from scratch, let's try something simpler. There's now a new option called Import from PowerPivot:

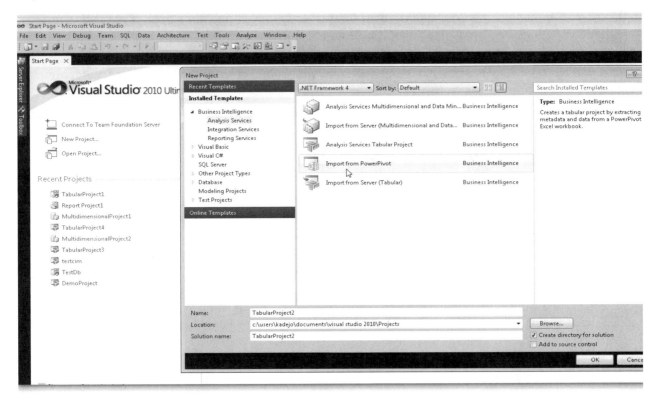

Figure 378 Import from PowerPivot

Guess what happens next? I browse for a PowerPivot workbook:

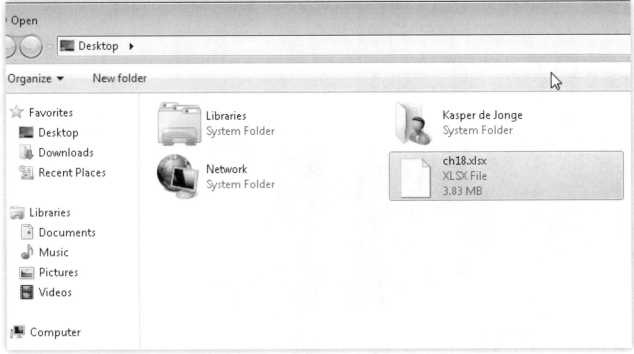

Figure 379 Just select a PowerPivot workbook

What we see next is a very, VERY familiar experience:

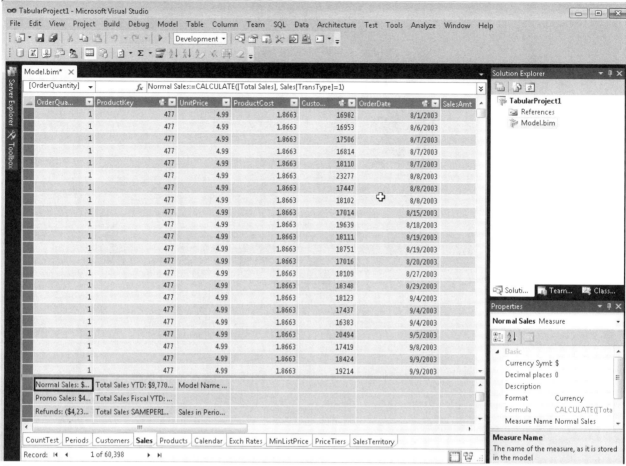

Figure 380 My PowerPivot model used in this book, now loaded in Visual Studio!

Other than the blue tint versus green tint, and the treeview docked on the right, this is precisely what we see in the PowerPivot window! Tables, sheet tabs, etc.

Zooming in a bit, we continue the "identical to PowerPivot" theme:

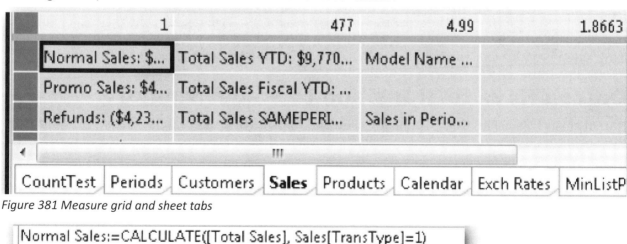

Figure 381 Measure grid and sheet tabs

Normal Sales:=CALCULATE([Total Sales], Sales[TransType]=1)

Figure 382 DAX formula is exactly the same

I can even toggle into diagram view, which again looks identical:

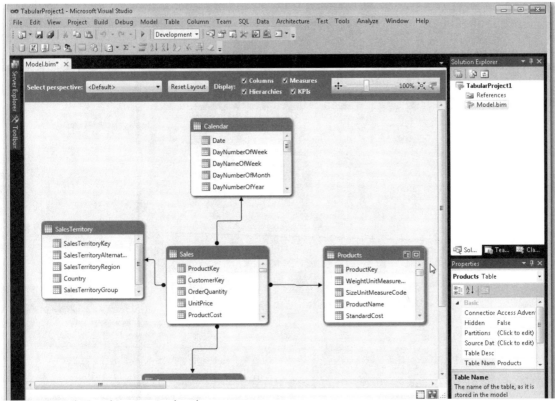

Figure 383 Relationship view is also the same

What This Means

In short, Microsoft has decided that the PowerPivot approach (DAX and tables) is a better way forward than the old SSAS language and approach (often referred to as "MOLAP" - MDX, Dimensions, etc.) PowerPivot – tables and DAX, which you will now see referred to as the "tabular approach" – is the future of their professional-grade product, and not just something for Excel Pros.

To be fair, that is really just my own analysis of the situation – Microsoft would not say it that way. They position it more along the lines of "the new Tabular (PowerPivot) model is now an equal to the traditional MOLAP approach, and both will be supported moving forward." But in my assessment, their actions indicate that "Tabular" is the future. There are significant new features in their BI ecosystem that were designed (at least initially) only to work with Tabular, not MOLAP. As a former engineering team leader at Microsoft, I can tell you that sort of decision is never an accident.

Do You Have to Transition to Visual Studio?

No, not at all. In fact, I have not. I probably will at some point – there are features that are available there that are not available in the Excel version. And the transition does not frighten me since I can import an XLSX and just keep cruising along.

But I don't really need to do that yet. The point is, it's good to know that it's there.

The two key takeaways I want you to digest here are:

1. The Excel-focused concepts and language covered in this book are now being adopted as **the** top-end analytical development approach for all of Microsoft. There is nothing more powerful. You are learning the most capable, most industrial-strength toolset in the entire world. You are becoming "Pro" in the strongest sense of the word.

2. If you ever need to "upsize" to a stronger tool – one that contains advanced security concepts or contains more data than the 2 GB file size limit of PowerPivot for instance – you can transition into Visual Studio without missing a beat.

A2- So Much Power, So Little Space: Further Capabilities

My original estimate for this book was 150 pages. Well it's turned out quite a bit longer than that, and yet the list of things I don't have space for is still quite sizeable.

I want to at least make you aware of these topics though, and in some cases point you to resources that I think could be helpful.

The first two of these, Power View and Cube Formulas, are the ones I most wish I'd had space for. That said, each of these has already been the subject of multiple entire books. So it was just a sensible decision to leave them out.

The rest of these don't feel so bad. None of them are things I use today. Maybe in the future I will, but I think it's fair to categorize them as "you can be extremely effective at PowerPivot long before you need them."

Power View

Power View is a new visualization surface (a new sheet type!) in Excel 2013 that can be used to display all kinds of modern stuff like maps, card views, and animated charts. (The 2013 version of Power View is actually Power View V2. V1 is not built-in to Excel, and exists purely as a SharePoint feature).

There's at least one post about Power View on the blog. This one shows off a few capabilities of Power View V1:

http://ppvt.pro/PowerViewCat

Cube Formulas

Any pivot you create with PowerPivot can be completely "exploded" into formulas – each cell in the pivot becomes a cube formula. This opens up limitless formatting possibilities, interaction between DAX and Excel's in-sheet calc engine, and some really creative things like the calendar chart.

There's actually quite a bit about cube formulas on the blog, under the cube formulas category:

http://ppvt.pro/CubeFormulasCat

GENERATE(), SUMMARIZE(), CALCULATETABLE(), ADDCOLUMNS(), KEEPFILTERS(), ROLLUP(), CROSSJOIN()

There are a lot of functions that help you work with entire "virtual" tables behind the scenes during a measure calculation.

I've yet to truly even attempt using them. David Churchward has used a few of these in guest posts to the blog, but really, this is a place where I recommend the Italians – Russo and Ferrari, plus our English friend Chris Webb. I believe they have a new book in the works for Excel 2013 and it's going to cover a lot of these more advanced things in great detail.

TOPN()

This one is new in PowerPivot V2 and I think I'm going to be using it a lot, but I have not had much time with it yet. It looks like a version of FILTER() that makes it easy to just return the top n rows. So you'd use this as a <filter> argument in a CALCULATE().

Hierarchies

The ability to link several fields in the field list together, so that all get added at the same time and in the proper order (think Country/State/City).

This feature doesn't interest me much, to be honest, since the vast majority of consumers don't ever want to see a field list, and this feature is really only useful for the person who *is* using the field list.

PATH( ) Functions

That said there are a number of PATH() functions added to DAX that all work with hierarchies, so there might be some usefulness to hierarchies yet :-)

HASONEFILTER(), ISFILTERED(), ISCROSSFILTERED()

The first two make semantic sense to me and should be easy to decipher. The third is still quite foreign to me.

USERELATIONSHIP()

PowerPivot V2 allows multiple relationships to exist between a pair of tables, whereas V1 restricted you to a single link. USERELATIONSHIP() lets you select which linkage you use in a formula, in the event there is more than one.

The multiple link feature is intended for cases such as where you have one Calendar table but two date columns in your Sales table – like OrderDate and ShipDate. Sometimes you want to show Sales data on your pivot according to order date, and other times you want to see it via ship date.

In the past you've had to have two Calendar tables to deal with that situation. It's unclear to me as of yet whether the USERELATIONSHIP() formula tradeoff will be valuable in my work, or whether I will keep using two different tables.

"Many to Many" Relationship Scenarios

Sometimes you have a pair of tables that you'd ideally like to relate, but it's not possible because there are duplicate values in each table. There is a DAX formula "workaround" for this situation however, but it is quite complicated.

Actually, it's not so much complicated as it is hard to understand. I have a few workbooks that use this technique, but I copied the technique from the Italians :-) I was able to modify the pattern to fit my needs but this technique strikes me as "not something Excel Pros need to learn in their first year of PowerPivot." Read Ferrari/Russo/Webb for more on this.

A3- Four Common Error Messages

There are a handful of errors that you will see from time to time – error messages that sound scary but ultimately mean very little. I wanted to dedicate just a quick page or two and cover these, so that you know what to do when you see them.

"Initialization of the Data Source Failed"

Figure 384 I see this one all the time

Simply put, you can completely ignore this error message. Click OK and everything is fine. I cannot recall a single instance where I clicked OK and something bad happened afterwards.

Quite literally, I have seen this popup thousands of times now, and it's never once indicated something was actually broken.

I wish we didn't see this popup at all of course. But it is not something to worry about, and it never happens on the server.

The Other Three

It makes sense to cover the remaining three as a group, because they all basically mean the same thing, and the steps you take to fix them are also the same.

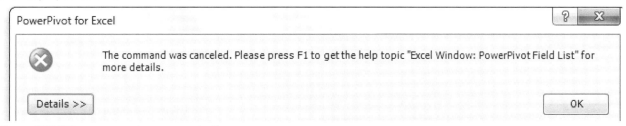

Figure 385 "The command was canceled"

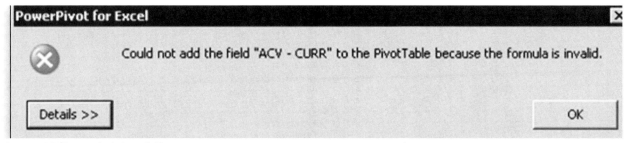

Figure 386 "Formula is invalid"

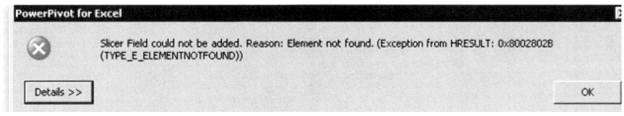

Figure 387 "Element not found"

All three of these indicate that the PowerPivot addin and Excel have gotten "out of sync" with each other. More speficially, PowerPivot knows about the field you are trying to add, but Excel does not think that field exists. This happens with fields you recently created – I have never seen this occur with a field that I have already used in a pivot.

235

The fix for this is essentially to "wake Excel up." Sometimes, Excel is a bit more asleep than other times, so here's a list of steps you can take, sorted from most convenient (try these first) to least convenient (try these if the others fail).

1. Make the pivot update somehow – click a slicer, add a different field, filter it, etc.
2. Right click a cell in the pivot and choose Refresh.
3. Add a calculated column in the PowerPivot window and then delete it
4. Save and close the workbook, close Excel completely (all Excel windows closed!), then reopen the workbook.

A4- People: The Most Powerful Feature of PowerPivot

PowerPivot is a pretty good piece of technology. It offers a lot of powerful new capabilities. But technology itself never changes the world – it's what *people* do with it that matters. The revolution, in other words, is not PowerPivot. The revolution is what *you*, the Excel Pro "army," are going to do with it (and are doing already).

In a similar vein, I started the blog in late 2009. Without the readership, questions, and feedback of the blog audience, this book never would have happened. Many of the names below have been with me for a long time. Their support, enthusiasm, and adoption have been a huge help to me over the years. They have validated, repeatedly, my beliefs about the future of data and Excel's role in it.

So here they are, some of the people on the very tip of the spear:

Index

Business Solutions from the MrExcel Library

Master Array Formulas in Excel

Ctrl+Shift+Enter

Mastering Excel Array Formulas

Mike "ExcelIsFun" Girvin

Summer of 2013 from Holy Macro! Books

Simulations in Excel

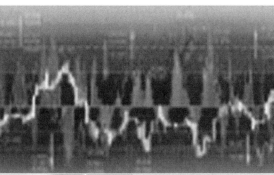
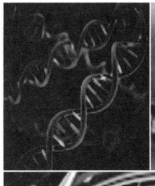

EXCEL SIMULATIONS

Solve Problems with Excel

Gambling

Statistics

Passwords

Genetics

Business Targets

Risk Analysis

Scenarios

Population Growth

Traffic

Exchange Rates

Monte Carlo

Using Excel to Model Risk, Investments, Genetics, Growth, Gambling and Monte Carlo Analysis

by Gerard M. Verschuuren, PhD

Fall of 2013 from Holy Macro! Books

PowerPivot for Excel:
How the DAX Engine Calculates Measures

=powerpivot(pro)

1

Total Sales	Year	
Model	2014	2015
Mountain-200		$807,309
Road-150	$2,601,402	$2,948,494
Road-250		$1,571,598

Detect Pivot Coordinates of Current Measure Cell:
Calendar[Year]=2015,
Products[Model]="Road-150"
Those are the initial filter context.

2 If applicable, apply <filters> from CALCULATE(), adding/removing /modifying coordinates and producing a new filter context.

3 Apply the coordinates in the filter context to each of the respective tables (Calendar and Products in this example). This results in a set of "active" rows in each of those tables.

4

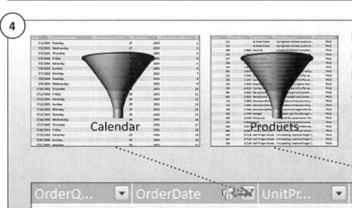

If the filtered tables (Calendar and Products) are Lookup tables, follow relationships to their related Data tables and filter those tables too.
(Only Data rows related to active Lookup rows will remain active).

OrderQ...	OrderDate	UnitPr...	ProductKey	SalesAmt
1	1/1/2015	3578.27	313	3578.27
1	1/2/2015	3578.27	312	3578.27
1	1/3/2015	3374.99	350	3374.99
1	1/3/2015	3399.99	345	3399.99
1	1/3/2015	3578.27	310	3578.27
1	1/1/2015	699.0982	338	699.0982
1	1/2/2015	3578.27		Data Table (Ex: Sales)

5 Once all filters are applied and all relationships have been followed, evaluate the arithmetic – SUM(), COUNTROWS(), etc. in the formula against the remaining active rows.

6 The result of the arithmetic is returned to the current measure cell in the pivot, then the process starts over at step 1 for the next measure cell.

PowerPivot for Excel:
Commonly-Used Functions and Techniques

CALCULATE() Function
CALCULATE(<measure expression>, <filter1>, <filter2>, ... <filterN>)

<measure expression>:	[MeasureName]
	SUM(T[C])
	Any measure name or valid formula for a measure
"Raw" <filter>:	Sales[TransactionType]=1
	Products[Color]="Blue"
	Calendar[Year]>=2009
	Sales[TransType]=1 || Sales[TransType]=3
Advanced <filter>:	ALL(...)
	FILTER(...)
	DATESBETWEEN(...)
	Any other function that modifies filter context
Notes:	Raw <filter>'s override (replace) filter context from pivot
	Raw <filter>'s must be T[C] <operator> <fixed value>
	Multiple <filter>'s arguments get AND'd together

DATESBETWEEN() Function
DATESBETWEEN(<date column>, <start date>, <end date>)

<date column>:	Calendar[Date]
	Column of type date
	Typically the main (or only) date column in your dates table
<start date>:	[AnyDateMeasure]
	FIRSTDATE(Calendar[Date])
	STARTOFMONTH(Calendar[Date])
	Any expression that returns a date
<end date>:	Same as <start date>
Notes:	Returns a table of dates
	<start date> and <end date> are included in the results
	More readable alternative to FILTER() with small differences

ALL() Function
ALL(<table>) or ALL(Table[Col1], Table[Col2], ...Table[ColN])

Basic usage:	As a <filter> argument to CALCULATE()
	Removes filters from specified table or column(s)
	Strips those tables/columns from the pivot's filter context
Advanced Usage:	Technically, ALL() returns a table
	So it is also useable wherever a <table expr> is required
	...such as the first argument to FILTER()

Time Intelligence with Custom Calendar
via "GFITW"

```
=CALCULATE(<measure expr>,
          ALL(<Custom Cal Table>),
          FILTER(ALL(<Custom Cal Table>), <custom filter>),
          <optional VALUES() to restore filters on some Cal fields>
          )
=CALCULATE([Sales],
          ALL(Cal445),
          FILTER(ALL(Cal445), Cal445[Year]=MAX(Cal445[Year])-1
          )
=CALCULATE([Sales],
          ALL(Cal445),
          FILTER(ALL(Cal445), Cal445[Year]=MAXCal445[Year])-1),
          VALUES(Cal445[MonthOfYear])
          )
```
More info at http://ppvt.pro/GFITW

FILTER() Function
FILTER(<table expression>, <single rich filter>)

<table expression>:	T or 'T' - name of table
	VALUES(T[C]) - all unique values of T[C] for current pivot cell
	ALL(Table) or ALL(T[C])
	Any expression that returns a table, such as DATESYTD()
	Even another FILTER() can be used here for instance
<rich filter>:	T[C1] >= T[C2]
	T[C1] = [Measure]
	[Measure1] > [Measure2]
	<true/false expr1> && <true/false expr2>
	Any expression that evaluates to true/false
Notes:	Commonly used as a <filter> argument to CALCULATE()
	Useful when a richer filter test is required
	Never use when a raw CALCULATE() <filter> will work
	Slow and eats memory when used on large tables
	Use against small (Lookup) tables for better performance
	Only SUBTRACTS rows from filter context, does NOT override
	Advanced usage: use anywhere a <table expr> is required

VALUES() Function
VALUES(Table[Column])

General:	Inspects "where" the current measure cell is in the pivot
	Returns table of values from current pivot filter context
	Sometimes returns a single-row table
IF tests on text:	Single row VALUES() tables can be used in an IF() test
	...IF(HASONEVALUE(T[C]),IF(VALUES(T[C])="Canada", ...))
	...useful for text fields since they have no aggregation fxns
Restoring a filter:	CALCULATE([M], ALL(Table), VALUES(Table[Col1]))
	...typically equiv to CALCULATE([M],
	ALLEXCEPT(Table,Table[Col1]))
Notes:	VALUES(T[C]) returns filtered list even if T[C] isn't on pivot
	...VALUES(Cal[Year]) always returns 2002 if Cal[Date] is
	...on pivot with current context Cal[Date]=6/1/2002
	VALUES() overrules ALL() if both are used on same column

Forcing Totals to Be the Sum of Their "Parts"
```
=IF(HASONEVALUE(T[C]),
    <original measure>,
    SUMX(VALUES(T[C], <original measure>)
    )
```

Calc Column That References "Previous" Row(s)
```
=CALCULATE(<measure expr>,
          FILTER(ALL(<table>), Table[Col]=EARLIER(Table[Col])-1)
          )
=CALCULATE(AVERAGE(Tests[Score]),
          FILTER(ALL(Tests), Tests[ID]=EARLIER(Tests[ID])-1)
          )
```

30 Day Moving Average
```
=CALCULATE(AVERAGE(Table[Column]),
   DATESBETWEEN(Cal[Date], LASTDATE(Cal[Date])-29,LASTDATE(Cal[Date]))
   )
```

RANKX() Function
RANKX(<table expr>, <arithmetic expression>, <optional alternate arithmetic expression>, <optional sort order flag>, <optional tie-handling flag>)

Simplest Usage:	RANKX(ALL(Table[Column]), <numerical expr>)
	EX: RANKX(ALL(Products[Name]), [TotalSales])
Ascending Rank Order:	EX: RANKX(ALL(Products[Name]), [TotalSales],,1)
"Dense" Tie Handling:	EX: RANKX(ALL(Products[Name]), [TotalSales],,,Dense)

Suppressing Subtotals/Grand Totals
```
=IF(HASONEVALUE(Table[Column]), <measure expr for non-totals>, BLANK())
```

Coming in Fall 2013

Simple, Impactful Techniques for the Data Professional

Bill Jelen and Rob Collie join forces to bring you dozens of magical, immediately useful and easily-applied techniques in a single reference. PowerPivot alchemy is a fast-paced guide to more than 50 techniques you can easily copy and apply to your work in minutes.

The results, however, often exceed what a team of programmers could accomplish in a month. Whether you let your colleagues in on your secret weapons is entirely up to you.